CATHOLIC WORSHIP
An Introduction to Liturgy

DONALD A. WITHEY

Reproduced by permission of
Kevin Mayhew LTD

Wipf and Stock Publishers
EUGENE, OREGON

About the Author

Dr Donald Withey is a member of the Committee for Pastoral Liturgy of the Bishops' Conference of England and Wales and of the Diocese of Clifton Liturgical Commission. He represents the Catholic Church in England and Wales on the Joint Liturgical Group, and is the Secretary of the Society for Liturgical Study. In addition to articles and reviews, he is the author of *Why Receive the Chalice?* (Kevin Mayhew, 1990), and has edited *Adult Initiation* (Alcuin/GROW Liturgical Study 10, 1989).

Wipf and Stock Publishers
199 West 8th Avenue, Suite 3
Eugene, Oregon 97401

Catholic Worship
An Intoduction to Liturgy
By Withey, Donald A.
Copyright©1990 Withey, Donald A.
ISBN: 1-59244-109-2
Publication date: December, 2002
Previously published by Kevin Mayhew LTD, 1990.

Reproduced by permission of the Publisher, Kevin Mayhew Ltd., Buxhall, Stowmarket, Suffolk, IP14 3BW, UK.

To my wife

'The most urgent task is that of the biblical and liturgical formation of the people of God, both pastors and faithful.'

'Much still remains to be done to help priests and the faithful to grasp the meaning of the liturgical rites and texts.'

'The time has come to renew the spirit which inspired the Church at the moment when the *Constitution on the Sacred Liturgy* was prepared.'

Pope John Paul II
4 December 1988

Acknowledgements

Excerpts from the English translation of *The Roman Missal* © 1973, International Committee on English in the Liturgy, Inc. (ICEL); excerpts from the English translation of *Holy Communion and Worship of the Eucharist Outside Mass* © 1974, ICEL; excerpts from the English translation of *Rite of Penance* © 1974, ICEL; excerpts from the English translation of *Rite of Confirmation*, Second Edition © 1975, ICEL; excerpts from the English translation of *Ordination of Deacons, Priests, and Bishops* © 1975; excerpts from the English translation of *Documents on the Liturgy 1963-1979: Conciliar, Papal, and Curial Texts* © 1982, ICEL. All rights reserved.

Extracts from *The Rite of Baptism for Children* (Geoffrey Chapman, 1970); *Rite of Christian Initiation of Adults* (ICEL/Geoffrey Chapman, 1988); *Documents of Vatican II*, edited by Walter M. Abbott (Geoffrey Chapman); *Pastoral Care of the Sick* (ICEL/Geoffrey Chapman) are reproduced by permission of Cassell.

Extracts from the *Jerusalem Bible*, published and copyright 1966, 1967 and 1968 by Darton, Longman and Todd Ltd and Doubleday & Co Inc, are used by permission of the publishers.

Extracts from the *General Instruction on the Liturgy of the Hours*, from *The Divine Office*, vol. 1 (Collins) are reproduced by permission of A.P. Watt Ltd.

Extracts from the Decree *Immensae Caritatis*, text taken from *Study Book for Special Ministers of Holy Communion* (CTS); Apostolic Letter *Vicesimus quintus annus*, English translation published by the CTS entitled *Love Your Mass* (Do 591, 1989); indirect quotations from Herbert McCabe *The Teaching of the Catholic Church: a New Catechism*, CTS, 1985, are reproduced by permission of the Catholic Truth Society.

The Imitation of Christ, by Thomas à Kempis, and *The Code of Canon Law* are published by Collins.

Contents

		page
Introduction		9
Abbreviations		13
1	Origins	15
2	The Eucharist During the First Three Centuries	29
3	Initiation in the Early Church	40
4	Growth and Consolidation of the Liturgy (4th c.–8th c.)	54
5	The Rites of Initiation in the Middle Ages	64
6	The Liturgy in the Middle Ages (9th c.-15th c.)	70
7	From Trent to Vatican 2	81
8	The Second Vatican Council	99
9	The Mass: The Introductory Rites	116
10	The Liturgy of the Word and the Lectionary	126
11	The Liturgy of the Eucharist	138
12	The Sacrament of the Holy Eucharist and Eucharistic Worship	156

13	The Liturgy of the Hours	167
14	The Sacraments of Initiation	190
15	Other Sacraments and Rites	209
16	People, Signs, and Sacraments	223
17	Space, Design, and Movement	235
18	Music, Speech, and Language	248
19	Time and the Liturgical Year	255
20	The Liturgy Today and Tomorrow	268

| Further Reading | 275 |
| Index | 276 |

Introduction

The twentieth century has been a time of unprecedented renewal and revision of the liturgy, especially since the Second Vatican Council. These developments are still continuing and at the present time a second round of revision is taking place.

This book is an introduction to today's liturgy. It offers a comprehensive survey of the Second Vatican Council's teaching on the liturgy and its decrees concerning liturgical revision and reform. It provides a guide to the revised forms of the Mass, the office, the sacraments and other rites. It discusses the principles of authentic participation and why we should make the most of the liturgy.

Above all it focuses on the meaning and significance of the liturgy, identifying what is essential to the rites and indicating why it was necessary for the Council to inaugurate a thorough revision. There is a critical assessment of the progress which has been made in implementing the aims of the Council and of those areas where more development is needed. In particular, it is suggested that both clergy and laity should be better informed about the liturgy and its place in the life of the Church.

In this I greatly welcome the lead given by Pope John Paul II in his recent Apostolic Letter on the 25th anniversary of the *Constitution on the Sacred Liturgy*.* The Holy Father referred to the need for 'an intensive education' in the liturgy and declared that 'the most urgent task is that of the biblical and liturgical formation of the people of God, both pastors and faithful'. I hope this book will help in this important programme of liturgical education.

Our approach to the liturgy should in the first place be spiritual: we are dealing with holy things, that sacred ground where man meets God in the profound relationship of worship and love. It should also be strongly pastoral in its concern for the spiritual well-being of God's people. Liturgy is not about the *minutiae* of ceremonies, but about bringing people closer to God in the official public worship of the Church and the sacraments.

At the same time, the basis of liturgical renewal today is thoroughly scriptural and patristic in character. It is traditional in that the Church has sought to retain or restore those elements which can be shown by an appeal to tradition to be of the essence of the rites. For this reason, considerable space has been devoted to the origins of the liturgy and its historical background as these are considered to be indispensable for an understanding of it.

Two other characteristics are considered important in the account of the liturgy offered in this present work. Liturgy is a branch of theology, and it is essential to consider the theological foundations of worship and the sacramental rites. For this reason, attention is given in this book to sacramental theology and doctrine, with particular reference to the meaning and significance of the Mass and the sacraments.

Finally, the account of the liturgy which follows is based firmly on the teaching of the Second Vatican Council and

---

*This Apostolic Letter is discussed more fully in Chapter Twenty.

Introduction

of the ensuing liturgical documents. The reader is urged to study these documents, for which comprehensive references and quotations have been provided for guidance.

It is hoped that the book will interest all who desire to know more about the meaning and structure of the liturgy. While the main part of the book is devoted to the rites and texts, I have aimed at what I call a 'total' approach to the liturgy, covering also, though more briefly, the place of music, art, architecture, speech, and movement in liturgy, and the significance of time and of signs and symbols.

I have kept in mind the needs of musicians studying for the Archbishops' Certificate in Church Music, giving particular attention throughout to the general principles of music and singing in the liturgy. There is also a section on the design and re-ordering of churches, which is an increasingly important issue today.

The book is designed to be complete in itself. It is hoped, however, that the reader will study the missal, the Liturgy of the Hours, the main rites, the *Constitution on the Sacred Liturgy*, and at least the more important of the Introductions and Instructions issued in conjunction with the rites. For those who would like to take the study of liturgy beyond the level of this basic text, some suggestions for further reading are given.

I am particularly grateful to my wife, Pam, for her great help and encouragement in the writing of this book. Her repeated checking of scripts and her criticism of the text and its presentation have been invaluable to me.

Abbreviations

CC	Dogmatic Constitution on the Church
CL	Constitution on the Sacred Liturgy
CTS	Catholic Truth Society
DL	Decree on the Apostolate of the Laity
DP	Decree on the Ministry and Life of Priests
ELLC	The English Language Liturgical Consultation
GICI	General Introduction to Christian Initiation
GILH	General Instruction on the Liturgy of the Hours
GIPCS	General Introduction to the Pastoral Care of the Sick
GIRM	General Instruction of the Roman Missal
GIWE	General Introduction to Holy Communion and the Worship of the Eucharist outside Mass
GN	General Norms for the Liturgical Year and the Calendar
ICEL	International Commission on English in the Liturgy
ICET	The International Consultation on English Texts
IRBC	Introduction to the Rite of Baptism of Children
IRC	Introduction to the Rite of Confirmation
IRP	Introduction to the Rite of Penance
JLG	Joint Liturgical Group
LMI	Lectionary for Mass: Introduction
RCIA	Rite of Christian Initiation of Adults
#	number

1

Origins

Prayer and the Christian

Jesus Christ left his Church an unmistakable legacy of prayer and worship. His own prayer life is an outstanding feature of the gospels. He prayed constantly, and his disciples noticed how he regularly sought solitude for prayer (Luke 5:16, 6:12). In prayer he entered into a close relationship with the Father, which so impressed his disciples that they asked for guidance on how to pray. He had already taught them to avoid making a public display of their prayer (Matthew 6:6): they should go to their private room to pray to their Father and he would reward them. 'Ask and it shall be given to you' (Matthew 7:7). Prayer is an indispensable element in man's relationship with God. Jesus puts great emphasis on personal prayer, and yet personal prayer has a communal dimension: they are to pray '*Our* Father ... give *us* this day *our* daily bread ... forgive *us* our trespasses ... lead *us* not into temptation ... deliver *us* from evil' (Matthew 6:9-13).

Personal and public prayer

In the Christian dispensation there is a continuity between personal prayer and public worship, and the relationship between the two aspects of prayer is an important principle of the liturgical life of the Church today. The distinction between them needs to be grasped clearly. There are certain difficulties in bringing about the participation in the liturgy which was advocated so insistently by the Second Vatican Council. One is the deeply rooted practice among some of the faithful of making private devotions during liturgical celebrations, and especially during the great eucharistic prayer.

The nature and necessity of public worship have to be understood if we are to take a full part in the Church's liturgy. 'Prayer expresses the very essence of the Church as a community ... The private prayer of the members of the Church is offered to the Father through Christ in the Holy Spirit, and as such is always necessary and to be commended. Community prayer, however, has a special dignity since Christ himself said "Where two or three meet in my name, I shall be there with them" ' [GILH (*General Instruction on the Liturgy of the Hours*) 9]. In the liturgy the members of the Church carry out the priestly work of Christ, the Head of the Church. This they do by virtue of being, through baptism and regeneration, a priestly people [cf. CL (*Constitution on the Sacred Liturgy*) 7].

While the official public worship of the Church is to be accorded a priority over personal prayer, the relationship between the two is important. Personal prayer is a foundation for public worship: it nourishes and is in its turn nourished by the liturgy. Our meeting with God in the liturgy does not end abruptly when we leave the church building. The divine love we encounter in the liturgy should spill out into our private lives, enriching our private prayer, just as it should spill out into the world around us.

Christ has left us an example, a clear mandate, of public

prayer and worship as well as of private prayer. He often went to the Temple, the 'house of God' (Matthew 12:4) and 'my Father's house' (John 2:17), a holy place sanctified by God who dwelt in it (Matthew 23:17, 21), and he was inspired to cleanse it (Matthew 21:12). [At the same time, Jesus taught that he was greater than the Temple (Matthew 12:7) and foretold its destruction (Mark 13:2).] Jesus also attended the synagogue regularly for the sabbath service of prayer and scripture, sometimes reading and teaching there himself (Mark 6:2, Luke 4:16-30). The importance Christ attached to public worship and prayer is reflected clearly in the practice of the early Christians. There is much evidence of this in Acts, where we read that the early Church in Jerusalem was 'joined in continuous prayer' (Acts 1:13-14) and often assembled in private houses for communal prayer (Acts 12:12). The epistles and Revelation also have much to say about the essential place of prayer in the life of the Church.

The liturgical Church

Christians are characterised, then, by their commitment to personal and communal prayer. But more than this, Christ established a Church which is fundamentally a worshipping society. By his institution of the eucharist and of the sacraments, the Son has made the Church a distinctively liturgical Church. The Church has a mandate to offer the eucharist in constant thanksgiving and remembrance of his death and resurrection, united with the Son in offering Christ's unique sacrifice of himself on the cross to the Father in the Holy Spirit. Christ's commands 'Take this and eat . . . take this cup and drink . . . do this in remembrance of me' give the Church a way of life in which the liturgy is predominant, first in the Mass, secondly in the sacraments, and then by extension in the Church's Office and in the other rites.

Christ left us a second mandate which determines the

liturgical structure of his Church, that concerning baptism (Matthew 28:19). Baptism[1] is the means ordained by God by which we are reborn and incorporated into Christ to live by his Spirit. We are freed from slavery to original sin, and receive sanctifying grace by which we share through faith in the life of the Spirit. It is the first sacrament of initiation into the Church and it is the gateway to the other sacraments. We belong to a sacramental Church, therefore, and so important is this principle that the Second Vatican Council taught that the Church herself is a sacrament, 'a sign of intimate union with God and of the unity of all mankind' [CC (*Dogmatic Constitution on the Church*) 1].

Origins of the Liturgy of the Word

The first part of the Mass is now known as the Liturgy of the Word. Its origin is the sabbath synagogue service which, as we have already noted, Jesus and his followers attended regularly.

The origin of the synagogue is uncertain. It is generally thought to have originated during the Exile. Before the Babylonian captivity, the centre for worship was the Temple in Jerusalem. Worship at the Temple became impossible during the Exile and so the synagogue was instituted. It was a meeting house for worship, study and instruction, and government of the civil life of the community. It was governed by elders. The chief officer was the Ruler of the Synagogue, and it was his responsibility to see that the services were carried out in accordance with tradition.

The sabbath morning service was devoted to prayer and scriptural reading. It began with the 'Shema', the Jewish profession of faith: 'Hear, O Israel: The Lord our God is one Lord . . .', consisting of three sections (Deuteronomy 6:4-9, 11:13-21, Numbers 15:37-41). Then a long prayer was recited by one of the congregation. Originally this had been an improvised prayer; later it was given a set form, and included

Origins

the Eighteen Benedictions. Then came a reading from the Law (Torah), the first five books of the Bible, on a three year cycle. It was read in Hebrew and then translated or paraphrased in Aramaic, the vernacular language. The second reading was from the Prophets, and in the time of Christ the reader was able to choose the passage to read. This was followed by an improvised homily. The service concluded with prayers and a blessing.

A good understanding of this service can be obtained from Luke 4:16-21. Jesus attended the synagogue at Nazareth and was called to read from the Prophet. Visitors and well-known persons were often given such an invitation. He was handed the scroll of Isaiah and chose his text from ch. 61, vv.1-2. Then they all waited for him to speak on the text, but his words first astonished and then enraged them. We know that Jesus took the opportunity to teach in synagogues throughout Galilee (Matthew 4:23, Luke 13:10), in and around Capernaum (Matthew 9:35, 13:54, Mark 1:21, Luke 6:6). Paul also taught in synagogues whenever he could, for example in Damascus (Acts 9:20), Antioch (Acts 13:14f), Iconium (Acts 14:1), Thessalonika (Acts 17:1), Beroea (Acts 17:10), Athens (Acts 17:17), Corinth (Acts 18:4) and Ephesus (Acts 19:8).

The early Christians who were Jewish converts still regarded themselves as Jews and continued attending the synagogue. Sometimes they held services similar to that of the sabbath in their own houses as well. When they no longer went to the synagogues, and especially when they were forbidden to enter them, they held their own service of prayer and readings in private houses. Sometimes this service was followed by the Lord's Supper. The first part of the Mass can be traced back to the sabbath service in the synagogue, and the basic pattern we follow today in the Liturgy of the Word is recognisably similar to the Jewish service. In this way the Church continues the Jewish reverence for the word of God.

Origins of the Liturgy of the Eucharist

We trace our eucharistic celebration back to Our Lord's actions and mandate at the Last Supper. This celebration was at first known as 'the breaking of bread' (Luke 24:35, Acts 2:42). The name 'eucharist' only became general in the second century among Greek writers and was only adopted by Latin writers towards the end of the second century. The name 'Mass' was even later. It is said to be derived from 'Ite, missa est' (Go, it is the dismissal), 'missa' being a later form of 'missio'. The earliest known use of 'missa' to signify not simply the dismissal at the end of the eucharistic celebration but the entire celebration is found in the works of Ambrose (fourth century).

The earliest account we have of the eucharistic rite is in 1 Corinthians 11:23-26, written probably in the spring of 57, although some commentators date it a few years earlier. We may regard it as an authoritative account. Paul is trying to check irregularities in the way the Corinthians celebrated the eucharist, and he is careful to point out that the rite he describes is that handed on to him 'from the Lord'. It consisted of a repetition of all the actions carried out by Jesus at the Last Supper.

Taking together the gospel accounts of the Last Supper (Matthew 26:26-29, Mark 14:22-24, Luke 22:15-20) and Paul's account, we can summarise the rite as follows: the president (1) took bread, (2) thanked God for it, (3) broke it, (4) said the words of institution, and (5) gave out the bread to be eaten; (6) the main meal was then eaten; after which the president (7) took the cup of wine, (8) thanked God for it, (9) said the words of institution, and (10) gave the cup to be drunk. In addition there would be, either explicitly or implicitly, a recognition of (11) Christ's commands 'Take this and eat' and 'Take this and drink', and (12) the command 'Do this in memory of me'.

In memory of me ...

What was Our Lord commanding his followers to do? They were to celebrate this meal, in the way he had celebrated it, and to do so in memory of him. He did not specify how often or when they were to 'break bread'. However, he left his gift of the eucharist to us so that he would continue to be present in his Church after his ascension into heaven. In our 'remembrance' in the eucharist of his death and resurrection, we make the redemption of mankind an ever-present and on-going reality in the world and in our lives.[2] Paul told the Corinthians 'every time you eat this bread and drink this cup, you are proclaiming his death' (1 Corinthians 11:26). The early Christians 'proclaimed' both the cross and the empty tomb. They were particularly conscious of the power and significance of the resurrection, and it was the risen Christ they 'recognised' in the breaking of bread (cf. Luke 24:35).

The Last Supper and the Passover

What sort of meal was the Last Supper? Traditionally it has been regarded as a passover meal, and this is perhaps the most commonly accepted view today. The passover meal in the time of Jesus had the same main features as it has today, although it has been considerably enlarged over the centuries:[3]

1 *Preliminary.* The blessing was said over the first cup of wine, which was then drunk; a small dish of green vegetables was eaten; and the main meal (the paschal lamb with bitter herbs and unleavened bread) was placed on the table.

2 *The narrative.* The president explained the significance of the lamb, the bitter herbs, the unleavened bread, etc., and told the story of the passover events; Psalm 113 was sung and the second cup of wine was drunk.

3 *The main meal.* The president took the bread, said the blessing over it, broke it and distributed it; the main meal was eaten and wine drunk with it; after the main meal, the president sang the long blessing over the third cup of wine, which was then drunk.

4 *Conclusion.* Psalms 114-118 were sung, and the president sang the blessing over the fourth cup of wine, which was then drunk.

The passover meal should not be thought of as if it were a solemn church service. It is normally a friendly, jolly occasion celebrated as a family meal, even though at the Last Supper the disciples were, understandably, sad and apprehensive.

The main support for the view that the Last Supper was a passover meal is that Matthew, Mark and Luke quite specifically say that it was. Moreover, the preliminary rituals appear to be mentioned in Matthew 26:23 and Mark 14:20; all the synoptic gospels and I Corinthians 11 mention the main meal ('supper') with the bread blessing before it and the wine blessing after it; and Mark 14:26 records the 'hymn' (psalm) at the end. It is, perhaps, surprising that there is no mention whatever of either the narrative of the passover or of the eating of the paschal lamb, but perhaps these features were taken for granted by the evangelists.

Recent writers have found other grounds for supporting this view. Joachim Jeremias[4] cites, among other things, the time of day (i.e. evening), the reclining at table, the prominence given to the drinking of wine, and the fact that Jesus gave an explanation of the rites he performed over the bread and wine.

Louis Ligier[5] argues for it not only from the gospel evidence but even more strongly from the appropriateness of the blessing over the third cup of wine for Jesus' act of institution. He highlights certain important themes of the eucharistic liturgy, namely the divine presence, the sense of sacrifice ratified and accepted, and the *epiclesis* (invocation), and argues that these could only have been accommodated in the solemn blessing used for the third cup of wine at the passover meal.[6]

Other explanations of the Last Supper

There are possible arguments against identifying the Last Supper with a passover meal. For example, John 18:28 places the Last Supper on the day before passover eve. Secondly, Mark wrote his gospel during the late 60s, and it is possible that his account of the Last Supper is coloured by the way the eucharist was understood in his time, namely a sacrificial view which might have lent itself to interpreting the Last Supper in terms of a passover meal. Thirdly, it is remarkable that, if the Last Supper was distinctively a passover meal, the early Church ignored or forgot its passover character. It did not have an annual celebration of passover, instead it held the breaking of bread frequently. Moreover, it dropped most of the passover rituals from the eucharist, leaving those elements thought to have derived from the blessings, namely the prayers of memorial and thanksgiving, in which was located the institution rite.

Alternative views have been proposed in the past. The Last Supper might have been a religious meal, with the customary blessings of food, held as an anticipation of the passover. Or, less likely, that Christ's blessing of the cup at the Last Supper was the Kiddush of the passover. The Kiddush is primarily the rite of sanctification of the sabbath: the household assembled for the evening meal on Friday afternoon, and at the beginning of sabbath the head said over a cup of wine and water the 'kiddush' or blessing of the day. A similar rite was observed on the eves of feasts. In support of this view, it is claimed that some of the early eucharistic prayers have phrases reminiscent of the kiddush. Linked with this theory is the suggestion that the Last Supper was a '*chaburah*' meal. A *chaburah* was a group of friends formed for religious purposes, but also serving social purposes. They held a weekly meal. If the Last Supper was a *chaburah* meal, assuming that Christ and his disciples had constituted themselves as a *chaburah* , then the blessing of the cup was either the kiddush (which *chaburoth* may have observed) or simply the usual blessings of bread and wine said at special meals.

The significance of the Last Supper

Whether the Last Supper was a passover meal or a *chaburah* meal, the early Church certainly did not follow the specific ritual of the passover seder in their celebration of the eucharist. The seder was too long and too complicated for frequent use. Many of its minor rituals were irrelevant to the Christian celebration of the breaking of the bread. In any case, it was against Jewish law to use the passover ritual except at the passover itself. But for a few decades the early Christians continued to celebrate the breaking of bread at an actual meal, with the blessing over the bread taking place before the main meal and that over the cup after it, as in the passover meal: for this we have the evidence of 1 Corinthians 11:23-26 written in the 50s and Luke 22:15-20 written about 85.

What is important is, firstly, that the Last Supper, whatever sort of meal it was, took place near and in the context of the passover, and that the paschal significance of the meal, though perhaps not fully understood by the disciples at the time, is unmistakable. Christ gave himself to his followers at the meal and on the cross in the new passover: 'Christ, our passover, has been sacrificed', Paul reminded the Corinthians twenty years later (1 Corinthians 5:7). Christ himself referred to the cup as 'my blood of the covenant' (Matthew 26:28, Mark 14:24), 'the new covenant in my blood' (Luke 22:20, cf. 1 Corinthians 11:25). Catholics see the Mass in terms of sacrifice and of oblation and this significance is traced back to the Last Supper.

Jewish blessings

Secondly, the Last Supper was an important meal and therefore included solemn blessings associated with the taking of bread at the beginning of the main meal and the taking of the cup at the conclusion. Such blessings were, and still are today, significant features of a Jewish meal. These blessings are not to be confused with modern blessings, such as the blessing of a rosary. In a Jewish blessing, it is God who is blessed, i.e. praised and thanked, for something. The blessing consists of the following elements: (1) the proclamation of the blessing, normally using the words 'Blessed are you, ...' which are followed by an ascription such as 'King of the Universe'; sometimes the words 'thanks' and 'praise' are specifically included here, but they are in any case implicit in the blessing; (2) a statement of what God is being blessed for, with an implication of making a remembrance also; (3) a petition, explicit or implicit, connected with what we are thanking God for, such as a prayer for the continuation of God's gift or for the grace it bestows.

There are numerous examples of these blessings throughout the scriptures and in Jewish prayer books, and this distinctive type of blessing is one of the many things we have inherited from the Jews. An outstanding example of these blessings is to be found during the Preparation of the Gifts at Mass, recited as the priest takes up the bread and wine:

Blessed are you, Lord, God of all creation.
Through your goodness we have this bread to offer,
which earth has given and human hands have made.
It will become for us the bread of life.

Blessed are you, Lord, God of all creation.
Through your goodness we have this wine to offer,
fruit of the vine and work of human hands.
It will become our spiritual drink.

We do not know the exact words which Our Lord used for the blessings at the Last Supper. To judge from later passover texts which are available to us, the blessing associated with the bread would probably have been similar to this:

Blessed are you, Lord our God, King of the Universe, who bring forth bread from the earth.

This is, however, a simple blessing or eulogy: it is known as the *birkat ha-mozi*. It is more likely that our eucharistic thanksgiving is derived ultimately from the blessing associated with the third cup of wine at the passover meal. This (the *birkat ha-mazon*) is a solemn and more elaborate blessing. In Our Lord's time it consisted of three parts (a fourth was added after the fall of Jerusalem in AD 40), and was similar to this:

1 Blessing of him who nourishes:

   Blessed are you, Lord our God, King of the Universe, who nourish us and the whole world with goodness, grace, kindness and mercy.

2 Blessing for the earth:

   We will give thanks to you, Lord our God, for having caused us to inherit the desirable, good and ample land, and the covenant, the law, life and food.

3 Blessing for Jerusalem:

   Lord our God, have compassion on your people Israel, on Jerusalem your city, on your sanctuary and the place where you dwell, on Zion the seat of your glory, and on the great and holy house which is called by your name. Restore the kingdom of David's house in our days and speedily build the holy city Jerusalem.

Origins

Then would follow:

Blessed are you, Lord our God, King of the Universe, creator of the fruit of the vine.

One can imagine Our Lord at the Last Supper adding some actions and words of his own. Instead of joining with the others in eating the bread, he commanded them to pass it round and eat from it, declaring that it was his body; and similarly with the cup of wine. One can also imagine the early Christian communities gathered together for the Lord's Supper using blessings similar to those quoted above, perhaps simplifying the Jewish references and inserting thanksgiving statements about Christ's resurrection and the new dispensation. A link between the bread nourished by the earth and the body of Christ which provides our spiritual nourishment is not difficult to postulate. Even more significant would be links between the Old and the New Jerusalem (the Church), the Old and the New Dispensation, and David (a 'type' of the Redeemer) and Jesus.

The possibility that our eucharistic prayer is developed ultimately from the Jewish meal blessings, and more specifically from the passover blessings over the third cup of wine, is very strong and is now widely accepted among liturgical scholars. The thanksgiving and remembrance themes of the *birkat ha-mazon* would have lent themselves most aptly to the Christian prayer of thanksgiving and remembrance. Ligier, as we have noted, worked in the opposite direction from the established eucharistic prayer back to possible sources, and argued that certain themes, such as the divine presence, sacrifice, and invocation of the Spirit, could only have been inaugurated in the context of the elaborate *birkat ha-mazon* and not in any other Jewish blessing.

Notes

1. Here and in other places I am indebted to the phraseology of Herbert McCabe's *The Teaching of the Catholic Church: A New Catechism*, (London: CTS, 1985)

2. This is discussed more fully in the chapter dealing with the Liturgy of the Eucharist.

3. There are numerous editions available today of the passover seder. The following are complete Hebrew-English versions and contain commentaries: Cecil Roth (ed), *The Haggadah* (London: The Socino Press, 1975); Nahum N. Glatzer (ed), *The Passover Haggadah* (NY: Schocken Books, 1979).
'Seder' is the name for the whole service, 'Haggadah' is the narrative of the passover events, but is customarily used to denote the whole celebration.

4. Joachim Jeremias, *The Eucharistic Words of Jesus* (London: SCM, 1966), ch. 1.

5. Louis Ligier, "From the Last Supper to the Eucharist", in *The New Liturgy* ed. Lancelot Sheppard (London: Darton, Longman and Todd, 1970), pp. 113-150.

6. There is a considerable literature on this subject. Two other articles can be recommended: Thomas Tally, "From 'Berakah' to 'Eucharistia': a Re-opening Question", *Worship* 50 (1976), pp. 115-137; and Raymond Moloney, "The Early Eucharist: The Jewish Background", *Milltown Studies No. 2* (Spring 1978), pp. 1-10.

2

The Eucharist During the First Three Centuries

Our knowledge of the eucharist in the first three centuries is necessarily rather sketchy, and it is only by piecing together the available evidence, much of it indirect and limited, that we can produce an outline of its development in the pre-Nicene church.

New Testament times

The primitive Church was Jewish in character and tradition. The early followers of Christ did not abandon Judaism. They regarded themselves as Jews and continued to practise as Jews. The teaching of Jesus was seen as a development of the Jewish dispensation, and the Christians remained an integral part of Jewry. Outsiders naturally saw them as a Jewish sect.

It is clear from Luke 24:53 and Acts 2:46, 3:1 that the early

Christians in Jerusalem continued to attend the services in the Temple, often daily. According to Acts 5:20-21, 42 the apostles taught in the Temple, and also in private houses. Paul and Barnabas frequently taught in the synagogues on their missionary journeys.

Passages such as Acts 13:14 suggest that the apostles and the other teachers went regularly to synagogues as a matter of observance as well as for the opportunities offered for preaching the Good News. Doubtless all the early Jewish Christians continued to attend the synagogue also, especially for the sabbath service.

Acts 2:42-47 gives a succinct account of the life of the early Christian community in Jerusalem. They were assiduous in communal prayer and 'met in their houses for the breaking of bread'. Before long they were less and less welcome in the synagogues. Paul's attack on the Law of Moses and his advocacy of faith in a crucified Messiah was a threat to Jewish belief and to Jewish identity. The admission of gentiles to what had begun as a Jewish sect aroused hostility and violence, which reached its culmination at the destruction of the Temple in AD70. Christians, both Jews and gentiles, were barred from the synagogues, and they therefore held meetings for prayer and readings in their own houses, often following this with the breaking of bread.

In the first century the eucharist was celebrated in 'house churches' (1 Corinthians 16:15; Romans 16:5; Philemon v.2; Colossians 4:15). The house of a well-to-do person was particularly suitable for this purpose. The *triclinium* (dining room) was presumably used in the earlier period when the eucharist was still celebrated as part of a meal. When, as we shall see later, the meal was discontinued, the *atrium* (central courtyard) might have been used for the people to stand in while the presbyter presided from a chair and table in the *tablinum* (study).

The New Testament writings provide only the scantiest information about these early eucharistic celebrations.

The Eucharist during the First Three Centuries

However, a detailed account of the rite cannot be expected, for it was not the intention of any of the New Testament authors to provide information of this sort for the benefit of outsiders and certainly not for twentieth century students of liturgy. For several centuries a full knowledge of the Christian mysteries was denied to pagans and even, as we shall see, to catechumens.

The valuable element for our purpose in the New Testament writings is what is implicit in them concerning the central points of Christian life and belief and the new concept of worship characteristic of Christianity. The breaking of bread was a centre of unity for the earliest Christians: as Paul reminded the Corinthians, 'the fact that there is only one loaf means that, though there are many of us, we form a single body' (1 Corinthians 10:17). Great importance was attached to communal worship, for which there would be regular assemblies, often in the face of hostility or even persecution.

While the Jewish converts continued to observe Saturday as the sabbath, all Christians observed Sunday as the Lord's Day, the first day of the week. Each Sunday was another Easter and thus a constant commemoration of the Resurrection. On the Lord's Day the people assembled with their presbyter for the breaking of bread. Easter Day was of supreme importance in the early Church. It could be argued that the chief contribution of the New Testament writings to an understanding of the early liturgy is their rich and varied exposition of the meaning of Easter. The eucharist cannot be understood except in a paschal context, that is in the context of the resurrection, which was a recent event to the early Christians. The eucharist consists of thanksgiving for what Christ had effected through his resurrection. This theological underpinning of the eucharistic liturgy is to be found particularly in the writings of John and Paul. According to Oscar Cullman the Book of Revelation is 'full of allusions to the liturgical usages of the early community'.[1] He also argues that John's first Letter can only be understood in terms of its liturgical interest and that in his gospel John 'regards it as one of his chief concerns to set forth the connection between the contemporary Christian worship and the historical life of Jesus'.[2]

It is tempting to think that John's account of the Last Supper, and in particular the High Priestly prayer, embodies an early eucharistic prayer, but it is difficult to be certain about this. Paul provides much information about the eucharistic beliefs and practice of the early Church, especially in 1 Corinthians 10 and 11. He also gives us many examples of greetings, doxologies, hymns and blessings, some of which may have been used at the breaking of bread as well as at prayer meetings.[3] 1 Corinthians 11 confirms that the eucharist took place, at least for a few decades, at an actual meal. The early Christians saw themselves as carrying out Christ's command by meeting for the breaking of bread in a manner reminiscent of the Last Supper. They met together in fellowship, bound by a common heritage of baptism and discipleship of the risen Lord.

They would not have used the actual ritual of the passover meal, because it was too complicated for frequent use and in any case it was against Jewish law to use the rite except at the passover itself. In the celebration of the eucharist, there was a blessing at the taking of bread before the main meal, and this was expanded to include the act of institution. Then would follow the meal. When it was finished there was a blessing at the drinking of the cup of wine, expanded to include the act of institution. The general pattern of the whole occasion would have resembled the *chaburah* meal rather than the passover meal, but at either or both of the blessings there would have been fuller thanksgiving statements concerning the paschal mystery. In this respect the eucharist derived its character from the *berakah* (solemn blessing) of the passover meal.

The abandonment of the meal

The accounts of the Last Supper in Luke 22:15-20 and 1 Corinthians 11:23-26 make reference to the main meal: the blessing of the wine takes place 'after supper', an expression which is missing in Mark 14:22-25 and Matthew 26:26-29. This might be evidence that it was during the fifties and early sixties of the first century that the actual meal was discontinued.[4] With the disappearance of the meal, the two 'consecrations' remained and were brought together into one sequence. The celebration of the eucharist then began to lose its outward appearance of being a meal, appearing more like a service. Instead of being simply picked up by the celebrant, the bread and wine were then placed on the celebrant's table, which marked the beginning of the so-called 'offertory'. The time previously taken up by the meal was gradually used for an enriched and expanded prayer of thanksgiving.

There were a number of reasons why the meal was abandoned. As Christian communities grew in size, it became increasingly impractical and difficult to organise every Sunday. Another factor militating against the meal was the change from evening to morning celebrations to avoid notice in times of hostility and persecution. A third factor was the growth of abuses, at least in Corinth, where people formed cliques, ate their own food instead of sharing it, talked too freely, took no notice of the presbyter when he began the eucharist, and sometimes even became drunk. When it ceased to be part of an actual supper, the eucharist developed into an assembly. The people no longer sat or reclined but stood in worship. There was then only a single table, the presbyter's, which became a focus of attention in the way the altar is today.

The typical meeting place was no longer a medium sized dining room but a hall or *atrium* big enough to accommodate a large congregation ranged in front of the 'Lord's Table'. The names 'breaking of bread' and 'the Lord's meal' gradually went out of use, while the term *eucharistia* (thanksgiving), brought in as the Greek version of *berakah* (solemn blessing), now became the name for the entire celebration. It was a common practice for consecrated bread to be taken away for the sick and for others absent from the eucharist, and also for consumption on the following days when there was no celebration of the eucharist. In addition to the communal celebration on Sunday, there were also private celebrations in family homes on particular occasions, in which case the practice of having an actual meal was probably retained after it had been abandoned for the Sunday celebration.

The Didache
One of the earliest non-biblical sources concerning the eucharist is *The Teaching of the Twelve Apostles* or, as it is usually known, the *Didache*. This document was rediscovered in 1873, but its date and origin are still unsettled. The exact nature of the document is also a matter of discussion. It may be a genuine Church Order issued in the latter part of the first century, but it could also be a later compilation making disputable claims to apostolic authority. What is interesting about the document is the meal ceremony described in chapters 9 and 10, which was probably a eucharist but may have been an *agape*. There are no words of institution, but an elaborate thanksgiving which bears a strong resemblance to Jewish *berakoth*.[5]

The second century
In the second century, *eucharistia* was commonly used by Greek writers as the name of the celebration, and by the end of the century Latin writers had adopted the same name. The separate blessings associated with the bread and the cup were now merged into a single prayer of thanksgiving. This was an extempore prayer composed by the presbyter, but there was a fixed theme which had to be observed, namely thanksgiving for man's creation and redemption, with particular reference to the death and resurrection of Christ,

of which the eucharist was a remembrance. From the second century we have two very significant texts which help us to understand how the eucharist was celebrated at that time.

Justin Martyr

Justin was a Syrian by birth, became a Christian in about 130, later moved to Rome and there wrote his book the *First Apology* (in defence of the Christians) in about 150. Chapters 65-67 of the latter contain two accounts of the eucharist.[6] The first (in chapter 65) is a baptismal celebration, in which the eucharist immediately follows the rite of baptism. The rite begins with the prayers of the community, the kiss of peace, and the bringing of the gifts (bread, water, wine mixed with water) to the president. The president 'takes them', 'offers praise and glory to the Father', 'gives thanks at some length' and at the conclusion the people 'give their assent by saying Amen'. The deacons then distribute the 'bread and wine over which thanks have been given' to the people. It is interesting to note the extempore eucharistic prayer, the emphasis on giving thanks, and the description of the consecrated elements as having been blessed by the giving of thanks, i.e. by a *berakah* type of blessing.

Chapter 66 contains a number of interesting references. The food is called *eucharistia* (thanksgiving), and is only to be given to one who has been baptised and who believes in the institution by Jesus Christ, namely that 'the food over which thanks have been given ... is both the flesh and blood of the incarnate Jesus.' Justin goes on to explain that this has been handed down from the apostles, and records that a similar ceremony has been imitated in the mysteries of Mithras: hence the strict supervision of those who are admitted to the eucharist.

In chapter 67 Justin describes a normal Sunday celebration. From this we learn that the service of readings is now regularly prefixed to the eucharist (unless it is replaced by a rite such as baptism). The 'records of the apostles or writings of the prophets are read for as long as time allows' and then the president gives a discourse on the readings. After intercessory prayers have been offered, the gifts are brought up and 'the president offers prayers and thanksgiving to the best of his ability'. The people assent with 'Amen', and the 'distribution' follows in which 'everyone participates in (the elements) over which thanks have been given'. The rite is still simple and unelaborated. There were apparently no prayers at the taking up of the bread and wine or in the preparation for the distribution. These are two areas of the Mass where the reforms of the Second Vatican Council, while not removing altogether prayers said during these two periods, have in our own time restored a certain degree of simplicity. Finally, the *First Apology* makes it clear that the eucharist was seen at that time as sacrificial and as a remembrance of the resurrection. The chapter finishes with a statement of the significance of Sunday.

Hippolytus

The third century has left us with the oldest extant text of a complete *anaphora* (or eucharistic prayer). This occurs in chapter 4 of *The Apostolic Tradition* supposedly written by Hippolytus in 215. This Hippolytus (there were others of this name) was a priest active in Rome during the early third century who was martyred with Pope Pontianus after 235 (feast: 13 August). The book was written to safeguard the tradition as handed down from apostolic times. In chapter 4 there is a description of an ordination Mass (to use modern terminology) in which a candidate has received bishop's orders.[7]

There is a complete text of an *anaphora*, and this with some amendment is now used today as Eucharistic Prayer II. Although it is a complete text, it must not be regarded as definitive for its time. In the third century the prayer was still extempore. It became a common practice for priests and bishops to write down a number of models for their own use. This is one which by chance has survived. Its adoption in the 1970 Roman Missal is a testimony to the excellence and simplicity of this model.

This text gives a clear and detailed indication of what were considered essential elements in a eucharistic prayer in the late second and early third centuries. The gifts (bread and wine) were brought to the altar by the deacons: no prayers were said at this stage. The bishop and the concelebrants extended their hands over the gifts and commenced the eucharistic prayer. This started with the introductory dialogue which is almost indentical with that still in use today. Then followed six parts as in the 'newer' eucharistic prayers of the 1970 Missal: thanksgiving statements, the institution narrative, a simple *anamnesis* (remembrance) and oblation (offering), an *epiclesis* (invocation of the Holy Spirit) asking for the gifts of the eucharist (specified as unity and faith)[8], and a final doxology with the people's Amen.

The eucharist was still celebrated with simplicity in the third century, even though the meal had been discontinued and there was an assembly rather than a domestic celebration. Some of the homely touches of a *chaburah* meal were retained, such as the spreading of the cloth on the table before the taking up of the gifts and the cleansing of the vessels before the dismissal. The only prayer (apart from the common prayers following the homily) was the *anaphora* itself, and this great thanksgiving prayer had not yet been broken up with the insertion of the *sanctus* and the intercessions for the living and the dead. The pristine simplicity of the early eucharistic prayer had not been spoiled by devotional or ceremonial accretions. There was a note of spontaneity as each presbyter prayed the thanksgiving extempore. While a basic framework was followed everywhere, there were obviously considerable variations in practice between different provinces and even between neighbouring communities. One is tempted to describe the third century eucharist as a 'living liturgy'. Whether or not this description is justified, it is surely indisputable that in order to understand our liturgy today we have to look at the practice of the early Church.

Notes

1 Oscar Cullman, *Early Christian Worship* (London: SCM, 1969), p. 7.

2 *Ibid.*, p. 37.

3 Some of these have been brought into use in the revised liturgy: e.g. the greetings at the beginning of Mass, the blessings at the end of Mass, and the canticles at Evening Prayer.

4 It is interesting also to consider the words used by the evangelists and Paul for 'blessing'. Mark and Matthew have *eulogesas* for 'he blessed' the bread. This reflects the *eulogia*, the simple blessing, recited over the bread at passover. They have *eucharistesas* for 'he gave thanks' over the cup: this reflects the more solemn blessing (*berakah*) recited over the third cup of wine at the passover meal. Mark wrote his gospel in about 65 and Matthew in 85-90. Luke and Paul use *eucharistesas*, that is, the solemn 'giving thanks', for both the bread and the wine. Luke, writing in about 85, might be reflecting the change in the ritual words since the time of Mark; but it is puzzling why Paul, writing to the Christians of Corinth in the fifties, should do this.

5. The text of chs. 9 and 10 is given in R.C.D. Jasper and G.J. Cuming, *Prayers of the Eucharist: Early and Reformed* (New York: Pueblo, 1987) pp. 23-24.

6 *Ibid.*, pp. 28-30 for the text of chs.65-67.

7 *Ibid.*, pp. 34-38, for extracts, including the eucharistic prayer in ch. 4. For a translation of the complete text see *Hippolytus: A Text for Students* tr. and ed. G.J. Cuming (Grove Liturgical Study No. 8) (Grove Books, 1976). See also *Essays on Hippolytus* ed. G.J. Cuming (Grove Liturgical Study No. 15) (Grove Books, 1978).

8 In the modern Eucharistic Prayer II, a 'consecratory' *epiclesis* has been inserted before the institution narrative.

3

Initiation in the Early Church

Institution by Jesus Christ

John the Baptist prepared the way for the institution of baptism by Our Lord. John's baptism can be regarded as an adaptation of Jewish ritual washing, influenced in particular by Qumran purification rites. He made it clear that his baptism was of a limited and preparatory nature: 'I baptise you in water for repentance, but the one who follows me is more powerful than I am: ... he will baptise you with the Holy Spirit and fire' (Matthew 3:11; cf Mark 1:8, Luke 3:16). 'It was to reveal him to Israel that I came baptising with water; ... he who sent me to baptise with water had said to me, "The man on whom you see the Spirit come down and rest is the one who is going to baptise with the Holy Spirit" ' (John 1:31-33).

John's baptism, then, was for repentance and forgiveness

of sins (Mark 1:4-5) and to prepare the way firstly for the revelation of Christ at his baptism by John[1] and secondly for the fullness of baptism as instituted by Our Lord. The baptism which Jesus Christ enjoined upon his followers entailed nothing less than total rebirth into new life by the infusion of the Holy Spirit. To be saved, man must believe and be baptised (Mark 16:16), and the baptism must be in water and the Spirit. 'Unless a man is born through water and the Spirit,' Jesus told Nicodemus, 'he cannot enter the kingdom of heaven' (John 3:5).

The relationship between baptism and the death and resurrection of Jesus was readily grasped by the early Christians. Paul taught it explicitly in his account of salvation (Romans 5 and 6; cf. Colossians 2:9-15, 3:11). Christ died to forgive sins; in baptism sins are forgiven, so in baptism we die to sin, we are 'baptised in his death' (Romans 6:3; cf. 2 Timothy 2:11). Just as Christ rose from the dead, in baptism we rise to new life in Christ . 'It is by faith and through Jesus that we have entered this state of grace' (Romans 5:2). Peter also taught this (1 Peter 3:18-22).

Baptism is necessary to salvation. Jesus commanded his followers not only to teach all men, but to baptise them (Matthew 28:19). The words 'in the name of the Father and of the Son and of the Holy Spirit' may be an amplification of Christ's mandate, reflecting the actual formula used in the baptismal rite at the time Matthew wrote his gospel (around the year 80) and anticipating a later, more explicit, conceptualisation of the Trinity. Baptism is taking on new life in Christ, a true initiation (cf. Galatians 3:27), and therefore there was an emphasis on being baptised in the name of Christ. Peter proclaimed this on the day of Pentecost (Acts 2:38) and repeated it in the house of Cornelius (Acts 10:48). Philip and Paul also emphasised it in their teaching on various occasions (Acts 8:12, 19:5, 22:16). Some commentators have concluded that in apostolic times there was a baptismal formula specifying only 'Jesus' or 'Christ';

others have argued that baptism in the name of Jesus only refers to the mandate and power of Christ, not to the formula used. It was probably the case that for a century or more there was some variation in the ritual wording used, but the intention to baptise in accordance with Our Lord's institution was always embodied in the administration.

The laying on of hands and anointing
The New Testament books do not provide us with definitive accounts of the rite of baptism in the first century. As with the eucharist, the details have to be carefully deduced from the references made to baptism in other contexts. It seems quite clear that in every baptism by water in the New Testament administered under Christ's institution the Holy Spirit was given, and it is this which distinguishes Christ's baptism from John's. The action of the Spirit is integral to baptism. What, then, are we to make of the two cases in Acts (8:17,18, 19:7) when the Spirit was imposed separately, after baptism by water, and by the imposition of hands?

The separate infusion of the Spirit is to be explained by the exceptional nature of the two cases. It would seem that the Samaritan believers had not received the fullness of baptism. This may have been because of the separatist Jehovistic worship which the Samaritans had maintained for centuries, and the possibility that they may have wished to carry the schism over to the Church; or perhaps because of their connection with Simon the Magician. Peter and John discerned that they had not received the Spirit, and laid hands upon them.[2] In the case of the disciples at Ephesus, the explanation is easier to establish: they had specifically received only John's baptism.

An even more obvious example of exceptional circumstances is the baptism of the first pagans at Caesarea recorded in Acts 10. These pagans received the Spirit before baptism, but this lends no support to the view that the bestowal of the Spirit is separable from normal baptism. It is important not to 'read back' from later liturgical practice, even that of the second or third century, to that of the first. There is no evidence that the laying on of hands to bestow the Spirit originated in the first century. The Spirit was bestowed then as now in baptism by water.

Similarly the practice of anointing with oil in connection with the bestowal of the Spirit did not originate in apostolic times. There are two New Testament references to anointing in connection with the Spirit (2 Corinthians 1:21, 1 John 2:20, 27), but they are almost certainly to be taken figuratively and without reference to baptism. Unction was a common practice in connection with bathing in the Roman Empire and beyond, and it would not be remarkable to find it used without any spiritual significance after baptismal immersion.

The references to 'being sealed' in the Holy Spirit in Ephesians 1:13 and 4:30 likewise have no connection with the 'sealing' which later formed part of the baptismal rite.

The Didache

The earliest post-biblical source concerning baptism in the early Church is the *Didache*, which, as we saw in Chapter Two, may have been written around 100. Chapter 7 of the *Didache* deals very briefly with baptism. The baptiser and the candidate had to fast for one or two days before the ceremony. The latter began with a recital of the moral and spiritual precepts given in the previous chapters of the *Didache* concerning the Way of Life and the Way of Death. Then the candidate had to be baptised in running water using the Trinitarian formula. If running water was not available, then water had to be poured thrice upon the head.

Justin Martyr's Apology

We have already noted the value of this work, written in about 150, concerning the early eucharist. Justin described the nature and rite of baptism in chapter 61 and a baptismal eucharist in chapter 65. This is the earliest detailed description of the second century rite which is available to us. Justin described baptism as a rebirth and an enlightenment. It conferred forgiveness of past sins and the promise of eternal salvation if the candidate persevered in goodness.

After fasting, repentance and prayer, the candidate was bathed while someone named over him the persons of the Trinity, which may have been a form of credal questioning since attributes were added to each person of the Trinity. Having given his assent to being baptised, the candidate was introduced into the assembled community, prayers were said and the kiss of peace was given. The eucharist then followed immediately.

Tertullian

Tertullian (c.160-c.220) was born in Carthage and joined the Church there in 195 or 196. He wrote many works, including a treatise *On Baptism*. His account is of a much fuller rite than that described in the *Didache* and in Justin's *Apology*. After preparatory fasting, prayer and confession of sins, there is a triple baptismal immersion with a threefold act of faith. Then follows an anointing, a signing with the cross and an imposition of hands to confer the Spirit. In the eucharist which follows, a drink of milk and honey is given[3], possibly signifying the Promised Land which the candidate had attained by baptism, but possibly being a relic of the actual meal which had formerly formed part of the eucharistic celebration.

Tertullian is the first author to mention an anointing, a signing, and the bestowal of the Holy Spirit by imposition of hands. In another work[4], he described baptism in terms of a fivefold action:

> 'The flesh is washed that the soul may be spotless: the flesh is anointed that the soul may be consecrated: the flesh is signed that the soul too may be protected: the flesh

is overshadowed by the imposition of hands that the soul also may be illumined by the Spirit: the flesh feeds on the Body and Blood of Christ so that the soul as well may be replete with God.'

Hippolytus

Hippolytus' account of baptism in his book *The Apostolic Tradition* written about 215 may be taken as a basis for reconstructing the general practice in Rome and much of the western Church in the third and fourth centuries. The liturgical norm was for adult baptism and no adaptation for infant reception was made in the rite for centuries. However, we know from Hippolytus and from other evidence that both infants and adults were admitted to the sacrament. Tertullian had made some strong objections to infant baptism[5], from which we may infer that it was a common practice. Hippolytus enjoined the parents to answer the credal questions on behalf of an infant. Certain classes of persons were to be debarred from baptism. Adults had to undergo a three year catechumenate. This was not only a period of careful preparation, both catechetically and spiritually, but also a period in which the mysteries of the faith, normally kept strictly secret from outsiders, were gradually revealed to the catechumens.

The rite began early on Easter Day with the Easter Vigil of readings and prayers. At cockcrow the bishop prayed over the water, which was to be pure and flowing. The candidates took off their clothes. Little children were to be baptised first, then the men, and finally the women, who were to loosen their hair and remove all gold ornaments. No one was to go down to the font* with any alien object.

> [* 'Font' is to be understood as something like a tank in size (one of the manuscripts of Hippolytus uses the Greek word *kolumbethra* = swimming bath, tank), usually arranged so that the candidates went down into the water to be immersed and climbed up on the opposite side. This was to preserve the symbolism of dying

to sin and rising to new life as Christ died and rose from the dead, and of going down into the tomb with Christ and rising again with him (cf. Romans 6:3-4).]

After the candidates had undressed, the bishop proceeded to bless ('gave thanks over') the Oil of Exorcism and the Oil of Thanksgiving, and gave them to the deacons standing on either side of him. The candidates then renounced Satan and were anointed with the Oil of Exorcism, probably as a sealing of the renunciation. The candidates went down individually for the immersion accompanied by a deacon. The baptism was then performed by a priest, who put the triple credal questioning, and then dipped the candidate into the water three times, once after each section of the questions. This credal questioning was the origin of our creeds. After the threefold baptism the priest anointed the candidate in the name of Jesus Christ with the Oil of Thanksgiving, probably over the entire body. The candidate got dressed and rejoined the assembly.

When all the candidates had been baptised in the water individually, they presented themselves as a group to the presiding bishop who laid his hands on them and invoked over them the Holy Spirit. He then anointed each of the newly baptised individually by pouring the Oil of Thanksgiving on the head and performing the laying on of hands. After sealing the newly baptised person on the forehead, presumably with the sign of the cross and oil, he gave to each the sign of peace. Then came the kiss of peace and the eucharistic prayer was begun, as described in the previous chapter.

Baptism in the third century

From this account by Hippolytus we can note certain important features about the developed rite of the third century. First of all, there was a unity about the rite of initiation which was later to be lost in the western Church. The immersion (or affusion), the laying on of hands and anointing, and the eucharist were a single initiating rite, and commonly referred to (for example by Tertullian) in its totality as 'baptism'. Each of the three sequential elements, including the first participation in the eucharist and the first reception of holy communion, was regarded as initiatory.

Secondly, there is a great significance liturgically in the pattern of the rite. In the early Church the bishop normally presided over liturgical celebrations. He was *the* priest of the diocese, so to speak: in him resided the fullness of priesthood. When the eucharist was celebrated, he presided as the celebrant, accompanied by presbyters and deacons, each with their own functions. Most of the local community attended this celebration. Only as dioceses became larger was it necessary to have other churches some distance away with a local priest celebrating the eucharist. In principle the bishop's eucharist was the main celebration: priests in outlying districts were seen, to some extent, as deputising for the bishop. This principle can be discerned today in the Chrism Mass on Holy Thursday. In the same way, baptism was a corporate rite, presided over by the bishop who blessed the oils, performed the laying on of hands, and was the chief concelebrant at the eucharist. He was assisted by presbyters, who performed the baptismal immersion at the font, and by the deacons. The rite could only be conducted in its entirety if the bishop was present. In cases of emergency only the baptism by water was carried out by a priest.

The third feature to be noted is the community aspect of the rite. Baptisms today are still often completely private functions carried out in an almost empty church. In the early centuries initiation was a function of the whole worshipping community. The faithful assembled to support and receive the new members, and this unitive aspect of the rite was brought to completion by the celebration of the eucharist, which itself is a centre of unity for Christians. One can amplify this by saying that the rite of initiation was recognised as a liturgical action, not a private conferring of a sacrament.

We are trying today to regain a sense of the community and liturgical aspects of initiation by encouraging the holding of baptisms at main gatherings of the faithful, especially at the Easter Vigil, otherwise at a Mass on a Sunday or great feast. Programmes of preparation for baptism are designed to involve the local Christian community as much as possible. The RCIA (Rite of Christian Initiation of Adults) also locates the baptism of adults in its community and liturgical setting, and it should be noted that in the initiation of an unbaptised adult today the original unitary sequence of water baptism, bestowal of the Holy Spirit, and first communion has been restored.

The catechumenate

In the early Church great care was taken in admitting new members. Christian communities were often illegal or at least regarded with suspicion and disfavour. At certain periods there was persecution. Spies and informers had to be excluded. Harlots, magicians, and certain undesirable occupations also had to be kept out. The sincerity of new members was of the greatest importance: they had to have the gift of faith, show themselves responsible and steadfast, and be well instructed. Their spiritual formation and preparation was as important as their catechesis. They had to cast off all attachment to pagan religion, to purify themselves, and in some cases to dissociate themselves from the influence of evil spirits. Finally it was necessary to ensure that the mysteries of the Christian faith were kept completely secret from outsiders, both to preserve their sacred character and to avoid attention from unfriendly authorities.

These objectives were met by the catechumenate, which in addition was based on sound teaching and developmental principles. This can be seen especially in its insistence on progressive learning and development, and on the growth of learning with understanding and commitment. This development took place in phased and meaningful stages, each leading to a sense of attainment. The completion of each stage was marked by a communal liturgical rite and the admission of the prospective new Christians into a new category.

To become a Christian at this time was an intense experience of conversion and enlightenment. At its best it constituted a total change in one's life, and the notion of regeneration was taken seriously. The gradual revelation of the Christian mysteries and the gradual initiation into Christian practices played an important part in rendering this a profound experience, as did the scrutinies, exorcisms, washings, renunciations and other awe-inspiring rites.

The catechumenate was a system of organising the preparation of adults for baptism which emerged in the second century, and reached its most extensive form in the third, fourth and fifth centuries, but began to decline in the different conditions which existed after the Peace of the Church. Brief allusions to early forms of the catechumenate are to be found in the *Didache*, in Justin Martyr's *Apology*, and in the writings of Tertullian.

The first fuller account is given by Hippolytus. In *The Apostolic Tradition* the catechumenate was in two phases. There was a lengthy training in doctrine and morals lasting three years, followed by a brief period of intensive preparation before the baptism at Easter. During the latter period, the candidates received exorcism every day, they fasted on the two days before Easter, and observed the Easter Vigil. The catechumenate was the chief factor in the development of the season of Lent as we know it.

Much more information is available from the fourth century. The catecheses of Ambrose in Milan and Augustine in Hippo are useful sources. A particularly rich source is the catechetical instructions of Cyril of Jerusalem, eighteen of which were to be given during Lent to the candidates for baptism and five during the period after Easter to the newly baptised. Egeria, a Spanish nun who made a pilgrimage to

Jerusalem in the 380s, recorded in considerable detail the developed catechumenate system she found there. It would seem that the text of Cyril's catechetical talks was still in use when she arrived in Jerusalem, some forty years after they were first given by Cyril, so her evidence fits in well with that derived from Cyril's catecheses. John Chrysostom and Theodore of Mopsuestia have also left us their catecheses: these also are informative, both on the catechumenate and the rite of baptism and on the current understanding of baptism.[6]

The typical catechumenate of the fourth and fifth centuries can be summarised as follows, although it must be realised that there was much variation in different places and at different times. For particular reasons, the catechumenate of an adult could be shortened.

OUTLINE OF THE CATECHUMENATE

1 ADMISSION TO THE CATECHUMENATE

Rite (in some places):
  Signing with a cross
  Salt on tongue [this signified healing, preservation, and the seasoning of wisdom]
  Laying on of hands
  Exorcism

Thereafter the catechumens were allowed to attend the first part of the Mass, which was known (until the new Missal of 1970) as the 'Mass of the Catechumens'. They left after the prayer said for them at the General Intercessions.
The period of instruction during this time could last up to three years.

2 THE PERIOD OF CANDIDATURE (Lent)

1. *Enrolment* as a candidate at beginning of Lent. The candidates were known as the COMPETENTES or ELECTI.
2. *Scrutinies*: investigation of the candidate's suitability in a ceremony held in the bishop's presence.
3. *Exorcisms*: usually repeated frequently.
4. *Instructions* daily throughout Lent.
   1st part of Lent: scripture, the resurrection, and faith.
   2nd part of Lent: the Creed and the Lord's Prayer.
5. *Fasting*, often for the 40 days of Lent.

3 THE RITE OF BAPTISM
At the Easter Vigil.

1. *Preparatory rites*, especially renunciation.
2. *The Effeta* or opening of ears and nostrils.
3. *Undressing*, for the anointing.
4. *Pre-baptismal anointing*.
5. *Renunciation* of the devil.
6. *Contract*: pledge of loyalty to Christ.
7. *Blessing of baptismal water*: usually consisting of an exorcism, an epiclesis (invocation of Holy Spirit to come down on the water), and the sign of the cross made in or over the water.
8. *Baptismal immersion*: usually threefold with the naming of the three persons of the Trinity in a credal questioning.
9. *Post-baptismal anointing* with olive oil or myron.
10. *Washing of the feet*.
11. *Gift of the White Garment*.
12. *Gift of the Holy Spirit*: various forms.
13. *Lighted candle* given to candidate.

14 *Procession* into church, candidates dressed in white and carrying candles.
15 *Eucharist*: candidates admitted to the eucharist and receive communion for the first time.

4 MYSTAGOGIA
During the Easter season: special catechesis for the newly baptised as they became fully involved in the mysteries of the Christian faith.

The decline of the catechumenate

From the middle of the fifth century, infant baptism became normal. As a result, the observance of the post-baptismal mystagogia and the secrecy (the *disciplina arcani*) lapsed, even for adults. Soon the pre-baptismal catechumenate was to be shortened and curtailed until only a few vestiges of it remained. The spread of the Church also brought profound changes in the pattern of initiation in the west.

Notes

1 This is one of the three manifestations of Our Lord celebrated in the feast of the Epiphany.

2 There are other possible explanations. Peter and John may have gone to Samaria to commission prophets and teachers (not to complete Philip's baptism), and the apostles' prayer and imposition of hands may have

been carried out so that the gift of prophecy and tongues might come down on the Samaritan believers: a Samaritan Pentecost, so to speak.

3 This is recorded in Tertullian's *Concerning the Crown of Soldiers*, ch.3. Extracts from the texts cited in this chapter are given in E.C. Whitaker, *Documents of the Baptismal Liturgy* (SPCK, 1970).

4 *On the Resurrection of the Flesh*, ch.8.

5 *On Baptism*, ch.18.

6 For an insight into the teaching and preparation given to catechumens during Lent and to the newly baptised after Easter, the following is strongly recommended: Anne Field OSB, *New Life: What it meant to become a Christian in the Early Church* (Oxford: Mowbray, 1980). The author has reconstructed a course of instruction by paraphrasing the teachings of Ambrose, Augustine, Cyril, John Chrysostom, and Theodore of Mopsuestia. Those who recite the Office of Readings will find extracts from catecheses in the following second lessons: *Ambrose*: week 15 of the Year; *Cyril of Jerusalem*: Advent week 1 Sunday, Eastertide week 7 Monday, March 18 (own feast day), Week 4 of the Year Thursday, Week 13 Saturday, Week 17 Wednesday and Thursday, Week 31 Wednesday and Thursday; *Jerome*: Week 13 of the Year Thursday; *John Chrysostom*: Lent week 2 Monday, Good Friday; *Unknown ancient author*: Easter Octave Thursday to Saturday.

4

Growth and Consolidation of the Liturgy
(4th c. to 8th c.)

Introduction

Liturgy should be a living experience, rooted in the present. However, in our liturgy we are linked through Christ with the worship offered to the Father until the end of time, in heaven and on earth, in the past and the present, in our own community and throughout the world. Our liturgy must have a past, and not to know our past is to risk losing our sense of identity. Through the incarnation, the second person of the Trinity entered into human time. Our rites and sacraments stem from their institution by Christ at a particular point in time.

For this reason we cannot avoid looking back in time to seek the roots of our liturgy. We look first at the acts of Christ during his ministry on earth. We look also at the developments of the early centuries and from them we gain an insight into the fundamentals of liturgy. We need to look, albeit briefly and selectively, at certain factors which have been significant in the later history of our worship, right up to the present. Only in this way can we assess in a relevant way the liturgical reform and revision set in motion by the Second Vatican Council.

The fourth century

The fourth to eighth centuries can be regarded as the 'classical' period of the western liturgy[1]. The fourth century was a particularly important time in this development, starting with the year 313 which saw the end of the persecution of the Church in the Roman Empire.

During the first three centuries the growth of the Church had been mainly within the provinces of the Roman Empire. There had been intermittent persecution of Christians, varying considerably in intensity and effect, culminating in the brutal persecution under Diocletian (284-305). Finally in 313 the western and eastern emperors, Constantine and Liberius, met in Milan and made an agreement that in future there would be freedom and toleration for pagans and Christians alike. The years which followed, in which the Church was under imperial protection and Christianity became virtually the established religion of the Empire, were by no means an unmixed blessing, however.

But the new situation, usually referred to as the Peace of the Church, meant that Christians could for the most part practise their religion openly without fear of legal or physical restrictions. Christians no longer had to celebrate the eucharist unobtrusively or in great secrecy in private houses. As a result, the Church grew rapidly in numbers, and the catechumenate developed to its high point in the fourth and early fifth centuries. At the same time, this rapid increase led in some places to a less thorough preparation for baptism.

(a) Church buildings

Places set apart for worship could now be built quite publicly, and the provision of church buildings not only stimulated many liturgical developments but also led to more formality and ceremonial in services of worship. Congregations became larger in size, and this was a factor both in the architectural design of the new purpose-built churches and in changes in the structure of the liturgy. Some control was needed and this was achieved in various ways.

The church was a formal building compared with the simple informal halls and domestic rooms in which the faithful had previously met for the eucharist. Space was now demarcated into the nave for the people and the sanctuary for the ministers. Roles were respected and reinforced by features such as the altar, the presidential chair, the *ambones* for the readings, stalls for the choir, and aisles for processions, so that ministers could reach and leave the sanctuary in a dignified fashion. The role of the deacon developed considerably in terms of directing the people and this function of the deacon can still be seen in the eastern rites today.

(b) Changing roles and functions

The role of the priest also began to grow. No longer could the bishop preside at all or most celebrations, as he once did in the small communities spread around the Mediterranean. He became a remote figure. The priest, on the other hand, was now the usual celebrant at Mass and the normal officiant at most of the sacramental rites. His role in the Mass became increasingly clericalised and formalised, until the stage was reached in the middle ages when he became the one who performed the main liturgical action, with supporting roles carried out, usually exclusively, by specialist ministers such as deacons, acolytes and singers. The larger congregations and the spacious churches stimulated developments in the structure of the eucharist and a growth of formality and ceremonial in its celebration. Nevertheless the people continued to participate fully in the liturgy throughout most of the period covered by this chapter.

(c) *The development of the liturgical year*
In the early Church there had been a single celebration of the paschal mystery on Easter Sunday which extended over Eastertide. Throughout the rest of the year, Sunday, the Lord's Day, was celebrated as a miniature Easter, so to speak. By the end of the fourth century much of the Proper of Time as we know it had developed. There was now Christmas, Lent (which lasted forty days from the Monday of the first week to Maundy Thursday), Ascension as a separate feast, and Pentecost as a distinct feast and not simply as the end of Eastertide.

(d) *Other fourth century developments*
The fourth century also saw other developments. Hitherto there had been a degree of liturgical uniformity among the local churches in the general pattern of the eucharist, as typified by the *anaphora* of Hippolytus. By the end of the fourth century the diversification of the liturgy into the differing rites of east and west had begun [see Appendix A to this chapter]. In the west, Latin replaced Greek as the language of the liturgy during this century, and the Roman Canon almost certainly emerged, supplanting the *anaphora* of Hippolytus (that is, in Rome and certain parts of the west). Ambrose, bishop of Milan 375-397, was an outstanding figure of this century. It is probably incorrect to ascribe the Milanese (or Ambrosian) rite to him, but he has left us the earliest evidence of the Roman Canon. His mystagogical instructions were outstanding and to him we owe the introduction of the office hymns, some of which he wrote himself in the distinctive style named after him.

Fifth-eighth century developments

(a) Bishops and baptism

In the next four centuries the liturgy, and especially the eucharist, continued to become more structured and to respond to changing situations. Trends already apparent in the fourth century continued, such as the growing importance and function of priest and deacon, and the diminution of the bishop's liturgical role as he became more remote from his widespread parishes. The newly baptised had to wait for the bishop to visit the area where they lived for the rite of laying on of hands and anointing with chrism. Some never received it at all, others waited for many years. As we shall see from the fuller survey of the history of initiation in Chapter Five, the original unity of the rite of initiation was now broken up. Baptism and confirmation were eventually defined as separate sacraments, and admission to first holy communion ceased to be regarded as part of Christian initiation. Bitter Christological disputes left their mark on the liturgy: for example, the creed, which first evolved as part of the baptismal rite, was eventually moved into the Mass (sixth century) for the benefit of the imperfectly converted and to combat the Arian heresy.

(b) The silent canon

Another significant change in this period was the practice of saying the canon of the Mass silently, which probably began in the seventh century. As we shall see in Chapter Six, this was part of a process that was to reach its height in the middle ages, in which the congregation was reduced from a full participative role in the liturgy to a somewhat secondary role, distanced from the celebration in the sanctuary and largely spectatorial. The Second Vatican Council has led us in our own day to re-examine the proper relationship between celebrant and people, the nature of liturgical participation, and the correct understanding and design of worshipping space in our churches.

(c) *The growth of liturgical books*
This period saw the growth of liturgical books.[2] At first there were 'booklets' *(libelli)*, with limited texts for particular occasions. Then more specialised books were produced, especially sacramentaries which provided Mass texts for celebrants, lectionaries, choir books, and 'orders' *(Ordines Romani)* directing the conduct of services. Most of these were produced locally in a diocese or religious house, and there was therefore much diversity and variation in the celebration of the liturgy. Papal Masses had considerable influence on liturgical practice throughout the west, especially the papal 'stational' Masses. The first of the 'orders', the *Ordo Romanus Primus*, compiled about 700, gives a detailed account of a papal stational Mass of that time. [There is a summary of this in Appendix B to this chapter.] From this it is certain that the main structure of High Mass, as it existed until the Second Vatican Council and without the various additions and accretions of later centuries, was achieved by the seventh century.

(d) *The emergence of the Roman rite*
The Gregorian Sacramentary was the most significant of the liturgical documents. Although named after Gregory (Pope 590-604) because he ordered its compilation, probably only a part of it was his work. In this document the Roman Canon assumed its final form, and the sacramentary later played an important part in the evolution of the missal. Gregory had a great interest in the liturgy. He made a number of alterations to the Mass: (e.g. he moved the Lord's Prayer to its present position) and composed some of the texts which later appeared in the Roman Missal (e.g. the prefaces for Christmas, Easter and Ascension).

In the sixth and seventh centuries the liturgy observed

in Rome spread to the Frankish lands north of the Alps and to the Rhineland. It there assimilated many Gallican elements. This was the beginning of the constant intermingling of rites which eventually produced the official Roman Rite, and it should be noted that this rite was in no way a 'pure Roman' rite, but very much a hybrid rite. As Cyrille Vogel put it:

> 'The entire process was one of osmosis, amalgamation, and hybridization; liturgies were never simply substituted for one another; they influenced and modified one another, and even the dominant Roman liturgy issued from the process changed and enhanced'.[3]

APPENDIX A: Liturgical Rites

By the end of the fourth century certain of the main centres of the Church had begun to develop characteristic usages of their own, including forms of worship. Several factors, such as language, culture and outlook, brought about the diversification of liturgical rites. Churches within the Roman-Byzantine Empire enjoyed more freedom to develop their own customs after the 'Edict' of Milan of 313. The liturgical rites or families are as follows:

1 Eastern rites:
   (a) Antiochene (or Syrian):
      (i) East Syrian: more Jewish in style and thought; developed in Edessa, Mesopotamia, and Persia; surviving today as the Chaldean and Nestorian churches.
      (ii) West Syrian: more Greek in style and thought; the primitive rite of Antioch and of fourth century Jerusalem; very rich heritage of eucharistic prayers

today represented by the Syrian Jacobites who use the Syrian rite and the Melchites who use the Byzantine rite.
(iii) Maronite: in Lebanon.

(b) Byzantine (Orthodox), using mainly the Liturgy of St John Chrysostom; today widespread in Russia, Greece, USA, Australia, UK, and in various countries to which its adherents have migrated in the course of history and in the twentieth century.

(c) Armenian rite: Syrian and Greek influences.

(d) Alexandrian: the original Greek liturgy of Alexandria was translated into Coptic; today represented by the Coptic rite and the Ethiopic rite.

2 Western rites:
  (a) Gallican rites:
      (i) Mozarabic: Spain; today this rite is only celebrated in Toledo cathedral.
      (ii) Celtic: superseded by the Roman rite.
      (iii) Milanese (Ambrosian): still used in Milan.
      (iv) Gallican rite or rites: superseded.
  (b) Roman-African.

APPENDIX B:
The Papal 'Station' Mass as in the *Ordo Romanus Primus* (c. 700)

[The custom of the Pope going in solemn procession to various churches in Rome on specified days to celebrate Mass is said to have been initiated by Gregory the Great (c. 540-604). It fell into disuse during the exile of the Popes at

Avignon (1309-1377). The stational days and the stational churches continued to be indicated in the Roman Missal until 1970.]

After various preliminaries, the Pope arrived on horseback accompanied by ministers and officials at the stational church. After vesting, the Pope processed solemnly through the church, during which time the *schola* sang the Introit. He prayed silently before the altar, gave the kiss of peace to certain of his assistants, kissed the gospel book and the altar, went to his throne in the centre of the apse, and stood facing eastwards. The *schola* sang the *Kyrie eleison* until the Pope signalled them to stop, and then the Pope intoned the *Gloria in excelsis*. The epistle and gospel, with the accompanying chants, were sung. There was no dismissal of catechumens. After the homily, the Pope sang *Oremus*, but there were no prayers. The creed was not sung: it was not to be introduced in Rome until the eleventh century.

There were no prayers during the offertory. The preface and eucharistic prayer were similar to those of the later Roman Canon, but without the elevation of the host and chalice and without the commemoration of the dead. At the end of Mass there was no blessing, but the Pope blessed the people as he walked out. The Mass ended with *Ite missa est* intoned by the deacon.

It should be noted that there was much ceremonial at different parts of this Mass which has not been mentioned here. This ceremonial was proper to the papal Mass, and allowances must be made for this in trying to reconstruct what Mass was like in ordinary churches. At the same time there were fewer prayers. The text of the Mass still retained something of its original simplicity.

Notes

1 For this classification and for much of the historical survey, especially in Chapters Four and Six, I am indebted to Mr William Jardine Grisbrooke, from whose lectures at The Queen's College, Birmingham, I derived many insights into the history and the nature of the liturgy. He is not, of course, responsible for any shortcomings in this present book.

2 A detailed and systematic reference work on these texts is Cyrille Vogel's *Medieval Liturgy: An Introduction to the Sources* (Washington: The Pastoral Press, 1986).

3 *Ibid.*, p. 3.

5

The Rites of Initiation in the Middle Ages

The effects of the Peace of the Church
After the year 313 Christian communities grew in size, especially as there were now no civil or social deterrents to joining the Church. From the mid-fourth century to the mid-fifth century adult baptism reached its peak both as a rite and in terms of the number of adults seeking baptism. By the end of the fifth century probably the majority of adults in the main centres of the western Empire had been baptised. Children had always been admitted to baptism along with adults, despite discouragement from churchmen such as Tertullian and Augustine, but gradually adult baptism became less common and child baptism the usual practice. In any case the solidarity of family life in the early centuries and throughout the middle ages was such that it seemed quite proper for parents to commit children in baptism and to make responses and promises on their behalf.

The Rites of Initiation in the Middle Ages

The children to be baptised were given token instruction and exorcism during Lent, and at the Easter Vigil they were carried to the font. There they replied by proxy to the credal questioning, received baptism, the laying on of hands, signing with chrism, and holy communion from the cup. Despite the unsuitability of the rite for use with children, no major adaptation was made for their benefit. However, one notable change was made in the rite at this time. The triple profession of faith was moved so as to precede the pouring of water, and the latter was then administered with the formula copied from the east 'I baptise you in the name of the Father,' etc. One unfortunate effect of this change was that the profession and the affusion were now separated. This weakened the link between baptism and personal faith, and increased the likelihood of the sacrament being regarded as magical.

The Peace of the Church and the spread of the Church to the northern European lands brought about extensive changes to the rites of initiation. In the countryside, in the large cities and among the peoples of the north, the pattern of initiation which had existed in the closely-knit local church of the town could no longer be maintained. Increasingly it became impossible to bring the majority of children to the bishop for baptism. Many of the bishops, because of their education, were involved in affairs of state. Baptism carried out by the priest of the parish became the regular practice, the priest doing this in his own right, not (as in the days when the bishop presided and concelebrated) by delegation. The parish priest now carried out the blessing of the water, the profession, the baptising, the anointing, and the baptismal eucharist. But the laying on of hands and the signing with chrism were reserved to the bishop, and as early as Jerome's time (c.342-420) many persons in country districts never received the bishop's ministration at all.

In the east the unity of the rite of initiation was preserved by delegating the anointing with chrism to the priest, who carried out the complete rite of initiation, as he still does today. In the west two diverging practices existed for a time. In Spain, Gaul and northern Italy, where the Gallican rite prevailed, bishops could not travel round their dioceses frequently enough to preside at every baptism. In addition it was necessary in these areas to administer baptism more frequently than just at Easter and Pentecost. The priest therefore baptised, anointed and gave communion to the candidate. There was no separate chrismation, and the gift of the Spirit was attributed to the anointing, as in the eastern Church. On the other hand, in Rome and in places which followed Roman practice, the rite was administered only once or twice a year, normally by the bishop himself, who in any case kept to himself the laying on of hands and chrismation.

Confirmation a separate sacrament

In time, the Roman rite spread over most of western Christendom. When Charlemagne set out to impose the Roman liturgy on his dominions, the two traditions clashed. To the followers of the Gallican rite it had to be explained why a prayer for the coming of the Spirit with an accompanying laying on of hands and chrismation was necessary in a ceremony which had already in their eyes given the Spirit in the anointing after baptism. It had always been believed that the candidate received the Holy Spirit in baptism. Baptism brings about rebirth. It also bestows sanctifying grace, and with it the Holy Spirit. As Cyprian had taught, 'there cannot be baptism without the Holy Spirit'.

In the late fifth century, Faustus, who became Bishop of Riez (Rhegium) in Provence in about 459, had preached a sermon which was later to provide a basis for clarifying the distinction between the bestowal of the Spirit in baptism and in confirmation, as it came to be called. He taught that the Holy Spirit restores to innocence at the font, and in confirmation confers an increase in grace. Aquinas and other theologians later extended the latter notion to include 'strengthening'. The Council of Florence declared (in 1439): 'By confirmation we are increased in grace and strengthened in faith'.

The Roman practice eventually prevailed over the Gallican, but it was impossible in most dioceses either to retain the bishop as the normal officiant at baptism or to ensure that the newly baptised child was brought to the bishop fairly soon after baptism by the priest. Baptism and confirmation were recognised as distinct and separable sacraments, with often an interval of many years between them. Neither confirmation nor the first reception of communion any longer had any initiatory significance, and the original unity of the rite of initiation with its sequence of three parts was now finally wrecked. Some restoration of this unity has been achieved in our own time in the RCIA.

Contraction of the rite of baptism

With the discontinuation of the catechumenate and with infant baptism becoming a universal practice in the west, the rite of baptism was somewhat abbreviated in the middle ages. The preparatory prayers, exorcisms and other ceremonies previously performed during Lent were now compressed into a short service in the church porch. In the font, water was always ready for use, kept under lock and key to prevent its theft for witchcraft. The water was blessed by the parish priest. The link with the bishop was retained by the requirement that the oils used for the anointing in baptism should have been blessed by him. This practice is still observed on Holy Thursday in the Roman rite.

The child was brought to the font, the devil was renounced, and the child anointed with oil. After the act of faith had been made by the godparents, the child was baptised with water and anointed with chrism, clothed in a white robe and given a lighted candle. The practice of giving communion to the newly baptised infant had virtually disappeared in the west by the end of the thirteenth century. Because of the delay in receiving confirmation, it became necessary to admit the faithful to communion before confirmation.

By the thirteenth century the practice was for baptism within eight days of birth (this was enjoined by the law of the Church), communion to follow when the child was old enough to consume the host safely, and confirmation when (and if) the bishop was available. Augustine had been among those who did not favour child baptism, but ironically it was his teaching on original sin which perhaps more than anything led to the almost universal demand for babies to be baptised as soon as possible after birth. There was a great dread of babies dying unbaptised. Not surprisingly, during the middle ages the popular understanding of baptism put more emphasis on baptism as remission of original sin than on baptism as new life.

Confirmation

Confirmation as a separate rite was necessarily rather truncated, originating as a brief element in the middle of the total rite of initiation. It consisted only of the prayer for the coming of the Spirit with the laying on of hands and the signing with chrism. A final prayer and blessing could be added. The rite was not always celebrated in church. Sometimes it was administered in houses or at the roadside as the bishop passed through a village; it was not unknown for bishops to officiate on horseback. Thomas Cantilupe, Bishop of Hereford 1275-82, used to wear his stole when travelling on horseback so that people might stop him by the wayside to present their children for confirmation.

During the middle ages such a casually administered sacrament was not always held in high regard by the laity, despite the teaching of the Church that confirmation conveyed an increase of the Spirit to strengthen the recipient to fight sin and to bear witness in the world. In England it was laid down by the Council of Lambeth in 1281 that no one could be admitted to communion who had not been confirmed. This was an attempt, not particularly successful at the time, to ensure universal confirmation, and the Church of England has retained this requirement ever since the Reformation.

6

The Liturgy in the Middle Ages
(9th c. to 15th c.)

The Middle Ages
The brief historical sketch begun in Chapter Four can now be resumed with an overview of the main developments of the ninth-fifteenth centuries.

(a) Consolidation
As we have seen, in the centuries following the Peace of the Church, the Church had enhanced its position and importance in the world. The consequent developments in the structure of the liturgy continued in this period. By the eleventh and twelfth centuries the Roman and Byzantine liturgies had become predominant in the west and east respectively. This reflected not only the importance attached

The Liturgy in the Middle Ages

to the liturgies of the two capital cities but also the outstanding qualities of these rites and forms.

At the beginning of this period, Charlemagne (Holy Roman Emperor 800-814) pursued a policy of liturgical uniformity throughout his lands. He suppressed the Gallican rite and introduced the Roman rite, but grafted on to this austere rite some more elaborate Gallican elements. Alcuin and Benedict of Aniane were also associated with liturgical reforms at this time.

(b) *The emergence of the missal*

From the fourth century celebrants had been increasingly expected to pray the eucharistic prayer from a prepared written text. This led the way to the production of liturgical books. As was noted in Chapter Four, the earliest of these were small booklets *(libelli missarum)*, produced mainly in the sixth century, containing the celebrant's formulae for one or two Masses. They did not contain the invariable canon, or the readings or parts to be sung by choir or *schola*. Readings were given in lectionaries, which at first contained simply lists of references and only later the full text of the readings. Sung parts were given in various books such as the *antiphonale* and *graduale*.

During the eleventh and twelfth centuries two other types of liturgical books were significant: sacramentaries and *ordines*. The sacramentaries were larger collections of Mass texts for the use of celebrants. The *ordines* supplemented the sacramentaries by providing detailed descriptions of the ritual organisation. Needless to say, the *libelli*, the sacramentaries, and the *ordines* are invaluable sources for studying the development of the liturgy.[1]

At this point, it is necessary to revert to the most important of the sacramentaries, namely the Gregorian Sacramentary. As we have seen in Chapter Four, it was named after Pope Gregory, who may have had a hand in the original version.

Towards the end of the sixth century he had ordered the compilation of a better and more convenient sacramentary. The resulting document contains the canon of the Mass in its final form. When Charlemagne (Holy Roman Emperor 800-814) wanted to bring about more uniformity in the liturgy throughout his domains, he asked the Pope (Adrian I) for a sacramentary. He was sent a copy of the Gregorian (known as the Hadrianum). Being a papal sacramentary, it was not complete: for example, it lacked texts for ordinary Sundays. But it had other valuable features, including an informative introduction (which is also useful to the historian of liturgy). Towards the end of the eighth century this sacramentary was revised either by Alcuin or Benedict of Aniane, and a famous supplement added to supply the missing parts. This has always been regarded as an excellent piece of liturgical development, and it was the chief foundation for the later Roman Missal.

Alongside these books, a newer sort of Mass book evolved, the *missale plenarius* (plenary missal, literally 'fuller Mass book') which combined in one volume the texts previously found in the sacramentary, the lectionary, and the antiphonal. The new book was already overtaking the sacramentaries numerically in the tenth century, and by the twelfth century the sacramentaries were now in a small minority. The plenary missal superseded the sacramentary firstly because of the convenience of having all the texts in one volume, especially with the multiplication of private Masses, and more importantly because from the end of the eleventh century the celebrant became obliged to say all the parts of the Mass, even if the deacon, sub-deacon and choir were present and performing their parts. This anomaly remained a requirement at High Mass and Sung Mass until the new rubrics of 1964.

The complete missal containing all the required texts came into being sometime in the twelfth century and became general only in the thirteenth century.

(c) *Individualism*

From the ninth to the twelfth century significant changes took place in the relationship of priests and people to the eucharist. The structure and content of the eucharist did not undergo any fundamental change. But there was a fundamental change in the understanding of the eucharist and in the devotional expression of this understanding. It was an age when the corporate spirituality which had characterised the celebration of the eucharist in the earlier centuries gave way to an individual spirituality. As far as the Mass was concerned, spirituality tended to be subjective rather than objective. The role of the congregation at Mass became largely spectatorial, and minimally participatory.

A number of factors accounted for this. In the first place, as the Church spread to the northern lands of Europe, rapid mass conversions of large numbers of people took place. Some of these new Christians were insufficiently instructed and perhaps not far advanced in the process of conversion. Secondly, the liturgy was in Latin, a barrier to participation and an incentive for the Mass to be accorded an inappropriate sense of mysteriousness.[2] Thirdly, the silent canon (a practice which can be traced to the late eighth century in the west, earlier in the east: see Chapter Four) and the physical distance between priest and people in a large church heightened this sense of mysteriousness and diminished further the sense of corporate liturgy.

(d) *Professionalisation of the rites*

It required a professional, with a knowledge of Latin (often in practice minimal), to celebrate the rites of the Church. The Mass became something the priest carried out, rather than a functional celebration of the whole people of God. The priest performed almost the whole action of the Mass himself, especially at Low Mass where the parts intended for other ministers and for the people were no longer differentiated. This clericalisation of the Mass was marked by the addition of private prayers in the first person singular throughout the rite and by the requirement that the celebrant had to say every prayer and text himself, whether or not there was a *schola* for the sung parts or a deacon to proclaim the gospel. The availability of plenary missals from the thirteenth century reinforced this practice and also played a part in the growth and multiplication of private Masses.

It must be emphasised that lay people for the most part attended Mass with great devotion and prayerfulness in the middle ages: there is much contemporary evidence of this. But they tended to make their own devotions alongside the action of the Mass rather than associating themselves fully with the liturgical action. The liturgy was a performance by the celebrant in the presence of a passive congregation: the priest was seen in practice as almost a substitute for the congregation. Those parts of the Mass which in principle belonged to the people had been appropriated by clerics and singers.

(e) Holy Communion

The absence of an authentic participation in the liturgy was reflected also in the decline of lay reception of communion. Inadequate understanding of the Mass, a misplaced sense of guilt and unworthiness, and a certain scrupulosity about irreverence towards the consecrated species were all factors in this. It is often said that the Church forbade the laity to receive the chalice. It is nearer the truth to say that the laity withdrew themselves from receiving the chalice, a process completed by the twelfth century. Communion even under one species became so infrequent that the Church in 1215 enacted the law that is still in operation, that communion must be received at least once a year.

(f) Propitiation and worship

The strong note of individualism which was a feature of medieval spirituality affected the priest as well as the people.

Both celebrant and laity said private personal prayers at various stages in the Mass, and the liturgy was, as it were, a background to this. There was a general lack of understanding of what constituted authentic liturgy, and a somewhat distorted view of the Mass. It was not that the teaching of the Church had altered, but rather that the popular view of the Mass was out of balance. Because of the obsessive concern with penance, especially in northern Europe, the eucharist was seen less as thanksgiving and more as propitiation.

The emphasis in the general approach to the Mass was not so much on the act of worship and the act of offering made by the Church; rather it was on God's gift to his people, his coming not for communion but in order to be adored. The moment of consecration was accorded almost disproportionate importance in relation to the rest of the *anaphora*, and the elevation was a high point, often *the* high point, in the Mass. For the people's benefit, a bell was rung.[3] People made a particular point of seeing the host at the moment of elevation, and this seemed to be of more importance than receiving the host at communion.

Christ's presence was not seen as an integral element of the eucharistic liturgy: instead he was seen as coming from outside the liturgical action in response to people's prayers. It was as if Christ was worshipped *through* the Mass, not *in* the Mass. This perspective on the Mass reinforced infrequent reception of communion, while the concept of the Mass as the eucharistic banquet receded even further as the use of unleavened bread and the kneeling posture to receive the host became general.

(g) *The end of the Middle Ages*
In the late medieval period these tendencies continued. During the thirteenth, fourteenth and fifteenth centuries devotional response to the liturgy remained highly subjective. The minor ceremonial and the music used at Mass were

greatly enriched, rather like the final flowering of Gothic architecture. The liturgy had to be celebrated with as much richness of form as possible, for it was regarded as a sphere in which God alone was active, not man.

The private Mass (that is, a Mass celebrated without a congregation) was by then a firmly established and widespread practice, and although the celebration of the private Mass was brought under a degree of control after the Reformation, it was not until the Second Vatican Council that the undesirability of this practice was fully realised. The private Mass was out of harmony with the public dimension of liturgical celebration: it also supported the attitude current in the late middle ages that the Mass was a personal act of the priest rather than an act of the Church. In this period votive Masses and Masses for the dead multiplied, especially after the Black Death. Finally it can be noted that the sign element in the sacrament of the eucharist was largely lost sight of, and the host and cup were popularly regarded as objects to be worshipped rather than as sacramental signs.

APPENDIX A: The Sarum Use

In liturgy, 'use' is not another term for 'rite', but denotes a local modification or variant of the standard rite. England had at least five 'uses' in the middle ages: Hereford, York, Lincoln, Bangor and Salisbury, each differing in detail only from the parent Roman rite. The only one of any importance was the Use of Sarum (or Salisbury).

This was developed in the first instance for use in the cathedral church of Salisbury and has been traditionally ascribed to St Osmund, bishop 1078-1099, who built the cathedral at Old Sarum and founded the Cathedral Chapter. But the Sarum Use was almost certainly developed by Richard Poore who was Dean of Sarum 1197-1217 and Bishop 1217-1228. In 1219 he removed the see to its present site (New

Sarum, or Salisbury) and began the erection of the present cathedral. He drew up the Salisbury Constitutions and a complete directory of services. He probably gave the Sarum Use its definitive form. There was a revision in the fourteenth century (the 'New Use of Sarum'), but this was mainly of the Calendar.

The constitution and chapter of Salisbury became a model for many other foundations, as did its liturgy. In the later middle ages the Sarum Use was increasingly used in other dioceses. It was apparently used in nearly the whole of the British Isles in 1457. In 1543 the Sarum Breviary was imposed throughout the Province of Canterbury. There was a complete set of Sarum liturgical books and these were produced in large numbers. Cranmer made much use of them in compiling the first Book of Common Prayer (1549).

Poore borrowed many northern French customs for his service books. The Sarum Use, therefore, was a twelfth and early thirteenth century variation of the Roman Rite to which were added French and other elements. The Roman Rite reached its developed state a little later, so the Sarum Use therefore reflects slightly earlier Roman forms, and has similarities with the Dominican and Carmelite uses. It was an exuberant liturgy, and in the cathedral and collegiate churches where it was carried out fully it was a complicated liturgy with much ceremonial. For example, at High Mass there were as many as seven deacons, a similar number of acolytes, and Rulers of the Choir vested in copes. During the canon the celebrant stretched out his hands in the form of a cross. A description of the Sarum Mass is given in Appendix B below.

APPENDIX B: The Sarum Mass
(As a convenient point of reference, comparisons are made with the Roman Missal of Pius V, i.e. that in use from 1570 to 1970.)

During the vesting in the sacristy, the priest recited the prayers 'Come, Holy Ghost...' and 'O God, to whom every heart is open...', followed by Psalm 42 (43):1-6 with antiphon and *Kyrie eleison*. He began the Our Father and Hail Mary, which were completed at the foot of the altar.

The priest, deacon and subdeacon recited the mutual confession, the *Confiteor* being shorter than the later version. The priest then kissed the deacon and subdeacon. The Introit had been sung by the *schola* during the entry procession, and was not repeated by the priest. The priest ascended to the altar, said the prayer *Aufer a nobis* and 'In the name of the Father,' etc. He incensed the altar. The *Kyrie eleison* and *Gloria in excelsis* were sung, the latter being intoned by the celebrant, who recited the rest privately.

Collects, epistle, gradual, alleluia, sequence, gospel and creed followed. There were many lengthy and not particularly attractive sequences in the Sarum Missal, as in most medieval missals. During the gradual the chalice was prepared by the deacon.

The priest greeted the people with *Dominus vobiscum* and added *Oremus*, but there were no prayers; these had dropped out of use much earlier. Offertory prayers and prayers during the incensing were slightly different from those of the Roman Missal. The priest recited a prayer, not a psalm, during the washing of the hands. He recited the prayer *Suscipiamur a te*, but there was no *Veni, sanctificator*. The response to *Orate Fratres* was different from the Roman version. Then came the Bidding of the Bedes, lengthy petitions in English, after which the sermon was preached.

The secrets, preface and canon were mostly as in the Roman Missal. There was a mention of the King after that

The Liturgy in the Middle Ages

of the Pope, and after the consecration the priest bowed and elevated the host and chalice, but there were no genuflections. The Mass continued as in the Roman Missal up to the *Agnus Dei*. The prayers at the commixture and before the Kiss of Peace were slightly different from those of the Roman Missal. For the kiss, a wooden implement (the 'Pax') was used. The priest recited three private prayers before communion, the second and third of which were those in the Roman Missal. The three prayers said during the priest's reception of communion and the second and third prayers at the ablutions were different from the Roman.

The choir sang the communion antiphon and the priest the postcommunion prayer. There was a greeting and dismissal, but no blessing. The priest then said privately the prayer *Placeat tibi, sancta Trinitas* and went out in procession, reciting privately John 1:1-14.

Notes

1 Cf. Cyrille Vogel's *Medieval Liturgy: An Introduction to the Sources* (Washington: The Pastoral Press, 1986).

2 In recent years there have been complaints from some who do not like the revised Mass of the 1970 Missal, and especially the use of English and the eucharistic prayer said aloud, that the 'sense of mystery' has been lost. This view will be discussed in a later chapter. It is in order to avoid confusing authentic with spurious notions of 'mystery' that the term 'mysteriousness' has been employed here.

3 The distance from the altar in larger churches, the screens and choirs coming between sanctuary and

nave, the silent canon, and the priest celebrating with his back to the people made it difficult to follow the course of the Mass. The custom of ringing a small bell (the 'Sanctus' bell or 'sacring' bell) at the elevation so that the people should not miss it began at least in the thirteenth century (the earliest record of this is from Cologne in 1201). Later this was supplemented by another ringing by way of preliminary warning when the priest spread his hands over the offerings at the *Hanc igitur.* The ringing at the *Sanctus* probably developed also as yet another preliminary warning. In the centuries following the Reformation, these bells became in many cases less necessary, but they remained a familiar feature of Mass, especially low Mass, right up to the 1960s. They served to tell the people what part of the Mass the priest had reached, and they were also to some extent signals, e.g. to kneel down at the *Sanctus* and to come up to receive communion after the *Domine, non sum dignus.* Some churches today are still ringing the sanctuary bell at the traditional points, but the practice is quite obsolete and, under present conditions, pointless.

7

From Trent to Vatican 2

The eve of the Reformation
In about the year 1500 a member of the Venetian embassy drew up a profile of the English people. He remarked on their devoutness:

> 'They all go to Mass every day, and in public recite many Our Father's. The women carry long rosaries in their hands. Those who are able to read carry the Office of Our Lady with them and with a companion recite it in a low voice in church, verse by verse, like monks. On Sunday, however, they always hear Mass in their parish church. They give alms generously because they are not allowed to offer less than a coin worth one fourteenth of a golden ducat. They do not neglect to observe any form which marks out a good Christian. Nevertheless, there are many who hold differing opinions about religion.'[1]

This is not the only evidence for the general piety of the English at that time, and in particular their great devotion to the Mass. To a varying degree people in the other countries of Christendom were devoted to the Mass. In view of this, why was it necessary in the sixteenth century to consider changes and reforms in the worship of the Church?

The popular view of the Mass and of holy communion which prevailed in the late middle ages has already been noted in the previous chapter. There was a misplaced emphasis on the eucharist as propitiation rather than thanksgiving, as a gift from God rather than as an action of God's people under Christ their High Priest. Importance was attached to Christ's coming to them, from outside the eucharistic action, so to speak, and coming so that the faithful might worship him rather than receive him in holy communion. In as far as the eucharist was seen as a remembrance (*anamnesis*), the general practice was to emphasise Christ's suffering on the cross rather than to recall the salvific significance of his death-resurrection-ascension.

It cannot be said that the imbalance in these popular attitudes was completely rectified during the sixteenth century, although the Council of Trent clarified the Church's teaching on the sacrificial nature of the Mass and restated her teaching on the sacraments.

Liturgical formation takes time to develop. Even today, a quarter of a century after the Second Vatican Council issued its *Constitution on the Sacred Liturgy*, we are making only gradual progress in liturgical education. In the sixteenth century it would seem that people went to Mass frequently but received communion infrequently. Here again progress has been slow. It is only in the twentieth century that frequent communion has been achieved, thanks largely to Pope Pius X and also perhaps to changes in the law of fasting. Even so, the popular tendency has been to see the reception of communion more in sacramental terms than as an integral part of the Liturgy of the Eucharist.

Little or nothing was done in the sixteenth century to encourage the participation of the people in the liturgy. In general, this liturgical principle would not have been readily understood at the time. It is interesting to note, however, that an embryonic form of participation was advocated in the year 1502. John Burchard of Strassburg, the papal master of ceremonies, published an *Ordo Missae* which contained a schema for the rubrics of the Mass. In this he directed that the people were to join in the responses with the server. They were to follow the prayers and actions of the priest, and not say their own prayers instead. Burchard's *Ordo* became widely known and formed the basis for the rubrics which prefaced the Missal of 1570. But his modest references to participation were not repeated in the Missal.

There were numerous practices which called for reform or abolition. Some people tried to hear as many Masses as possible each day. Some priests said as many Masses as possible in order to collect stipends and to meet the great demand for Masses for the Dead. There was a sub-class of priests who did little else but say such Masses. An excessive number of private Masses, said by the priest alone or often with no one present except a single server, were offered. This practice militated against the communal dimension of the liturgy. These were mostly Masses for the Dead or votive Masses, the frequent celebration of which deflected attention from the course of the liturgical year.

There were superstitious practices associated with the Mass, such as the belief that Masses offered every day for a specified number of days (such as seven or thirty) would bring particular blessings, or that to attend Mass would be rewarded with the gift of not becoming ill that day or of not growing any older that day. The Mass was seen as sacrificial, but in a distorted sense: it was seen by many as a sacrifice which would obtain specific favours, in other words it was treated as one of the 'good works' by which man could 'buy' merit. This view was one of the targets for Luther's attacks on the concept of 'good works', and the distorted sense of the sacrifice of the Mass had to be rectified by the Council of Trent.

The Reformation

The Catholic Church received two main lines of attack during the Reformation. The first was directed against abuses in the organisation of the Church and the conduct of some of its clergy. The historian must not generalise too sweepingly in listing these abuses, but some of them were sufficiently widespread to merit criticism. These included worldly prelates, neglect of pastoral duties, insufficient preaching, pluralism, absenteeism, superstitious practices connected with the Mass, scandals connected with indulgences, ignorant and uneducated priests, and laxity in some religious houses. Considerable progress was made in the sixteenth century and after in tackling these abuses, many of which, such as inadequate clerical training, had had significant repercussions on the liturgical life of the Church.

The other line of attack, doctrinal, also had important implications for the liturgy. As new doctrines were propagated, many traditional doctrines were impugned. They included the sacrifice of the Mass, transubstantiation, the sacraments, the nature of the priestly ministry, episcopacy, the place of the scriptures in the life and services of the Church, and fundamental questions concerning justification, grace and the forgiveness of sin. It is not difficult to see the profound changes to the liturgy which could have resulted from the new doctrines, especially if we study the new structures of worship which developed in the reformed churches. The challenge of these doctrinal attacks was met firmly by the teachings of the Council of Trent, by the establishment of new orders such as the Jesuits, by the founding of seminaries, and by other improvements in clerical and lay education.

Some of the attacks on the worship of the Church were

not without justification. The use of Latin, the ignorance of many of the laity of what was taking place in the sanctuary, the subsidiary role of the laity in church services, the unsatisfactory presentation of the scriptures in church, the excessive complexity of missals and breviaries and of the services they contained, and the unsuitability of many elements in the Mass, the office and the sacramental rites were subjected to criticism. Modern liturgists would tend to sympathise with these criticisms.

The chief criticism at the time, among those who desired liturgical reform, was of the many variations of texts and ceremonial which existed. The basic pattern of the Mass and office was common to most of the western Church, but there were numerous variations for particular countries, regions, dioceses, religious orders, and even for particular churches. There were variations in prayers, proper parts, prefaces, sequences, hymns, and ritual. There were outstanding variations in calendars, each calendar having many feasts and saints' days of its own. This played havoc with the course of the liturgical year, and especially the seasons, and it multiplied the number of commemorations which had to be made because so many feasts concurred on the same day. In fact, commemorations had to be limited to seven in number on any one occasion!

As long as liturgical texts had to be written by hand and as long as there was no central body in continuous existence to control and supervise liturgical matters, the prolixity of texts and variations was virtually inevitable. Churches depended upon *scriptoria* for their books. Particular sources for books and particular bishops who authorised the books had therefore considerable control over the details in them, including the many variations. Of the numerous examples which could be quoted, one could cite the influence of Arles and Lérins in the sixth and seventh centuries in parts of south-east France and that of Salisbury over much of England in the later middle ages.

There was a case for tidying-up the liturgy in the western Church, though less of a case, perhaps, for the rigid uniformity which was eventually achieved. But uniformity had to await the opportunity provided by the printing press and the reform of the central government of the Church. These conditions were established to some extent by the Council of Trent.

The Council of Trent

The Council met at a troubled time. Its opening had been several times delayed, and its meetings were interrupted and influenced by outside events and pressures. There were 25 sessions altogether, the first being held on 13 December 1545, the last on 3-4 December 1563. The main objectives of the Council were to re-establish discipline within the Church, to renew its spiritual life, and to provide a clear formulation of doctrine to meet the growth of Protestantism and the demands of the reformers. Although the Council fathers were aware of the need to consider liturgical reform, this was not the most urgent matter needing attention, and little time was given specifically to the Church's liturgy.

However, some of the Council's other decrees had a considerable bearing on the liturgy. This was particularly the case with the Council's teaching on the sacraments, and especially baptism, confirmation, and the holy eucharist: these are, as we have seen, constitutive elements of the liturgy. The teaching of the Council of Trent on these matters was systematic and definitive, and forms the basis of the study of the Mass and the sacraments which we shall be undertaking in subsequent chapters. It is important, therefore, to review in some detail the conciliar decrees which are of concern to the student of liturgy.

(a) *The sacraments*

At the 7th Session (3 March 1547) the Council defined (or re-affirmed) the Church's teaching on the sacraments, mainly in response to teachings of the Reformers. The bishops issued 13 canons on the sacraments in general. The chief definitions were as follows:

(i) That all seven sacraments were founded by Christ: some Reformers taught that the sacraments were human inventions.

(ii) They are necessary to salvation, though not all are necessary to every man: the necessity of the sacraments was reaffirmed against the Reform doctrine of justification by faith alone.

(iii) They contain the grace they signify, and confer it *ex opere operato*[2]: this also was a refutation of the 'faith alone' doctrine, according to which the sacraments do not of themselves confer grace but merely excite and confirm fiducial faith in the recipient.

(iv) Baptism, confirmation and holy orders confer an indelible character and cannot therefore be repeated: the sacramental 'character' had been denied by the Reformers.

(v) A priest is ordinarily required for the administration of the sacraments: that is to say, the Council condemned the doctrine that all Christians have power to administer the sacraments.[3]

(vi) The celebrant must have the intention at least of doing what the Church does: the Reformers denied the necessity of intention as they held that sacraments have only a subjective, psychological efficacy.

(vii) The validity and efficacy of the sacrament is independent of the minister's orthodoxy and state of grace: this was a refutation of a doctrine taught by various heretical groups.

(In the teaching of the Council of Trent on the eucharist, it was affirmed that the Church has power to make changes in the administration of the sacraments, but not to change their substance. Hence the Church has the power to revise its sacramental rites, as it has done following the Second Vatican Council, provided the matter and form are unaltered.)

(b) Baptism and Confirmation

There were 14 canons on baptism and three on confirmation. The main teachings on baptism were that it must be administered with water and in the threefold name of the Trinity. Baptism remits original sin and is necessary for salvation. We have seen how confirmation came to be a distinct and separate sacrament. The Council of Trent refuted the teachings of the Reformers that confirmation was unbiblical and not commanded by God, condemning the doctrines that confirmation of baptised persons is an unnecessary ceremony, that it is merely an occasion for young people to give an account of their faith, and that it is not a true and proper sacrament.

(c) The eucharist

We can now pass to Session 13 held on 11 October 1551 when important decisions were reached on the eucharist. The Council was confronted with three types of heretical teaching concerning the eucharist, those of Luther, Zwingli, and Calvin. The Fathers accordingly issued a Decree on the Eucharist in eight chapters, teaching among other things the doctrines of transubstantiation and the real presence, and 11 Canons on the Eucharist in which particular errors were condemned.

(d) Penance and extreme unction

Session 14 (25 November 1547) issued decrees and canons on the sacrament of penance and the sacrament of extreme unction. The Council reasserted that the Church has received from Christ the power of forgiving sins. This power involves not simply the power of preaching the gospel of the forgiveness of sins, as the Reformers argued, but the full power of actually remitting sins. The Reformers who preached justification by faith alone not only rejected the power to forgive sins, but claimed that absolution is not a true release from sin but simply a declaration that sins are forgiven on the grounds of faith. They held that penance was fundamentally one and the same sacrament as baptism: it is a 'regression' to baptism in that the sinner remembers the assurance of the forgiveness of sins given in baptism and renews the act of faith made in baptism, and thereby the sins committed after baptism are remitted.

The Council condemned this view of justification and the remission of sins, reasserted the necessity of sacramental absolution, and taught that baptism and penance are separate and distinct sacraments. Sacramental confession was declared to be necessary for salvation and the priest acted judicially in pronouncing absolution: he did not simply 'declare' that sins were, through faith, remitted. The Council also specified what was necessary for the sacrament to be bestowed validly.

The sacrament of extreme unction was similarly declared to be a distinct sacrament, instituted by Our Lord, by which sins were forgiven and sometimes health restored to the body where the health of the soul required it.

(e) *The laity and the chalice*
Session 21 (16 July 1562) is of particular interest to liturgists. It issued a decree on the reception of the chalice and four canons condemning errors. Protestants had attacked the Church for withholding the chalice from the laity, which they considered contrary to the command of Our Lord in the New Testament. The Council Fathers came to the conclusion that it would be inopportune to restore the chalice to the laity.

They affirmed that communion under both kinds is not of obligation or divine command, that the Church has authority to regulate the way in which the sacraments are to be administered, that Christ is whole and entire under either species, and that little children are not bound to sacramental communion.

(f) *The sacrifice of the Mass*

The Council Fathers then proceeded to consider the sacrifice of the Mass, and their decrees on this were ratified during Session 22 (17 September 1562). There was much discussion of whether Christ offered himself as a sacrifice for us at the Last Supper or only upon the cross. There was a heated debate, but it concluded with unanimity. The Council declared that at the Last Supper Christ offered himself simply, but not as propitiation, whereas he offered himself as our propitiation only on the cross. The Mass was defined as a true and proper sacrifice, essentially linked to the sacrifice on the cross. Christ left a visible sacrifice to his Church in which the bloody sacrifice which was once offered on the cross should be made present, its memory preserved to the end of the world, and its salvific power applied to the forgiveness of sins. In the sacrifice of the Mass the victim is the same as in the sacrifice of the cross: he is the same who now offers himself through the ministry of his priests and who then by himself offered himself on the cross: the difference lies only in the mode of offering.

The Council also declared that the Mass was not merely a sacrifice of praise and thanksgiving, but also a propitiatory sacrifice. The Mass is offered for sins, for punishments for sins, and for expiation; it is offered as an impetratory ('asking') sacrifice for other necessities. The sacrifice of the Mass does not remit the guilt of sins immediately as do the sacraments of baptism and penance, but mediately by conferring the grace of repentance. The Council taught that God is propitiated by the offering of this sacrifice and, by granting the grace and gift of penance, he remits sins.

Although the Council provided a fairly comprehensive treatment of the doctrine concerning the eucharist, we must remember that throughout they were refuting contrary teaching proposed by the Reformers. It was to this end that the Council Fathers went on to reassert that Mass can be offered for both the living and the dead, and that it could be celebrated in honour of the saints. They decreed that while it was desirable that the faithful should communicate at every Mass (something which has only been re-established in recent years in the twentieth century), Mass without communicants was lawful. Finally they decreed that Mass was to be said in Latin and they retained the practice of saying the canon of the Mass and the words of consecration in a 'low voice'.

These last two enactments were disciplinary in character. They may seem very conservative or even reactionary decisions to us in the late twentieth century when, thankfully, they have finally been abolished. It has to be remembered that many reforms which one would like the Council to have carried out, such as the restoration of the chalice to the laity, the introduction of the vernacular, and a more thorough restructuring of rites in accordance with what today would be considered the correct liturgical principles, were considered inopportune and likely to be construed as surrender to the principles of the Reformation.[4] One of the Council's decrees on the sacrifice of the Mass which will doubtless find favour with liturgists today is that there should be frequent instruction of the people on the Mass.

(g) *The sacrament of orders*
In Session 23 (15 July 1563) the doctrine and canons on the sacrament of orders were passed. The necessity of the hierarchy, the legitimate authority of bishops, and the episcopal character of the bishops created by the Pope were

reaffirmed. Seventeen canons for the reform of abuses connected with the sacrament of orders had been discussed for some two months by the Council during the previous session. A decree was passed enforcing the residence of bishops in their sees. Another decree, which was of the greatest significance for the subsequent history of the Church, established seminaries for the training of priests. This did more, perhaps, for the elimination of abuses, for the training and enlightenment of the clergy, and for the revival of true religion in the Church than any other measure during the Counter-Reformation.

(h) Matrimony
Session 24 (24 November 1563) dealt with the sacrament of matrimony. It was declared to be a genuine sacrament, founded by Christ, and not, as some reformers claimed, purely a human institution.

(i) Revision of the Breviary and Missal
The final Session, 25, (3-4 December 1563) passed a decree which referred the revision of the breviary and the missal to the Pope. It may seem strange that the revision of these two fundamental service books was hardly discussed by the Council but simply ordered to be carried out. However, we have seen why liturgical reform could not have been expected to claim much attention during the Council sessions: there were more pressing and urgent questions to settle. Consolidation seemed more important than development.

(j) Abuses in the Mass and the sacraments
The Fathers did consider lists of abuses concerning the Mass and the sacraments, but rather than deal with each in detail they issued a general condemnation of superstitious practices and liturgical abuses. Their restatement of sacramental and eucharistic doctrine and the issuing of decrees concerning

the administration of the sacraments played a considerable part in rectifying malpractices and in removing misunderstanding and ignorance. The better education of the clergy, and especially their more systematic instruction in theology, resulting from the establishment of seminaries, also contributed eventually to this improvement.

The Roman Breviary 1568

As with the Mass, the daily office of the Church was for centuries carried out with the use of a variety of books. In the thirteenth century the process began of reducing these different books into a single volume, which eventually was called the breviary. Although some shortening of texts took place in this process, especially in the readings, the office went on expanding and became so elaborate that it was excessively time-consuming and burdensome. A notable attempt to shorten and simplify the office was made in 1533 with the reformed breviary of Cardinal Quiñones. But this was too drastic and radical to be generally acceptable at the time, although it became very popular with busy clergy, and it was suppressed in 1568.

Pope Pius IV carried out the decree of the Council of Trent by setting up a commission to reform the breviary. We have little detailed knowledge of the workings of this commission, and have to deduce what we can about their policy and methods from the finished product, the *Breviarium Romanum* issued by Pius V in 1568. They restored rather than reformed the office. In this breviary we have the old Roman office stripped of some of the accretions of the middle ages. Thanks to the printing press, the new breviary was imposed uniformly on the Church. The great variety of local usages was demolished, with exemption for usages which could claim an unbroken history of two hundred years.

There was a need for tidying up the office, but with uniformity came rigidity. The resulting office was marked by a certain nobility, but despite the abolition of much surplus material, such as the lesser offices which had to be said in addition to the main office, it was still far too long: for example, on Sundays (for many priests the busiest day of the week) matins still had eighteen psalms and twelve lessons and lauds eight psalms. Not only was the office burdensome; it was governed by complicated rubrics. The office as a whole was still monastic in character and highly clericalised: nothing was done to reconstitute the office as the prayer of the whole Church, including the laity.

The Roman Missal 1570

Pius IV also set up a commission for the reform of the missal. The first printed missal had been issued in 1474, and the commission based their missal on this, with minor changes. Their revised missal was accepted and promulgated as the Roman Missal by Pius V in 1570. It was imposed on the whole of the Church (that is, the Latin rite) in a similar way to the new breviary, and with similar effects. There was now great uniformity not only of texts but also of rubrics governing both what was to be said and the actions to be performed by the priest. As with the breviary, the missal represented a very conservative reform. Accretions were stripped away and the number of saints' days reduced, especially during Lent. But some anomalies remained in the rite, such as the Introit antiphon said by the priest not at the beginning of Mass but after various other prayers and actions, and the dismissal which did not come at the end of Mass.

Both the new breviary and the new missal missed many opportunities for an effective, living and pastorally-based liturgy; but they provided a stability in the next few centuries when conditions did not favour reform.

The Congregation of Rites 1588

To carry out the decrees of the Council of Trent regarding uniformity of public worship, Pope Sixtus V established the

Congregation of Rites in 1588. Its task was to ensure that throughout the Latin rite the prescribed manner of celebrating Mass and carrying out other parts of the liturgy was strictly observed. The Congregation also gave judgment in matters of doubt referred to it, issued dispensations and privileges, and formulated new rules and texts for new feasts when required. This Congregation remained in existence until after the Second Vatican Council.

The Roman Pontifical and Ritual

The Council of Trent had enacted that authentic and, where necessary, revised editions of the liturgical books were to be prepared and published. As we have seen, this was carried out with regard to the Roman Missal and the Roman Breviary. The liturgical reform and revision ordered by the Council of Trent was eventually completed by the publication of the *Pontificale Romanum* by Pope Clement VIII in 1595 and the *Rituale Romanum* by Paul V in 1614.

The pontifical contains the sacramental rites carried out by the bishop. The new one of 1595 was strictly enforced by Clement VIII with no exemptions. All bishops were obliged to use it and all pontificals of local churches were abolished. It is to the Roman Pontifical, which underwent various amendments up to 1962, that we have to look for the official post-Tridentine rites of confirmation, ordination, the consecration of churches, and other episcopal functions.

The ritual contains the rites of the sacraments and other functions performed by priests. It was revised several times after 1614, the final edition being that of 1962. It provided the official texts of such rites as baptism, penance, marriage, visitation of the sick, extreme unction, viaticum, funerals and certain blessings. It was not, however, exclusively enforced, and some local rites remained in use until the present century: for example, the marriage rite used in England.

From the time of Trent to that of Vatican 2, the Church's

liturgy was contained, in essentials, in four books: the missal, the breviary, the pontifical and the ritual. Since Vatican 2, a new missal and office book have been published. All the other rites, however, despite having 'The Roman Pontifical' or 'The Roman Ritual' inscribed on their title pages, are at present in separate books.

Subsequent changes to the liturgy

Despite the good intentions of Pius V and the activity of the Congregation of Rites, changes did take place in both Mass and office in the next few centuries. New feasts were constantly added, so that once again the course of the liturgical year was obscured. Clement VIII and Urban VIII both made considerable changes to the rubrics. The latter had the Latin breviary hymns 'revised' to accord with 'classical' taste. For a time, alternative liturgical books were issued in France, known as 'neo-Gallican' because of claims to exercise 'Gallican liberties': for example, the Parisian Breviary of 1736. These were eventually suppressed. The Roman Breviary was given a new psalter in 1911. Otherwise the breviary and missal underwent no major change until after the Second Vatican Council.

The Liturgical Movement

The Liturgical Movement is the name given to various initiatives, especially in the twentieth century, to restore active participation of the people in the worship of the Church. It had its origins in the work of Dom Prosper Guéranger who refounded Solesmes Abbey in 1832 as a centre for the revival of Gregorian chant and of liturgy in general. Although his work was marked by a certain degree of medievalism, it greatly stimulated a new interest in liturgy and in liturgical studies. This has been sustained by scholars such as Cabrol and Battifol, and by monastic communities such as Maredsous in Belgium and Maria Laach in Germany.

The Movement proper dates from the first decade of the

twentieth century. Pope Pius X advocated the active participation of the laity in worship. In 1903 he issued his famous *motu proprio* on music which encouraged congregational singing of plainchant. He also promoted more frequent communion. In England the Society of Saint Gregory (founded 1929) promoted (and continues to promote today) much interest in liturgy and liturgical music.[5] In 1909 an important conference was held in Malines in Belgium, the main theme of which was the pastoral and spiritual importance of liturgical understanding and participation. Between the two world wars the Movement developed strongly in Germany and in the USA. It also developed in the Anglican Church.

After the second world war, the Movement spread widely. There was seen to be a fundamental need not merely for participation and understanding, but even more so for a reform and revision of the liturgy. The Movement bore some fruit in these years: Pius XII's encyclical *Mediator Dei* of 1947, the restoration of the Paschal Vigil in 1951, the new order of Holy Week in 1956, the relaxation of the eucharistic fast, the permission for evening Masses, and the simplification of rubrics in 1955 and 1960. These developments, together with a growing literature on the liturgy and its renewal, formed the prelude to the liturgical reforms of the Second Vatican Council.

Notes

1 Anon. *A Relation of the Island of England.* Camden Society, 1st series, xxxvii (1847), 23. My translation.

2 The Church teaches that the sacraments operate by the power of the completed sacramental rite (*ex opere*

Catholic Worship

operato), not by the subjective disposition of the recipient (*ex opere operantis*).

3 The ordinary minister of baptism is a bishop, priest, or deacon; in the absence of an ordinary minister, a catechist or other deputed person may baptise; in case of necessity, any person may confer baptism (Code of Canon Law, 861). In matrimony, the contracting parties administer the sacrament to each other. The other sacraments can only be conferred by an ordained minister.

4 Cf. recognition of these difficulties in GIRM 7.

5 Cf. J.D. Crichton, H.E. Winstone, J.R. Ainslie (eds.), *English Catholic Worship: Liturgical Renewal in England since 1900* (London: Geoffrey Chapman, 1979).

8

The Second Vatican Council

Introduction

It was on 25 January 1959 that Pope John XXIII surprised everyone by announcing his intention to call a council. There followed four years of busy preparation. On Christmas Day 1961 the Pope officially ordered the council to convene in 1962 on a date to be fixed. He wrote [in the Apostolic Constitution *Humanae Salutis*] 'while humanity is on the edge of a new era, tasks of immense gravity and amplitude await the Church ... It is a question in fact of bringing the modern world into contact with the vivifying and perennial energies of the gospel.' He went on to speak of the present vitality of the Church, saying 'This (Council) will be a demonstration of the Church, always living and always young, which feels the rhythm of the times and which in every century beautifies herself with new splendour, radiates new light, and achieves new conquests, while remaining identical in herself, faithful to the divine image impressed on her countenance by her Spouse.'

Liturgy and renewal

This dynamic and vibrant view of the Church awakened exciting prospects of renewal throughout the Church. Looking back we can see that this was the spirit which underlay and informed the renewal of the Church's liturgy. The keynote of the Council was to be *aggiornamento*: renewal, updating, revision. It would probably be fair to say that the laity in general were largely unaware of the need for any renewal of the liturgy. Since the Reformation period, and in particular since the publication of the Roman Breviary of 1568 and the Roman Missal of 1570, the forms of worship had been static and highly regulated. So much so that many Catholics gloried in the unchanging and unchangeable nature of the Church's liturgy.

The period between the two missals, 1570 to 1970, has been described by Theodor Klauser as 'the epoch of changelessness or rubricism'.[1] By this he meant that, thanks to printing and the authority of the Congregation of Rites (created in 1588), the liturgy was tightly codified, performed with uniformity throughout the Latin rite, and subject to strict centralist control and regulation in the greatest detail. During this period the rubricist emerged as the expert on the liturgy, thus reflecting the legalistic view which governed the implementation of the liturgy until recent times. For a quick indication of how the Second Vatican Council has changed this situation, one only has to compare the introductory matter which prefaces the two missals. The 1570 Missal begins with a conglomeration of intricate and tedious rubrics and legalistic matters. The 1970 Missal begins with the *General Instruction of the Roman Missal*, a highly readable account of the significance and structure of the Mass.

It would seem that many of the Council Fathers were similarly unaware of any need to renew the liturgy. Liturgy was placed first on the Council's agenda: it was expected by many to be an uncontentious subject and not likely to result in more than a few modest changes.

The Second Vatican Council

Was reform needed?

Since some Catholics still seem unconvinced about this, it might be just as well to ask whether there was any real justification for changing the Church's liturgy. The answer has to be 'yes', despite the incomparable riches of the liturgy, its dignity, its venerable character, its impressive music and ceremonial, and its air of unchanging mystery and tradition. The sad fact is that the basic simplicity of the original Roman liturgy had been lost for over a thousand years. From the ninth century much additional material had been added to the liturgy in France and the Rhineland. The effectiveness and authenticity of the primitive liturgy were submerged under the elaborations and accretions of later ages.

It may be asked at this stage whether the liturgical reform set in motion by the Council of Trent had been a failure. In general, it had not. It resulted in the promulgation of four carefully revised books, the missal, the breviary, the pontifical, and the ritual. Many accretions were removed, and more unity and uniformity brought about. Abuses, especially in connection with the Mass, were stopped. Lay people attended Mass with great devotion, despite the lack of overt participation and the use of Latin, and reforms in the Church in the sixteenth and seventeenth centuries, especially in the education of priests, largely brought to an end the fanciful beliefs and distorted views associated popularly with the Mass.

There had been, then, much improvement, but the Tridentine reforms were very cautious and conservative. Perhaps that was all that could have been achieved in the circumstances of the time. But Trent left behind much unfinished business as far as the liturgy was concerned, and by the time of Vatican 2 another and more radical revision was long overdue.

It is not suggested that contemporary liturgical renewal should take or has taken the form of restoring primitive or ancient forms. But the early liturgy shows us clearly the essential characteristics of liturgy, such as the roles and relationship of ministers and people, the nature of the Mass and especially the structure of the *anaphora* or eucharistic prayer, and the appropriate posture, response and mode of participation of the people. In the early liturgy we discern the essentials, and this indicates where revision and simplification are appropriate.

Over the centuries the Mass had become overladen with numerous minor accretions, and these tended to conceal or camouflage the essential elements. Private ministerial devotions had been added to the beginning and end of Mass, and private prayers for the priest were inserted in various places. There were some absurd rules: for example, until the new rubrics of 1960 the celebrant at High Mass had to repeat all the parts said or sung by the choir, deacon and subdeacon, the requirements of Low Mass having been thrown back on to High Mass. There were many elements which were no longer meaningful, such as the *oremus* before the offertory, and many superfluous gestures of little significance such as kissings, bowings, blessings with the hand and with the host, and unnecessary genuflections.

The Liturgy of the Word was proclaimed in Latin, and only on Sundays and great feasts were the readings repeated in the mother tongue. There was no response by the people to the readings. Very few Masses had a homily, and often the homilies were not on the readings. Indeed the sermon was not technically regarded as part of the Mass. The lectionary was limited. The people did not necessarily follow all that was done in their name, but mostly made their own devotions.

The latter comment applied even more to the Liturgy of the Eucharist. The eucharistic prayer was said not only in Latin but also silently. Consequently it did not clearly appear to be what it was meant to be, the great prayer of thanksgiving, memorial, and offering, pronounced by the priest in the name of Christ and the assembled people. Some people followed the eucharistic prayer, but many made their own parallel devotions. In either case the great eucharistic prayer tended to be seen as an exclusively priestly action. Until quite recently reception of communion was not the norm at every Mass, and then only under one kind. Distribution of communion often took place before or after Mass, or even outside Mass altogether, and the laity were given hosts from the tabernacle rather than hosts consecrated at the same Mass.

The proper of the Mass also needed overhauling. In particular, the calendar was overloaded with saints' feasts. The rubrics allowed the liturgical seasons to be interrupted too frequently by feasts. The many classifications of liturgical days were absurd and complicated, and there was a gross excess of commemorations. This affected both Mass and office, and it was perilous to embark on the saying of Mass or the office without an *ordo* to tell you what to say.

So the Mass needed some reshaping and simplification to bring into clearer focus what was important and to bring the people into fuller participation. It had become over the centuries too clericalised and in externals too complicated.

A similar verdict can be passed on the daily office. In principle the official prayer of the whole Church, it was in practice mainly a clerical preserve. Centuries ago it had become thoroughly monasticised and clericalised. It was far too long and suited only to the initiated. It meant little to most of the faithful. Breviaries were something carried around by priests because they had to spend much time every day reciting the office, but to the laity in general the contents of the breviary were largely a mystery.

The sacramental rites also needed reordering to make them more meaningful and pastorally effective. The rite of baptism included a clutter of truncated relics from the past, and was not very suitable either for children or for adults. To a lesser degree the other rites also needed some overhauling.

Before the Council
Some modest changes had been made in the twentieth century before the Second Vatican Council. Pius X simplified the calendar and partially reformed the missal and the breviary. His most notable change was the restoration of the position of the Sunday Mass and office so that it would not normally be supplanted by another celebration. He also published a new psalter for the office (1911) with a better (though still rather burdensome) distribution of the psalms. Pius X had envisaged further reforms of the liturgy, but these did not take place, mostly because of the two world wars.

In 1947 Pius XII published his important encyclical letter *Mediator Dei* on the liturgy. He stressed the need for understanding the liturgy and for liturgical development. In the following year he established a Pontifical Commission for General Liturgical Restoration. The Commission's work led to a revision of the rites of Holy Week (1955), a provisional simplification of rubrics (1955), the *Instruction on Sacred Music and the Sacred Liturgy* (1958) which dealt with music and participation, and the Code of Rubrics (1960). The latter introduced a modest simplification into the arrangement of the liturgical year, the calendar, the office and the Mass. With hindsight we can say that they were moves in the right direction, but not in themselves sufficient. They paved the way for the more thorough-going revisions set in motion by the Council, and prepared people's minds for change. Other significant changes took place at this time, such as the permission for evening Masses and the relaxation of the law governing the eucharistic fast.

The Council and liturgical renewal
The liturgy, the first item on the agenda, was debated for just over three weeks, and the original draft submitted to the Council was greatly amended. What had been expected to be uncontentious and more or less a formality turned out to be so important that the momentum of progress surprised

most of the Council Fathers. Surely the Holy Spirit was at work here. They suddenly realised the profound significance of the liturgy in the life of the Church. Great enthusiasm was aroused and the *Constitution on the Sacred Liturgy* was the first of the Council's sixteen documents to be promulgated (4 December 1963). It is one of the outstanding documents of the Council, and has been immensely important. It is also a very readable and stimulating document, and is seminal for any understanding of the liturgy today.

The Council Fathers did not content themselves with a few modest and predictable reforms, such as lightening the burden of the breviary or having the readings at Mass in the vernacular. They ordered nothing less than a total and comprehensive overhaul of the entire liturgy — Mass, office, sacraments, and other rites. There was to be a re-examination and revision, a simplification, and a restoration of the authentic meaning and significance of all the rites. The main principles of the revision can be summed up as follows.

The new forms were to constitute a genuine spiritual renewal; they were to be liturgical and pastoral in their impact, and firmly biblical; and they were to be ecclesial, keeping in mind the nature of the Church (this Constitution has been in effect the kernel of the *Constitution on the Church*). The fruits of the Liturgical Movement and the work of liturgical specialists (hitherto largely disregarded and often disapproved of) now became important. Many Council Fathers did not realise how much the ground had already been laid for liturgical reform.

The Constitution on the Sacred Liturgy
The opening sentence of this memorable document reiterates the main objects of the Council: to intensify the daily growth of Catholics in Christian living, to make the Church's observances more responsive to the needs of our times, to nurture unity, and strengthen those aspects of the Church

which can help to call all of mankind into her embrace. These are the special reasons for renewing and fostering the liturgy (1). (*Numbers in brackets refer to the sections of the Constitution.*)

Chapter 1 (General Principles for the Restoration and Promotion of the Sacred Liturgy) deals in considerable detail with the nature of the liturgy and its importance in the Church's life (5-13). Christ is always present in his Church, especially in liturgical celebrations. He associates the Church with himself in giving perfect praise to God and making men holy. The liturgy is therefore an exercise of the priestly office of Jesus Christ. Every liturgical celebration is an action of Christ and his Body (the Church), a sacred action surpassing all others (7).

The Constitution then decrees the promotion of liturgical instruction and active participation (14-20). The clergy are to be adequately instructed in liturgy and given a liturgical formation in their spiritual life. Seminaries are to appoint a professor of liturgy, and all students for the priesthood are required to take courses in liturgy. The people also are to be given catechesis on the liturgy, especially by their own pastors, who must also promote participation in the liturgy.

The reform of the liturgy (21-40) is to be undertaken in accordance with the relevant norms. Changeable and unchangeable elements must be carefully distinguished: the former ought to be changed if they are out of harmony with the liturgy or no longer functional. There are, firstly, general norms (22-25), such as the authority of the Church and the importance of scripture. Experts from various parts of the world are to be appointed to revise the liturgical books and the bishops are to be consulted on this. The second category of norms are those drawn from the hierarchic and communal nature of the liturgy (26-32): liturgical services are not private functions but celebrations of the Church, and celebrations with full and active participation of the people are to be preferred whenever possible.

The third category of norms refer to the educative and

pastoral nature of the liturgy (33-36). Rites are to be distinguished by a noble simplicity: they should be short, clear, and unencumbered by useless repetitions. They should be easily comprehensible and not need much explanation. There is to be more reading from scripture, and preaching is to be part of the liturgical service; Bible services are to be encouraged, and instruction on the liturgy is to be given in a variety of ways. Vernacular languages may be used and translations of the Latin texts must be authorised.

Finally, there are norms for adapting the liturgy to the genius and traditions of people (37-40). Local hierarchies can obtain permission for experimental rites to determine the most suitable forms of adaptation to local cultures.

Chapter 1 concludes with sections on the promotion of liturgical life in diocese and parish (41-42) and the promotion of pastoral-liturgical action (43-46). As the high priest of his flock, the bishop has a great responsibility for the celebration of the liturgy and for promoting good liturgy in the parishes. The liturgical apostolate is to be given considerable importance. Each diocese is to have a liturgical commission, and it is desirable that ecclesiastical territories should also have a commission and an Institute for Pastoral Liturgy. Every diocese should also have, where possible, commissions for liturgical music and art, working in conjunction with the liturgical commission.

The remaining chapters of the Constitution will be referred to in the subsequent sections of this book. Chapter 2 deals with the eucharist; Chapter 3 with the other sacraments; Chapter 4 with the divine office; Chapter 5 with the liturgical year; Chapter 6 with sacred music; and Chapter 7 with sacred art and furnishings. As we shall see, each of the chapters provides an exposition of these aspects of the liturgy and proposes important criteria for liturgical renewal and revision.

The implementation of the Constitution

The task of revising the liturgy was entrusted to the *Consilium ad exsequendam Constitutionem de Sacra Liturgia*. The Liturgy Consilium, as it was commonly called, with its various groups, began work before the Council ended. It was established by Pope Paul VI on 29 January 1964, and was international in character, consisting of some fifty cardinals and bishops and over two hundred experts. The Consilium came to an end in 1969, to be succeeded by the new Congregation for Divine Worship (which remained in existence until 1975 when it was reorganised). Wide consultation took place before new texts, which were drawn up by the Consilium or by one of the Congregations which succeeded it, were authorised.

The main new rites have been published (in the official Latin version) as follows: Holy Order (1968), Rite of Funerals (1968), Infant Baptism (1969), Lectionary (for Mass) (1969, new and revised edition 1981), Marriage (1969), Missal (1970), The Liturgy of the Hours (1971), Confirmation (1971), Christian Initiation of Adults (1972), Lesser Ministries (1972), Pastoral Care and Anointing of the Sick (1972), Penance (1973), Dedication of a Church and Altar (1977), Book of Blessings (1984), and Ceremonial for Bishops (1984). To this can be added two 'approved' books published by the Abbey of Solesmes: the *Graduale* (1974) containing chants for the Mass, and the *Liber Hymnarius* (1983) containing hymns and certain other chants for the Liturgy of the Hours.

Mention must also be made of various documents issued on the implementation of the new rites and norms. These include the *Instruction on Putting into Effect the Constitution on the Sacred Liturgy* (1964)[2], a second and third *Instruction* (1967, 1970)[3], and various others. In December 1988, Pope John Paul II issued an important Apostolic Letter to mark the 25th anniversary of the publication of the *Constitution on the Sacred Liturgy*.[4]

International Commission on English in the Liturgy (ICEL)

Episcopal conferences set up machinery for producing vernacular versions of the new rites. The *Constitution on the Sacred Liturgy* had laid down that, where it seemed appropriate, episcopal conferences were to consult with other conferences or regions employing the same language. Consequently the International Commission on English in the Liturgy (ICEL) was established on 17 October 1963 by the bishops' conferences of Australia, Canada, England and Wales, India, Ireland, New Zealand, Pakistan, Scotland, South Africa, and the United States of America. An eleventh conference, the Philippines, joined in 1967. There are also fifteen associate member conferences participating in the work of ICEL.[5]

The headquarters of this joint commission of Catholic Bishops' Conferences is in Washington. The work of ICEL is governed by the Episcopal Board which consists of eleven bishops representing the eleven member conferences. There are committees to deal with various functions, such as the Advisory Committee, the Sub-committee on Original Texts, and the Sub-committee on the Presentation of Texts. ICEL prepares translations and editions of all the rites of the Roman liturgy on behalf of the 26 conferences. It is now engaged on the comprehensive revision of all its translations in the light of two decades of use worldwide. So far the Order of Christian Funerals and the Rite of Christian Initiation of Adults have been completely revised, and the commission is now working on the revision of the Roman Missal.

The Congregation for Divine Worship and the Discipline of the Sacraments

This is the present name of the curial congregation in Rome responsible for liturgical matters, having undergone several reorganisations and changes of title. The first Congregation of Divine Worship replaced the former Congregation of Rites in 1969. It is headed by a Cardinal Prefect, assisted by a Secretary, an Additional Secretary (Divine Worship), an Under-Secretary (Sacraments), and an international staff. It is situated in the Palazzo delle Congregazioni, Piazza Pio XII, Rome.

In addition to examining and approving new texts and dealing with other liturgical business, the members of the Congregation are engaged at present on new documents on Holy Orders, Exorcisms, Adaptation of the Liturgy, and Young People and the Liturgy. It is also preparing a new edition of the Marriage Rite (for the universal Church), a Roman Ritual, volume 5 of the Liturgy of the Hours, an Order of Holy Week for Small Churches, and a new edition of the Roman Martyrology.

England and Wales, and Scotland

The work of the Bishops' Conference of England and Wales is now conducted through Departments. In the Department for Christian Life and Worship, three of the five committees have responsibility for liturgy. They are the Committee for Pastoral Liturgy, the Committee for Church Music, and the Committee for Church Art and Architecture. Each has a bishop chairman. These three committees are served by the Liturgy Office at 39 Eccleston Square, London. There is a priest Secretary to the three Committees who is also National Director of Liturgical Formation, and a lay Assistant Secretary. A National Liturgy Conference is held annually which is attended by representatives of the diocesan liturgical commissions and members of the three committees.

The Scottish Bishops' Conference has its own Liturgical Commission, the Secretary of which maintains contact with the committees for England and Wales. There is no national liturgical centre in these countries.

It may be of interest to mention the participation of the Catholic Church in ecumenical liturgical agencies.

The International Consultation on English Texts (ICET)
With a vernacular liturgy in the Catholic Church and with much liturgical reform taking place in other Churches, Christians have recognised that they share many prayers. ICET was set up to produce agreed translations of these common texts. It was an ecumenical body representing Christian Churches in all the major English speaking countries of the world. The best known achievement of ICET was the publication of *Prayers We Have in Common* (SPCK, 2nd revised edition 1975). This contained the agreed translations of the Kyrie, Gloria, Nicene and Apostles' Creed, Preface Dialogue, Sanctus, Lord's Prayer, Agnus Dei, Benedictus, Magnificat, Nunc Dimittis, Gloria Patri, and Te Deum. Many of these translations have been adopted in the Roman Missal. ICET has now gone out of existence.

The English Language Liturgical Consultation (ELLC)
This body has succeeded ICET. It first met in Boston in 1985. At present it is further revising the content of *Prayers We Have in Common*, and it is hoped that many Churches will adopt these revised texts in their own liturgies.

The Joint Liturgical Group (JLG)
This consists of members of various Churches in Great Britain. Its first meeting was in 1963. At present it has two members from each of the following: The Church of England, The Church of Scotland, The Baptist Union of Great Britain and Ireland, The United Reformed Church, The Episcopal Church in Scotland, The Methodist Church, The Roman Catholic Church, and one member from The Fellowship of the Churches of Christ. The JLG has produced a number of well-known publications, such as *The Calendar and Lectionary* (1967), *The Daily Office* (1968), *Holy Week Services*

(1971), *Initiation and Eucharist* (1972), *Worship and the Child* (1975), *Getting the Liturgy Right* (1982), and *The Word in Season* (1988).

What has been achieved?

The total revision of the entire liturgy was quite unprecedented in scale and in the quality of well-informed expertise available to the Consilium and to succeeding Congregations. With such resources to draw on, the revisers have achieved a corpus of new rites which are soundly pastoral, biblical and scholarly. They are designed to meet the needs of God's people today so that the Church's official worship can be truly authentic and meaningful. The main characteristics of the new forms are simplification, clarification, restoration, participation, and corporate celebration. The revision has been basically a conservative one, radical but not revolutionary.

The Church's year is now reordered so that the seasons are observed without interruption and the paschal Triduum stands out as the summit. The Calendar has been simplified and the number of saints' feasts greatly reduced. The arrangement and classification of celebrations, together with the rubrics governing these matters, have at long last been firmly and radically simplified. There are now only solemnities, feasts, and memorias, many of the latter being optional. There are no commemorations and only two octaves. It is now much easier to see which Mass and office texts are to be used without constant recourse to an *ordo*. Proper texts have been enriched so that through the seasons and through the course of 'ordinary time' the whole cycle of our salvation is celebrated and observed.

Particular importance has now been accorded to the celebration of Sundays. The lectionary has been totally reordered and expanded (twice), and the rubrics governing the choice of texts from the lectionary ensure that the course of scriptural readings, especially during liturgical seasons, is largely uninterrupted.

The daily office is now simple, short and manageable. It is designed to be more effective pastorally and spiritually. It can be celebrated either in Latin or in the vernacular, and is in a form which enables it to be used by the whole People of God and not simply the clergy. It can be said that the Church's daily office has now been restored to the people, although there is scope for further adaptation for use in parishes. The sacramental rites also have been simplified and reordered to make them more effective and meaningful.

In the reordering of the Mass, considerable opportunity has been given for participation, corporate celebration, and fuller understanding of the Liturgies of the Word and of the Eucharist. In the first of these liturgies, we now have a genuine proclamation of the living and saving word, in our own language. The homily has been restored to its rightful place and function, and there is provision for congregational response and participation. The restoration of the Prayer of the Faithful has been widely welcomed.

The reordering of the Liturgy of the Eucharist has been more fundamental than is generally realised. The outstanding change has been the restoration of the saying of the *anaphora* aloud. This is of far greater significance than the switch to the vernacular, important though that is, and arguably the greatest single liturgical change resulting from the Second Vatican Council. It is the key to the correct celebration of the great eucharistic action by priest and people together, with the people involving themselves and closely associating themselves with this liturgical action. Those who work in liturgical development often find that very few Catholics seem to understand this aspect of the Mass at all adequately, and they do not seem to have had it explained to them. It is surely one of the most urgent tasks of liturgical catechesis to address this need.

However, we have been given ample opportunity by the

Council and the Consilium to understand the spirit of the new liturgy. Many important liturgical documents and instructions have been issued, but two in particular merit commendation. In the *Constitution on the Sacred Liturgy* and in the *General Instruction of the Roman Missal* we have two magnificent and readable accounts of the liturgy. The task of liturgical renewal and development among both priests and people would be greatly assisted if these documents were more widely read.

The liturgical revision of the last quarter of a century has been extensive. Liturgical renewal is ongoing, but varies greatly from place to place. Progress in liturgical formation has been the least satisfactory feature of this period, and much more needs to be done in this area. However, the years since the Council have seen a growth in the study of liturgy, both among ourselves and our sister Churches. New journals have appeared, new liturgical societies, both national and international, and new degree courses. The Liturgical Institute and Athenaeum at Sant' Anselmo in Rome and the many centres and institutes in various countries bear witness to this.

Notes

1 Theodor Klauser, *A Short History of the Western Liturgy* (Oxford University Press, second edition 1979), ch. IV. The words quoted formed the title of ch. IV in the first edition (London: Mowbray, 1952), p. 49.

2 *Inter Oecumenici* (1964). Translation: CTS Do 348 (1966).

3 *Ecclesiae Semper* (1965) [which promulgated the Rite of Concelebration of Mass and the Rite of Communion under Both Kinds (1965)]; *Liturgicae Instaurationes* (1970). Translation: CTS Do 437 (1971).

4 Translation: *Love Your Mass* CTS Do 591 (1989).

5 The Antilles, Bangladesh, CEPAC (Fiji Islands, Rarotonga, Samoa and Tokelau, Tonga), Gambia-Liberia-Sierra Leone, Ghana, Kenya, Malaysia-Singapore, Malawi, Nigeria, Papua New Guinea and the Solomons, Sri Lanka, Tanzania, Uganda, Zambia, Zimbabwe.

9

The Mass: The Introductory Rites

The two liturgies

Since the promulgation of the new rite of Mass (known as the *Missa Normativa*) in 1969 and the new Roman Missal in 1970, the Mass has been designated as two liturgies, the Liturgy of the Word and the Liturgy of the Eucharist. The former is preceded by the Introductory Rites (unless these are replaced by another rite) and the latter is followed by the Concluding Rite.[1] To accompany the new Roman Missal, the *General Instruction of the Roman Missal* was issued in 1969 and an expanded second edition in 1975. This is an outstanding liturgical Instruction: it is informative, comprehensive, and straightforward in style. It is an indispensable source for any study of the Mass.

This twofold division of the Mass is not new. The first part of the Mass was sometimes referred to in the past as

The Mass: the Introductory Rites

the 'fore-Mass'. Another traditional distinction was to refer to the two parts as 'the Mass of the Catechumens' and 'the Mass of the Faithful' because at one time catechumens were dismissed at the end of the first part, not being admitted to the sacred mysteries of the eucharist until after baptism. The Liturgy of St John Chrysostom, which is used in the eastern Churches, still has a dismissal at this point: the Deacon proclaims three times 'All catechumens depart!' and then 'Let no catechumen remain!' Yet another title sometimes used in the past for the first part of the Mass was *synaxis* ('assembly' or 'meeting').

St Thomas à Kempis has left us in his spiritual classic *The Imitation of Christ* a well known description of the two liturgies as two tables:

> 'I perceive two things to be particularly necessary for me in this life ... To me, weak and helpless, you have given your sacred Body for the refreshment of soul and body; and your Word you have set as a lamp to guide my feet. Without these two I should not well be able to live; for the Word of God is the light of my soul, and your Sacrament the Bread of Life. These also may be called the two tables, set on the one side and on the other, in the treasury and jewel-house of the Holy Church.'[2]

This powerful imagery helps us to set the two liturgies in their proper relationship to each other. Both are to do with nourishing: we feed on the word, we feed on the Body of Christ. We are nourished both by the word and the sacrament. In our churches both the lectern and the altar should be well designed and accorded a place of honour and dignity. At Mass we incense the book as well as the altar.

At this point we can look at other similarities between the two liturgies. In both we have the presence of Christ. There are various aspects of Christ's presence. Christ is present always in his Church. He is present whenever we gather together to pray and worship. He is present in his word. He is present in the celebration of the eucharist. He is present in his body and blood in holy communion. All liturgy, indeed, is characterised by Christ's presence: 'Christ is always present in his Church, especially in her liturgical celebrations: ... every liturgical celebration is an action of Christ the priest and of his Body the Church' [CL (*Constitution on the Sacred Liturgy*) 7].

Although we are meant to learn more about the scriptures and deepen our understanding of them during the Liturgy of the Word, the main characteristic of this liturgy is not so much teaching but proclamation. We proclaim the word by which we have life.

> 'The Church has always venerated the divine Scriptures just as she venerates the body of the Lord, since from the table of both the word of God and of the body of Christ she unceasingly receives and offers to the faithful the bread of life, especially in the sacred liturgy' [*Dogmatic Constitution on Divine Revelation*, 21].

Other similarities between the two liturgies are also significant. Both are anamnetic, that is in both we recall Christ's saving work and make his death and resurrection a continued present reality in our lives. Finally, as we have seen in Chapter One, both these liturgies have a Jewish origin.

The Church teaches us that we are not to see the two liturgies as completely separate: 'Although the Mass is made up of the liturgy of the word and the liturgy of the eucharist, the two parts are so closely connected as to form one act of worship' [GIRM (*General Instruction of the Roman Missal*) 8]. Accordingly the Church prefers to talk, as we have seen above, of a single table rather than two tables. 'The table of God's word and of Christ's body is prepared and from it the faithful are instructed and nourished' [GIRM 8].

The Introductory Rites

Until the end of the fourth century in both east and west the eucharistic liturgy began with a call to order by the bishop or deacon, and then the reading of the lessons. Later the liturgy began with a greeting from the president and a prayer. We have seen in the appendix to Chapter Four that in a papal Mass about the year 700 the first action performed aloud by the Pope was to intone the *Gloria in excelsis*, and then he greeted the people and sang the prayer.

By the eleventh century preparatory prayers had become common, especially those of a penitential nature. The growing concern with sin affected clergy as well as laity, and private prayers for the priest began to be inserted into the Mass. In the thirteenth century, Psalm 42, the *confiteor* and the prayer *aufer a nobis*[3] were inserted in the Missal of the Roman Curia under Innocent III. During the next two centuries, the use of these prayers spread. They were originally said entirely in the sacristy. Then in many places they came to be said partly in the sacristy, partly during the entry procession, and partly in the sanctuary at the foot of the altar, with *aufer a nobis* being said as the priest ascended the steps.

Eventually all these private ministerial prayers were said at the foot of the altar steps, and in the Roman Missal of 1570 Psalm 42 and the other penitential prayers were officially incorporated into the Mass. These were still private prayers. When the server made the responses, he did not do so on behalf of the people but in place of the deacon and subdeacon. Rather anomalously, the congregation took over these responses in the dialogue Mass which became popular in the 1930s onwards.

When the Liturgy Consilium considered this part of the Mass, there was the possibility of suppressing the private penitential prayers, which were on a strict view unnecessary accretions which obscured the beginning of the Mass. Eventually it was decided to insert a public penitential rite into the *Ordo Missae* of 1969.

The Introductory Rites in the 1970 Missal are as follows [GIRM 24-32]:

(Entry chant or hymn)
'In the name of the Father ...'
GREETING
Penitential rite and Lord have mercy
(OR sprinkling with holy water)
(Glory to God in the highest ...)
PRAYER

The two fundamental items of the Introductory Rites are shown in block capitals, namely the greeting and the prayer or collect. The items in round brackets do not always take place.

(a) *The Entrance*

It is preferable for the priest to process through the body of the church to reach the sanctuary area. This signifies his link with his people and the unity of priest and people in celebrating the liturgy. It could also be seen as symbolising our journey to God. When the priest comes to the sanctuary by a 'short' route, especially if he appears through a door by the side of the altar, the impression may be given that the priest is like an actor coming on to the stage from the wings. It is important to avoid the impression that Mass is something which the priest carries out entirely by himself with the congregation watching or following but not really participating in.

During the entry procession and the incensing of the altar, music may be played or a piece may be sung by a group of singers. In that case, after the priest has greeted the people, priest and people together can sing an opening hymn. In this way, the hymn will be accorded its due importance. This opening hymn should be chosen to express either the gathering of God's people for eucharistic worship or the day or season.

The alternative arrangement, perhaps less preferable, is to have a hymn sung by the congregation during the entrance procession and continued during the incensing of the altar. There is a tendency in Catholic churches to have hymns sung while something else is happening in the sanctuary, thus giving the impression perhaps that the people are being kept usefully occupied. It is surely important that if hymns have an authentic and not simply an ornamental function, their integral part in the worship is reflected in their being sung by the entire community together, ministers and people, in appropriate cases. A similar point can be made about a communion hymn: it is suggested that this should be sung by priest and people together when the distribution of holy communion and all the routines which follow it have been completed.

When the priest (and concelebrants and deacons) have reached the altar, he venerates (with the concelebrants and deacons) the altar by kissing it. The altar may then be incensed. The former distinction between High Mass, Sung Mass and Low Mass is now abolished. Incense, music and singing can be used at any celebration of the Mass, and not simply at 'solemn' celebrations.

(b) *The Greeting*

Mass commences with the sign of the cross and the words 'In the name of the Father . . .' This is not a formality. It is significant that the Trinity is invoked at the beginning of worship. This trinitarian formula embodies the whole thrust of the eucharist as an offering *to* the Father, *through* the Son and *in* the Holy Spirit. By the greeting, 'the priest expresses the presence of the Lord to the assembled community. This greeting and the people's response manifest the mystery of the Church that is gathered together' [GIRM 28]. The priest may then briefly introduce the Mass of the day: the temptation to give a miniature homily at this point must be resisted.

(c) *The Penitential Rite*
The priest invites the assembly to repent of their sins and then uses one of several alternative forms: (a) a collective act of penance by means of a shortened version of the 'I confess'; (b) a short dialogue; or (c) invocations of a more supplicatory nature which incorporate the 'Lord have mercy . . .'. Under the provision for adaptations to suit local needs [CL 37-40], the English edition of the Missal has two additional introductory prayers and seven additional options under (c).

Options (b) and (c) may be sung, usually responsorially with a cantor. This may be meaningful on occasions, but care should be taken not to overload this part of the Mass with congregational singing. The emphasis should be on the opening prayer and the scriptural readings.

(d) *Rite of Blessing and Sprinkling Holy Water*
This may be celebrated at all Sunday Masses. It takes the place of the Penitential Rite, and the *Kyrie* ('Lord, have mercy') is then omitted. It is full of significance, reminding us of our baptism and asking for a renewal of baptismal grace and a cleansing of our sins. It is a link with the renewal of baptismal vows and sprinkling with water which takes place at the Easter Vigil. It is particularly fitting for the community, a priestly people by virtue of their baptism, to begin the celebration of the eucharist on the Lord's Day with this sprinkling, especially as each Sunday is a particular celebration of the Easter mystery.

(e) *Lord Have Mercy* [4]
If this has not been included in the penitential rite, it is now sung or recited, normally responsorially. In some churches

the Greek version is retained (*Kyrie eleison, Christe eleison*). Short verses (tropes) may be inserted between the acclamations.

(f) *Glory be to God on high*
(Gloria in excelsis Deo)
This is an ancient hymn, and should therefore be sung whenever possible. It is used on Sundays (except in Advent and Lent), solemnities and feasts. The English version used in England, Wales, Scotland and Ireland is that drawn up for ecumenical use by the International Consultation on English Texts (ICET).

(g) *The Opening Prayer or Collect*
'Next the priest invites the people to pray, and together they spend some moments in silence so that they may realise that they are in God's presence and may make their petitions. The priest then says the prayer which is called the opening prayer or collect. This expresses the theme of the celebration ...' [GIRM 32].

There is a long tradition in both east and west of singing or chanting the prayer, and this practice seems preferable. However, we are not accustomed to prayers in English being sung, and perhaps the English language does not lend itself to this practice.

The lectern and the presidential chair
The priest is more properly referred to as the 'president' during the Introductory Rites and the Liturgy of the Word because he presides over this part of the liturgy, whereas he acts as the priest during the Liturgy of the Eucharist. However, the title 'president' is unpopular. After kissing and incensing the altar, the priest should go to the presidential chair and remain there throughout the Introductory Rites and the Liturgy of the Word, except when he goes to the lectern for the gospel and homily. (The homily can be given

from the chair.)

The Introductory Rites of the Mass and the Liturgy of the Word should not be conducted from the lectern (except for the readings, gospel and homily) and certainly not from the altar. If needs be, a small stand can be placed by the chair for the use of the president (for books and other items). To use the lectern for the penitential rite or the opening prayer is to detract from the importance of the proclamation of the word, while the use of the altar as a desk detracts from the Liturgy of the Eucharist.

As we shall discuss in Chapter Seventeen, there are three distinct focal points in the 'sanctuary' — the altar, the lectern, and the chair, each to be used for specific parts of the Mass.

Notes

1 Titles such as 'Introductory Rites' and 'Concluding Rite' are those used in the official full version of *The Roman Missal* in English published by William Collins and joint publishers. This is the altar missal used in church. A photo-reduced reproduction edition is available entitled *Saint Luke's Daily Missal*, published by C. Goodliffe Neale Ltd. The latter is suitable for study purposes, and much less expensive. With regard to this and the next chapter, it is very much hoped that readers will study the complete edition of the Missal and the *General Instruction of the Roman Missal*. The latter is printed at the front of the above editions of the Roman Missal and is also available as a pamphlet (CTS Do 455).

   The division of the Mass into clearly specified sections is taken from the Latin version, which is, of

The Mass: the Introductory Rites

course, definitive. Here the four main divisions are entitled 'Ritus initiales', 'Liturgia verbi', 'Liturgia eucharistica' and 'Ritus conclusionis'.

2   Thomas à Kempis, *The Imitation of Christ*, Book 4, ch. 11, 4.

3   Psalm 42 was adopted because of v. 4. It was used widely from at least the twelfth century. The *confiteor* ('I confess') dates from the early middle ages and has existed in various forms, both longer and shorter. The prayer formerly said by the priest as he ascended the altar steps, *Aufer a nobis* ('Take away from us our sins, O Lord ...') is to be found in several of the early sacramentaries. The prayer said as he kissed the altar, *Oramus te, Domine* ('We pray you, Lord, through the merits of the saints whose relics are here and of all the saints to forgive all our sins') is a later prayer, dating from the eleventh or twelfth century.

4   It has been suggested that Pope Gelasius (d.496) replaced the Solemn Prayers (which were similar to the Good Friday prayers) with a litany of his own and then transferred this litany to the beginning of the Mass. It has also been argued that Gregory shortened this litany, the *Kyrie eleison* being the only thing to survive. There is little certainty about this. It is more likely that the *Kyries* were inserted at this point of the Mass by or under Gregory in the late sixth century.

10

The Liturgy of the Word and the Lectionary

Structure of the Liturgy of the Word [GIRM 33-47]
We have already seen how the general structure of the Liturgy of the Word still resembles closely the Jewish sabbath synagogue service from which it is derived:

    READINGS from scripture
    Chants
    (HOMILY)
    (Profession of faith)
    (Prayer of the Faithful)

(The two major parts of the Liturgy of the Word are in capitals. Parts in brackets do not always occur.)

The Church has ordered that in Masses with a congregation

present, the readings are to be proclaimed at the lectern [LMI (*Lectionary for Mass: Introduction*, second edition, 1981), 16]. The lectern (or ambo) should be a permanent and dignified structure, not a movable stand [GIRM 272; LMI 32-34]. Readings should be proclaimed from books of readings or the Book of Gospels, not from leaflets or other pastoral aids [LMI 37].

On Sundays, solemnities and feasts, there are two readings before the gospel. The first is from the Old Testament and is followed by the responsorial psalm. The second is from the New Testament letters or the Apocalypse and is followed by the gospel acclamation and *alleluia*.

On other days there is a first reading from the Old or New Testament, followed by the responsorial psalm and the gospel acclamation. The *alleluia* is not used during Lent. It is usually clear from the Lectionary what is to be read and what responsorial psalm and acclamation are to be used.

(a) Readings

'Reading the scriptures is traditionally considered a ministerial, not a presidential function. It is desirable that the gospel be read by a deacon or, in his absence, by a priest other than the one presiding; the other readings are proclaimed by a reader. In the absence of a deacon or another priest, the celebrant reads the gospel' [GIRM 34].

(a) *Deacons*
The normal reader of the gospel is the deacon: this is one of the traditional roles of the deacon, and he can also give the homily. The use of a deacon at Mass should be encouraged where one is available. Some parishes have the services of a so-called 'permanent' deacon; others occasionally have a deacon from a seminary attached for pastoral experience. It is important that deacons should exercise their liturgical roles [GIRM 61; LMI 49, 50].

(b) *Instituted Readers (Lectors)*
Instituted readers (or lectors) may read any of the readings except the gospel. Their ministry is conferred through a liturgical rite. This is known in Canon Law as a 'stable' ministry, unlike that of the lay minister who is commissioned for a period of time. At present this institution is mainly confined to students preparing for the diaconate and men preparing for religious vows in an order or congregation. It is, however, open in principle to laymen who are not seeking the diaconate or priesthood. (There is another instituted ministry, that of acolyte. See *Code of Canon Law* 230.1.) When instituted readers are available, they must carry out their office [LMI 51].

(c) *Lay Readers*
Catholics are now accustomed to hearing the scriptures (except for the gospel) proclaimed by a lay reader. It is important to note that a reader exercises this ministry by being commissioned. It is an authentic lay ministry, and not connected with a shortage of priests.

Lay people who are readers should receive training [GIRM 66; LMI 51-55]. On the practical side they need to develop skills in voice production and modulation. They should study and practise the passages they are to read so that they can proclaim them effectively and meaningfully. They should have some background knowledge of the Bible and of the theology of the word. Their style of reading should be related to the type of passage in question. Narrative passages, prophetic passages, psalms, poetic passages, and epistles require different stress and tone: they should not all be delivered in the same perfunctory way. Readers should bear in mind that 'in the readings, God speaks to his people of redemption and salvation and nourishes their spirit' [GIRM 33].

(b) *Responsorial psalm*

The responsorial psalm after the first reading is an integral part of the Liturgy of the Word. Its text is usually related to the readings of the day, and it is the community's response to the proclaimed word. It should be sung whenever possible. The cantor can sing each verse of the psalm and the people sing the response. Alternatively, the psalm can be sung throughout by the whole assembly. When spoken, the responsorial psalm often sounds dull and meaningless, because it is a song and should be sung. If it is recited, it should not sound like a fourth reading, which it often does: the reader should read the psalm as poetry, with appropriate expression. Readers should *never* prefix their reading with announcements like 'Responsorial psalm' or 'The response is . . .', nor should they give orders to the people such as 'Response!'.

(c) *The Gospel*

The gospel is treated with great reverence because it is the word of Jesus Christ himself, and he is present in his word. Everyone stands and sings with great joy the gospel acclamation and *alleluia*. The book is carried in procession with lights and may be incensed. It is fitting that the gospel should be sung rather than recited. At the end the book of gospels is kissed. The practice of repeating the acclamation and *alleluia* after the gospel is very effective. The acclamation is pre-eminently meant to be sung: it is less convincing and effective when merely recited. Understandably, the rubrics say that it may be omitted if not sung. There are now many attractive melodies available for the responsorial psalm and acclamation, and cantors and music leaders should use a varied and lively selection of these melodies or even compose their own.

(d) The Homily

The homily is 'an integral part of the Liturgy of the Word and a necessary source of nourishment of the Christian life' [GIRM 41]. The homily is to be given on Sundays and holy days of obligation at all Masses with a congregation, and it is recommended on other days, especially during the seasons of Advent, Lent and Eastertide. The homily 'explains the readings' [GIRM 33]: God speaks to his people in the readings, explained by the homily. The homily therefore complements the readings. 'It should develop some point of the readings or of another text from the Ordinary or the Mass of the day. The homilist should keep in mind the mystery that is being celebrated and the needs of the particular community' [GIRM 41]. The same Instruction enacts that the homily should ordinarily be given by the celebrant.

(e) Silence [GIRM 23]

Times of silence are as important as singing and music. They should not just be inserted at random moments but where they will serve a definite purpose in relation to the liturgical action. The following silences are suggested during the Introductory Rites and the Liturgy of the Word:

1. a brief examination of conscience during the penitential rite;
2. a brief moment of private prayer between 'Let us pray' and the opening prayer;
3. silent recollection at the end of the first reading: after a suitable interval of time the president to give a signal for the responsorial psalm to commence;
4. silent recollection after the second reading at the end of which the president to stand and the gospel acclamation to be sung;
5. silent recollection (preferably with president and assembly

The Liturgy of the Word and the Lectionary

  seated) after the gospel;
6 silent recollection after the homily, until president stands to begin the creed.

This schedule of silences will not be popular with everyone! Those who have attended a Mass where this is done will, however, appreciate the value of such silences. To rush on from reading to responsorial psalm and straight on to second reading and acclamation is an unsuitable practice: it turns the readings into perfunctory formalities and leads to complaints that the Liturgy of the Word is overloaded with readings. Above all, there should be a silence after the homily. The president should return to the chair and sit down to join in with the assembly in meditation on the readings and homily. To proceed at once to the creed creates an abrupt and distracting transition from the word to the profession of faith.

(f) *The Creed*

The profession of faith is said on Sundays and solemnities. In it the people respond and give assent to the word of God spoken to them in the readings and preached in the homily. The creed originated as the credal questioning at baptism. It began to be said in eastern liturgies from the fifth century to counteract Christological heresies. Its use spread to Spain and then to the Holy Roman Empire under Charlemagne, and was finally inserted into the Roman Mass by Pope Benedict VIII in 1014 at the insistence of the Emperor Henry II.

  The creed used at Mass is the Nicene Creed, or more accurately the Niceno-Constantinopolitan Creed because it contains articles of faith formulated at the Council of Nicaea (325) and the Council of Constantinople (381). Whereas the Latin Missal of 1970 has retained the singular version of the creed (*Credo in unum Deum*), the English translation has reverted to the plural form found in the original conciliar texts[1] ('We believe in one God . . .'). The singular form is more suited to a baptismal profession of faith made by an individual person; the plural form is appropriate to a corporate profession of faith by a community. The adoption of the plural form is not, as some people have supposed, a novelty imposed by the translators or by liturgists. It is one of the texts used ecumenically, having been prepared by the International Consultation on English Texts (ICET) and approved by the bishops of England, Wales, Scotland and Ireland.

Singing the creed does not seem appropriate, especially in English: a declaration of articles of faith is not particularly song-like. However, many Catholics retain an attachment, perhaps nostalgic, to the *Credo* sung in Latin. Some countries have obtained permission to use the Apostles' Creed instead of the Nicene, and the Apostles' Creed may be used in Masses with children.[2]

(g) *The Prayer of the Faithful*

The Prayer of the Faithful or General Intercessions (styled *Oratio universalis*, universal prayer, in the Latin Missal) now follow, when they are to be said. They are to be regarded as appropriate in all Masses with a congregation [GIRM 45].

'As a rule the sequence of intentions is:

   (a) for the needs of the Church,
   (b) for public authorities and the salvation of the world,
   (c) for those oppressed by any need,
   (d) for the local community.

In particular celebrations, such as confirmation, marriages, funerals, etc., the list of intentions may be more closely concerned with the special occasion' [GIRM 46].

The Liturgy of the Word and the Lectionary

The priest invites the people to pray; the intentions are announced by the deacon, cantor or other person, and the congregation either makes a common response after each intention or prays silently. The latter option, allowed by GIRM 47, never seems to be used: it could on occasions be very suitable. The practice of singing the response seems unobjectionable, but the possibility of prolonging this part of the Mass unduly should be considered. After the intentions, the priest says the concluding prayer. In England and Wales it is customary to include a prayer to Mary (usually the 'Hail Mary') or a reference to 'joining our prayer with hers'. However, a Marian invocation, direct or indirect, is, on a strict view, inappropriate in the General Intercessions, which like all the prayers of the Mass, are addressed to the Father through the Son.[3]

Spontaneous intentions from individuals in the assembly are made on occasions, but in general the Church expects the intentions to be prepared beforehand and written out. It is preferable to prepare carefully worded intentions for each celebration, and not to rely solely on collections of ready-made prayers. The composition of these prayers could well be undertaken by the parish liturgy committee and other parishioners in conjunction with the priest. To be effective the prayers should be brief and simple.

Care must be taken that the intention sounds like an intention and not a miniature homily; it should have a form equivalent to 'Let us pray for ... Lord hear us' or 'We pray for ...' or simply 'For peace in the world ...' etc. The response must be in the form of petitionary prayer, such as 'Lord hear us' or 'We pray to the Lord'. Responses such as 'We are your children, O Lord' or 'You are always with us, O Lord' are inappropriate and lack any intercessory character. The response should, of course, relate to the petition which has just been proclaimed, and not introduce new petitions, as in this example from one of the printed collections: at the end of each petition the reader is required to say 'Lord, have mercy' and the people to reply 'And forgive us our trespasses'. Here a misconceived attempt to be imaginative has resulted in the people not praying for the main petitions at all, and instead reader and people have made two extra petitions!

The Prayer of the Faithful is not a novel feature of the Mass but a felicitous restoration of an ancient practice. In the old Roman Missal, the priest used to turn to the people after the creed (or after the gospel when the creed was not said), greet them with *Dominus vobiscum* (The Lord be with you), turn back to the altar and say *Oremus* (Let us pray). However, no prayers followed. This is all that had survived of the General Intercessions (rather like those of Good Friday) which used to be said at this point but were supposedly suppressed by Pope Gelasius in the sixth century.

The Lectionary for Mass

On 25 May 1969, the *Ordo Lectionum Missae* (Order of the Readings for Mass) was published, thus completing the revision of the eucharistic liturgy. This document consisted of a list of scriptural references. From it, the lectionary was compiled, at first in Latin and later in the vernacular. The *Lectionary for Mass* and the accompanying *Instruction* were reissued in a second edition in 1981, both lectionary and instruction having been considerably amplified. It is now in three volumes. The *Instruction* is an important source of information about the revised lectionary for Mass, dealing with the theological and liturgical significance of the lectionary and the structure of the order of readings.

The Second Vatican Council ordered the revision and extension of the lectionary. 'In sacred celebrations there is to be more reading from holy Scripture, and it is to be more varied and suitable.' 'The treasures of the Bible are to be opened up more lavishly, so that richer fare may be provided for the faithful at the table of God's Word. In this way a more representative portion of the holy Scriptures will be read to

The Liturgy of the Word and the Lectionary

the people over a set cycle of years' [CL 35, 51].

The new lectionary was the result of extensive consultation and study. It provided the following categories of readings:

(a) Thematic readings for Sundays (three year cycle) and weekdays (single cycle) in the seasons of Advent, Christmas, Lent, and Easter; the Easter Triduum; Ascension and Pentecost.
(b) A three-year cycle of readings for Sundays in Ordinary Time.
(c) A two-year cycle of readings for weekdays in Ordinary Time.
[(b) and (c) are independent of each other]
(d) Thematic readings for Solemnities of the Lord occurring in Ordinary Time: Holy Trinity, Corpus Christi, Sacred Heart.
(e) Readings for the Proper and Common of saints.
(f) Readings for ritual Masses, Masses for various needs and occasions, votive Masses, and Masses for the dead.

On Sundays and solemnities there are three readings: from the Old Testament, from an apostle (i.e. a letter or the Apocalypse), and from the gospels.

For Sundays in Ordinary Time, Year A (1989-90, 1992-93, etc.) has semi-continuous gospel readings from Matthew, Year B (1990-91, 1993-94) from Mark and sections of John, Year C (1991-92, 1994-95) from Luke. The Old Testament readings have been selected to harmonise with the gospel themes. The second readings are a semi-continuous reading of the Letters of Paul and James, as set out in Table II of the lectionary.

[In the case of Sundays, the lectionary year is the ecclesiastical year: it commences on the First Sunday of Advent and concludes on the Last Sunday of the Year (Christ the King): e.g. readings will be taken from Year A from Sunday 3 December 1989 and throughout 1990 until Sunday 25 November (Christ the King); from Sunday 2 December 1990, readings will be taken from Year B, and so on. See Table I in the lectionary.]

On feasts, memorias, ferias and other occasions, there are two readings. The first is from the Old or New Testament, the second from a gospel.

For weekdays in Ordinary Time, the first readings for each of the two year cycles (Year 1: 1991, 1993; Year 2: 1992, 1994) are as set out in Table III of the lectionary. The gospel readings are repeated each year, with selected passages and some semi-continuous reading first from Mark, then Matthew and finally Luke.

[In the case of weekdays in Ordinary Time, the Weeks of the Year in the lectionary commence on the day after the First Sunday of the Year (Baptism of the Lord): e.g. in 1991 (Year 1), the First Week of the Year will commence on Monday 14 January; Weeks of the Year will continue for five weeks up to the day before Ash Wednesday (13 February) and resume on 20 May with Week 7 and continue until Week 34 commencing 25 November. See Table I in the lectionary.]

The revised lectionary for Mass[4] has been widely praised for its distribution of the readings, and some non-Catholic Churches make use of it. Catholics are now able to hear most of the scriptures read in church, and the revised lectionary is a great improvement on the limited readings previously available. In this its compilers have admirably carried out the task set them by the Fathers at the Second Vatican Council. Scripture now plays a full and meaningful part in every liturgical rite, and particularly so in the Liturgy of the Word at Mass.

The Liturgy of the Word and the Lectionary

Notes

1 Cf. Greek and Latin texts in C.A. Heurtley, *De Fide et Symbolo* (Oxford: Parker, 1889), pp. 20, 25; and H. Denzinger, *Enchiridion Symbolorum* (Barcelona: Herder, 1948), pp. 29, 41.

2 Cf. *Directory for Masses with Children*, 49. [CTS Do 459].

3 I am told that some years ago the Congregation for Divine Worship intimated that the inclusion of the 'Hail Mary' or any other prayer to Mary was not permissible.

4 There is a separate lectionary for the Office of Readings. This will be discussed in the chapter on the Liturgy of the Hours.

11

The Liturgy of the Eucharist

Preparation of the Gifts [GIRM 48-53]
This preliminary section of the Liturgy of the Eucharist consists of the preparation of the altar and the placing on it of the gifts of bread and wine. This is essentially a practical element in the liturgy, and in the early centuries it was carried out without any prayers. In time prayers came to be said and various ceremonies added.

The Liturgy Consilium set up after the Vatican Council decided to make a complete revision and a certain simplification of this part of the Mass. The only prayer which has been retained is the *Orate, fratres* ('Pray, brethren, that my sacrifice . . .'). Opportunity has also been taken to bring out certain symbolic references which enrich the act of preparing the gifts.

The bread and wine are referred to in the rite specifically

The Liturgy of the Eucharist

as 'gifts', thus reviving a title found in some of the earliest liturgies. It designates the bread and wine not simply as elements to be provided for the eucharistic rite, but as gifts offered to God by his people: hence the stress in the rite on the offerings being brought forward. 'It is desirable for the faithful to present the bread and wine, which are accepted by the priest or deacon ... The rite of carrying up the gifts continues the spiritual value and meaning of the ancient custom when the people brought bread and wine for the liturgy from their homes' [GIRM 49]. In presenting the bread and wine, we are presenting ourselves also, bringing to God our needs, our good intentions, our faith, hope and love.

In this way our daily life and work is linked to the liturgy, and the spiritual nourishment of the eucharist is related to the physical nourishment of earthly food. This is echoed in the Jewish-type blessings said by the priest as he takes in his hands the gifts on the altar: 'which earth has given and human hands have made' and 'fruit of the vine and work of human hands'. The bread and wine begin as God's gifts to us: 'through your goodness we have this bread/wine to offer'. We fashion them, so to speak, and present them to God for the eucharist. He gives them back to us, in the 'divine exchange', transformed into the body and blood of his Son.

There is a stark contrast between the little we have to offer to the Father and the infinite grace which flows from the sacrifice of Christ on the cross. So just as we give back to the Father the gifts of nature which he has given to us, so we offer back to the Father the Son's offering of himself.

This part of the Mass used to be called the offertory. There is some difference of opinion concerning the significance of this term. Does it refer to the 'bringing up' of gifts by the people to the altar? Does it refer to the prayers which used to be said by the priest at this point: 'Receive, holy Father, this spotless host which I offer unto you ...' and 'We offer unto you, O Lord, the chalice of salvation ...' Does it refer, as seems most likely, not to *bringing* up or to *offering* up, but to *taking* up (in one's hands)? The priest is told in both the old and new forms of the rite to *take* the bread and the cup of wine into his hands; and this seems to come from the Jewish blessings where the president signifies the bread and wine over which the *berakoth* (blessings) are to be pronounced by taking them up in his hands (some books say holding them a hand's breadth above the table).

The term 'offertory' is no longer used as the name of the whole rite. This is to be welcomed as there was a tendency to confuse 'offertory' with 'offering'. At this point, we only have the bread and wine to offer; but during the eucharistic prayer, following the act of remembrance (*anamnesis*), we make the offering (or oblation) of the sacrifice of Christ (made once and for all). The title 'Preparation of the Gifts' avoids any possible ambiguity. However, the term 'offertory' has not entirely gone out of use: GIRM 50 refers to the 'offertory song' and in popular usage there is the expression 'offertory procession'. It is to be hoped that the word 'offertory' is now used with understanding of its correct meaning.

The Preparation of the Gifts consists of the following:

> Preparation of altar
> [corporal, purificator, chalice and missal]
> OFFERINGS (or GIFTS) BROUGHT UP
> [preferably by the people] AND TAKEN UP BY PRIEST
>
> (Collection of gifts or money for the poor and for the Church)
> (Incensing of gifts and altar)
> Priest washes his hands
> Invitation to pray with the priest
> PRAYER OVER THE GIFTS

(The principal parts of the Preparation of the Gifts are in capitals. Parts in round brackets do not always take place.)

Music and singing during the Preparation of the Gifts

There is no need to have any music or singing at all during this part of the Mass. By watching the practical actions, the people might best be able to ponder on the spiritual significance of the 'divine exchange' mentioned above. Too much music might prolong this part of the liturgy unduly. More importantly it might highlight these minor actions out of all proportion, so that the eucharistic prayer might seem less important because it is merely spoken by the priest. Finally, the temptation (1) to equate 'participation' with 'hymn singing', (2) to fill in silences and gaps with music, (3) to keep the people occupied with hymn singing as much as possible must be guarded against here and elsewhere in the Mass.

However, some music and singing seems to be a popular practice during the preparation of the gifts. It is quite fitting to have a song or hymn or chant as the gifts are brought up [GIRM 50]: this must be chosen so that its wording is relevant to the action. It should not begin until the procession begins. Instrumental music may be played as an alternative to singing. It could also quietly accompany the recitation of the blessings if these are said aloud. Apart from these suggestions, it would seem better to have silence during the preparation of the gifts rather than continual singing or instrumental background music.

The Eucharistic Prayer

The eucharistic prayer (or *Anaphora*) is the central part of the Liturgy of the Eucharist, indeed of the entire Mass. There seems to be less catechesis on the eucharistic prayer than on any other part of the Mass. This is to be regretted because there is a great need for more understanding among many Catholics of its nature and significance. A common failing seems to be not to see the eucharistic prayer as an integral whole. Some Catholics seem to see it as an accompaniment to the act of consecration and as a preliminary or formality leading up to the reception of holy communion. This is to perceive the eucharist in its sacramental aspects to the exclusion of its liturgical character.

In order to understand the Eucharistic Prayer, it is important to grasp why this part of the Mass is called a 'liturgy'. What is its liturgical character? How are priest and people involved in it? What is the relationship between priesthood and eucharist? We shall look briefly at these points before discussing the nature and structure of the Eucharistic Prayer.

Why 'liturgy'?

We talk of the 'Liturgy' of the Eucharist because it is a public, communal action, not an action pertaining exclusively to the priest. 'The Lord's Supper or Mass gathers together the people of God, with a priest presiding in the person of Christ, to celebrate the memorial of the Lord or eucharistic sacrifice' [GIRM 7]. Priest and people offer the liturgy together, while at the same time observing their distinctive roles.

Priesthood and the Mass

There are three aspects of priesthood in the eucharist.

(a) The first is that of Christ himself. 'The celebration of the Mass is the action of Christ and the people of God' [GIRM 1]. 'Christ always associates the Church with himself in the truly great work of giving perfect praise to God . . . Rightly, then, the liturgy is considered as an exercise of the priestly office of Jesus Christ . . . In the liturgy full public worship is performed by the Mystical Body of Jesus Christ, that is, by the Head and his members' [CL 7]. Christ offered himself to the Father on the cross. He is both priest and victim [Hebrews 9:10-12; and *passim* chs. 3-10]. In the eucharist, which is rightly called the sacrifice of the Mass, the unique and perfect sacrifice of Christ is sacramentally represented and enacted.

(b) The second dimension of priesthood is that of the

ordained priest who presides at the eucharist. He has received the sacrament of ministry (or order) which gives him authority to preside at the eucharist as the representative of the whole Church and to speak in the name of Christ and of the Church. He shares in the priesthood of Christ in a special way, acting as the minister 'of him who in the liturgy continually exercises his priestly office on our behalf by the action of his Spirit' [DP (*Decree on the Ministry and Life of Priests*) 5].

(c) The third dimension of priesthood is the priestly character of all the people of God, imparted in baptism. 'You are a chosen race, a royal priesthood, a consecrated nation, a people set apart to sing the praises of God who called you out of darkness into his wonderful light' (1 Peter 2:9). In our baptism we are consecrated to the worship of God, and so we share sacramentally in the priesthood of Christ, but in a manner distinct from that of the ordained priest. 'The ministerial priest moulds and rules the priestly people. Acting in the person of Christ, he brings about the Eucharistic Sacrifice, and offers it to God in the name of all the people. For their part, the faithful join in the offering of the eucharist by virtue of their royal priesthood. They likewise exercise that priesthood by receiving the sacraments, by prayer and thanksgiving, by the witness of a holy life, and by self-denial and active charity' [CC (*Dogmatic Constitution on the Church*) 10; cf. DP 2, DL (*Decree on the Apostolate of the Laity*) 3].

What is the Eucharistic Prayer?
It is a liturgical act consisting of three elements: giving thanks, remembrance, and offering:

(a) *giving thanks*
It is by Christ's mandate that we offer the eucharist: 'Do this . . .'. Christ had pronounced the *berakoth* over the bread and the wine, that is to say, he had 'blessed' God in the Jewish

sense of blessing, which means giving thanks and praise for something. Hence the word 'eucharist' which is Greek for 'giving thanks'.

(b) *remembrance*
Christ went on to say '. . . as a memorial of me'. He probably said this in Hebrew (rather than Aramaic) and used the word *zikkaron* for 'memorial'. The latter is translated in the Greek as *anamnesis*. Both words have a special meaning (there is no English equivalent in one word), namely remembering something not as an act of recalling but as making it a continuous present reality. Our Lord has ascended into heaven but he has left us his presence in the form of this ongoing and repeated 'memorial' or 'remembrance' of himself and of his death and resurrection. It is his death and resurrection which we (priest and people) remember and give thanks for in the eucharistic action. *Anamnesis* also implies a prayer that God's gift will continue. So Christ's death and resurrection, by which we have been saved and given new life, are remembered and their effects made present for us in the eucharist.

(c) *offering*
Christ offered himself to us at the Last Supper and to the Father on the cross. The Christ who is present to us in the eucharist is the Christ who died and rose again for us. In the eucharist Christ associates us with himself in offering his unique unrepeatable sacrifice to the Father. This sacrifice is continually recalled, re-enacted and offered to the Father in the eucharist. The sacrifice of the Mass, as the Council of Trent reaffirmed, is not only a sacrifice of praise and thanksgiving: it is a sacrifice of expiation for the sins of the living and the dead.

The Liturgy of the Eucharist

The structure of the Eucharistic Prayer [GIRM 54-55]

The eucharist prayer has a definite shape and structure. It is pronounced by the priest in the name of the Church, but the people offer it with the celebrant. Notice that the eucharistic prayer is in the plural throughout ('We . . .'). The congregation should therefore follow the eucharistic prayer as the priest is saying it and associate themselves closely with this act of thanksgiving, remembrance and offering. The people can be said to begin and end the eucharistic prayer (the Opening Dialogue and the Great Amen), and they have their parts in between ('Holy, holy', and proclaiming the Mystery of Faith). It should be noted that the eucharistic prayer begins at the dialogue, not after the 'Holy, holy'.

(a) Opening dialogue

This is one of the oldest parts of the eucharist. It occurs, for example, in the prayer of Hippolytus written in about 215. The theme of thanksgiving begins at this point with the words: 'Let us give thanks to the Lord our God'.

(b) Thanksgiving statements

The celebrant now recounts those things for which we are giving thanks in the eucharist. [By way of illustration, Eucharistic Prayer IV, the richest and fullest of the eucharistic prayers, will be quoted in this section.]

The first series of thanksgiving statements is called the Preface, which means 'proclamation', not 'foreword'. The preface is usually variable, which allows much choice to the celebrant. There are over eighty prefaces in the 1970 Missal, so that different mysteries of our faith can be emphasised at different times. Eucharistic Prayer IV, however, has its own preface, which cannot be replaced by another preface. This preface talks about God, the one true God, ever living, source of life and goodness, creator of all things, and so on. Then comes a note of praise (the Jewish blessing incorporated both thanks and praise) which leads to the *Sanctus* ('Holy, holy . . .').

The *Sanctus* was not inserted into the eucharistic prayer until the fifth century in the west. Before then the thanksgiving proceeded without interruption up to the consecration. It is a beautiful and striking acclamation; but it does tend to break the continuity of the eucharistic prayer by coming in the middle of the thanksgiving statements. This tendency is reinforced by the regrettable custom in this country of changing the posture of the congregation from standing to kneeling. This incidentally is against what is laid down in GIRM 21. Standing is a much more suitable posture for the proclamation of the eucharistic prayer. Kneeling is likely to encourage the unfortunate practice, inherited from earlier times, of making private devotions while the priest is saying the eucharistic prayer.

After the *Sanctus* the celebrant resumes the thanksgiving by recounting the history of salvation, starting with the creation, then mentioning the Fall, the covenants, the prophets, the sending of Jesus to be our saviour, the incarnation, the ministry, death and resurrection of Jesus, and the sending of the Holy Spirit 'to complete his work on earth'.

(c) The Consecration

The celebrant now says the first *epiclesis* or invocation of the Holy Spirit in which he prays that the Holy Spirit will sanctify the offerings (the bread and wine) that they might become the body and blood of Jesus Christ. This is known as the 'consecratory' *epiclesis*.' The priest then recites the Institution Narrative, the story of the Last Supper, during which the transformation of the gifts takes place. This is followed by the proclamation of the mystery of faith. There is a choice of four proclamations, each of which expresses succinctly (mostly in scriptural sentences) the paschal mystery of Christ's death and resurrection.

The Liturgy of the Eucharist

(d) The Remembrance
Although the entire eucharist is offered in memory of Christ, the celebrant now proceeds to make a specific act of remembrance, the *anamnesis*. In Eucharistic Prayer IV he prays:

> *Father, we now celebrate this memorial of our redemption.*
> *We recall Christ's death, his descent among the dead,*
> *his resurrection, and his ascension to your right hand;*

(e) The Oblation
The prayer runs straight on to the offering or oblation:

> *we offer you his body and blood,*
> *the acceptable sacrifice*
> *which brings salvation to the whole world.*

At this point a second *epiclesis* or invocation of the Holy Spirit is said. This is a 'communion' epiclesis in which the priest prays for the fruits of holy communion, especially for unity with Christ:

> *by your Holy Spirit, gather all who share this bread and wine into the one body of Christ, a living sacrifice of praise.*

(f) Intercessions
The priest now prays for all for whom the Mass is offered: the Pope and the Bishop, all bishops and priests, the congregation, all God's people, and all who seek God. Having prayed for the living, he prays for the dead. It is a cardinal point of Catholic doctrine that Mass is offered for both the living and the dead. He then prays that we may all 'enter into our heavenly inheritance', which leads into a note of praise once more.

(g) Final Doxology and Great Amen
This is taken up in the final doxology ('through him, with

him ...') to which the people respond with a resounding 'Amen', thus giving their assent to all that the priest has done in their name. This brings the eucharistic prayer (or *anaphora*) to an end.

Music and the Eucharistic Prayer

It is very desirable that the priest should sing (or chant), instead of reciting, the entire eucharistic prayer. In the eastern rites, much of the *anaphora* is chanted. This marks the solemnity of the eucharistic prayer and makes it stand out in importance. However, very few priests seem to do this, and it would be a strain if a priest has to say Mass several times during the weekend. Some priests sing the opening dialogue and the final doxology, and these are the parts which at least should be sung.

The people should join in the singing of the opening dialogue, the *Sanctus*, the proclamation of the mystery of faith, and the Great Amen: these are people's parts and are obviously meant for singing. They are less impressive when recited. The Amen should be sung with enthusiasm. There is no occasion for instrumental music during the eucharistic prayer, except to accompany the parts sung by the people: all attention should be directed to the priest's proclamation of the eucharistic prayer.

The Communion Rite [GIRM 56]

In earlier times, the celebrant then proceeded to the breaking of the consecrated bread and the distribution of holy communion. The fraction was a practical necessity as large loaves were used, and this was carried out by priests and deacons without any other rites.

Now, however, we prepare for communion by singing or saying the Lord's Prayer and by exchanging a sign of peace. In this way the people express their desire for unity with the Church and with all mankind before sharing the same bread.

The Liturgy of the Eucharist

Then comes an important function which is perhaps an overlooked feature of the Mass, the breaking of bread (or fraction). As well as being a practical necessity in earlier times, it has an obvious significance: the one loaf broken for many, the one sacrifice of Christ on the cross for all, the same communion with the whole Christ for all receivers. As Paul reminded the Corinthians, 'The fact that there is only one loaf means that, though there are many of us, we form a single body because we all have a share in this one loaf' (1 Corinthians 10:17).

GIRM 56(e) directs the singing or saying of the *Agnus Dei* (Lamb of God) during the breaking of the bread and the commingling which follows. It is best to avoid other activity at this time so that people are not distracted from the fraction. Ministers of Communion can leave their places and come to the sanctuary when the *Agnus Dei* is finished. Small ready-made hosts do not look much like bread, and their use reduces the fraction to a formality carried out on the celebrant's personal host. It is preferable for priests to use large hosts which can be broken into many pieces.

One occasionally sees priests breaking hosts just before the distribution of holy communion: this should, of course, have been done at the fraction. Another common practice which has been constantly deprecated by the Church is giving communion to the people at Mass from hosts in the tabernacle.[2] This is a most inappropriate practice. The host received in communion should have been consecrated at the same celebration of the eucharist, not at a previous one. Reception of communion is meant to be linked to the Mass in which it takes place, not to operate as a free-standing sacrament which happens to be received during Mass. There are occasions when hosts need to be taken from the tabernacle for communion during Mass, but this should not be the regular practice [GIRM 56(h)].

After the fraction, the celebrant says private prayers of

preparation for communion, and the people are recommended to pray in silence also. Music is inappropriate here.

Holy communion is now distributed. It is most desirable that the people should be able to receive the cup: this is now permitted at all Masses in England and Wales and it is the explicit wish of the Church that this should be made available [GIRM 56(h), 240]. Communion under both kinds and the use of Ministers of Communion will be discussed in Chapter Twelve.

The prayer after communion, which should be sung or said at the chair, not at the altar or lectern, begs God for the fruits of the eucharistic mystery; 'and by their acclamation, Amen, the people make the prayer their own' [GIRM 56(k)].

The Concluding Rite

The Liturgy of the Eucharist is now finished. The Roman Missal [Order of Mass 141] directs that any brief announcements are to be made at this point. In the Concluding Rite the priest greets the people and gives them a blessing, which on certain days and occasions can be expanded by the prayer over the people or by a solemn blessing.

The deacon, or if there is no deacon, the priest himself, dismisses the people 'to do good works, praising and blessing the Lord' [GIRM 57 (b)]. If any other liturgical service is to follow immediately, the rite of dismissal is omitted. The practice of adding other devotions on to the end of Mass after the dismissal has taken place is inappropriate, and it should be remembered that the accretions of several centuries had to be swept away from the Mass in the revision following the Second Vatican Council.

Music and singing during the Communion and Concluding Rites

Singing the Lord's Prayer seems preferable to saying it: 'The priest invites all the faithful to sing or say the Lord's Prayer with him' [GIRM 56 (a)]. A suitable and simple tune should be used so that no one is deterred from joining in. It is

The Liturgy of the Eucharist

important that it be sung by the whole assembly, not by the celebrant alone. It is appropriate also for the priest to sing the embolism[3] 'Deliver us . . .' and for the whole assembly to sing the doxology 'For the kingdom . . .', the latter in a tune corresponding to the Lord's Prayer.

Singing and music during the sign of peace are not recommended, and are not allowed for in the rite. During the fraction, the *Agnus Dei* (Lamb of God) is to be sung and can be repeated until the fraction is finished, surely an encouragement to have large hosts. It is better sung than said. It could be sung by the choir alone while the people meditate on the significance of the fraction and the coming of Christ in holy communion.

During the distribution of holy communion there are often too many hymns. Sometimes these hymns have been chosen at random and are quite irrelevant to holy communion. It may be better not to have hymns at all, but to have one piece sung by the choir, which can be the communion antiphon given in the Missal. A single Taizé chant (or similar) can be inspirational. Continuous organ playing or continuous hymn singing is an unwelcome intrusion into a time of silent prayer and meditation.

When the distribution of communion is finished, the celebrant should return to the chair for a period of silence. This is most important as the gathered community requires an opportunity after communion for prayer and recollection by both priest and people. When an adequate period of silence has been observed, the celebrant can rise and announce the hymn. A hymn is appropriate after the silence, and it should be one of thanksgiving for the eucharist. It is important that the priest should join in singing this hymn with the people and not give his attention to other matters during it, such as looking at notes or finding the place in the missal. Too often hymns are sung by the people alone while the priest does something else, and we should avoid giving the impression that we undervalue hymn singing or regard it as a 'stop-gap' activity or 'silence filler'.

The prayer after communion should be sung if the collect and the prayer over the gifts were sung. To sing these prayers is to give them their due solemnity: they are important presidential acts. The blessing is best said, while the dismissal can be sung at a more solemn Mass.

It is important that the celebrant and ministers leave the sanctuary after the dismissal. The Roman Missal does not allow for any further singing. It is suggested, therefore, that if a hymn is pastorally desirable, it is sung as the priest processes out. Alternatively, the choir could sing a chant or organ music could be played. A recessional hymn should, in the spirit of GIRM 57(b), be a hymn of praise or rejoicing.

Eucharistic Prayers in current use

Eucharistic Prayer I
In the Roman rite there was only one eucharistic prayer, known as the Roman Canon, which dated back to the fourth century. It was revised by Gregory I (Pope 590-604), and from then on only very slight changes were made. In 1962 John XXIII ordered Joseph to be added to the list of saints in the Canon.

The Liturgy Consilium set up by the Second Vatican Council considered carefully the possibility of either revising or replacing this prayer. Eventually it was decided that neither of these courses would be easy or acceptable, so it was left with a few minor changes and called Eucharistic Prayer I. At the same time it was decided to issue three additional alternative prayers.

Eucharistic Prayer II
This prayer is that of Hippolytus (c.215) with some modifications and additions (e.g. a *sanctus*). It has its own preface, but other prefaces may be used in place of it. It is a short prayer, and was expected to be used on weekdays.

However, it is widely used on Sundays as well, and is a popular prayer.

Eucharistic Prayer III
This prayer was composed by the committee set up to revise the Canon of the Mass[4], although it owes much to one man.[5] It is an attractive, balanced and well-rounded prayer.

Eucharistic Prayer IV
This is the longest of the new prayers. It must be used with its own preface, and is therefore not available for use on Sunday. It has been inspired by eastern eucharistic prayers, especially that of St Basil. It is a beautiful prayer, skilfully encompassing the whole of salvation history.

Eucharistic Prayers for Masses with Children
These three prayers for use in Masses where children are in a majority (e.g. school Masses) were first authorised in 1974. It is hoped they will be incorporated in the new edition of the missal which will be published in a few years' time. They are written in a simple direct style and make considerable use of acclamations by the children.

Eucharistic Prayers for Masses of Reconciliation
These two prayers were issued for use during Holy Year (and after) when the theme of Mass is that of reconciliation. Each must be used with its own preface.

Masses in Latin
While most Masses are now celebrated in a vernacular language, Mass can still be celebrated in Latin, using the *Missale Romanum* (1970). In accordance with liturgical principles, such Masses should be celebrated participatively, and in England the scripture readings have to be in English. However, for the celebration of Mass in Latin using the older missal (1962 edition), permission has to be obtained from the bishop of the diocese.

Notes

1 *Epiclesis* means 'invocation'. The word is usually used with reference to an invocation of the Holy Spirit, either on the gifts, or the people, or both. Most historic *anaphorae* have an *epiclesis*, usually after the consecration. The Orthodox Churches believe that the Holy Spirit effects the transformation of the gifts, while the Catholic Church teaches that this takes place through the words of consecration. There is a long-standing difference between east and west on this point.

The historic Roman Canon (now Eucharistic Prayer I) appears not to have an epiclesis, at least not one with a mention of the Holy Spirit. However, many liturgists believe that the Roman Canon contains an elaborate epiclesis, petitioning for consecration, in the two prayers following the anamnesis and oblation: *Supra quae propitio* ('Lord, look with favour on these offerings') and *Supplices te rogamus* ('Almighty God, we pray that your angel may take this sacrifice to your altar in heaven'). It is also claimed by some that the prayer before the consecration *Quam oblationem* ('Bless and approve our offering ... let it become for us ...') is an epiclesis.

It was decided to include two *epicleses* in Eucharistic Prayers II, III and IV, probably in recognition of the long-standing tradition, especially in the eastern Churches, and probably also in recognition of the operation of the Holy Spirit in every action of the Church, including its liturgy. By placing the first *epiclesis* before the Institution Narrative, it was made clear that it was a petition that the consecration might take place, but that it did not in itself effect the consecration. The *epicleses* are a

The Liturgy of the Eucharist

very striking and significant feature of the new eucharistic prayers.

2 The practice has been condemned, for example, by the Council of Trent; by Pope Benedict XIV in the encyclical *Certiores effecti* (eighteenth century); by Pius XII in the encyclical *Mediator Dei* (Christian Worship) (1947); by the Second Vatican Council [CL 55]; and in the Instruction *Eucharisticum Mysterium* (25 May 1967).

3 The embolism is the name given to the prayer which occurs between the Lord's Prayer and the Rite of Peace, *Libera nos, quaesumus, Domine* ('Deliver us, Lord, from every evil'). By derivation the word implies 'insertion' or 'intercalation'. It is connected with the Greek word *embolos*, a plug or wedge: hence the medical term 'embolism' meaning the obstruction of an artery by a clot of blood.

4 The Liturgy Consilium was divided into various groups. Coetus X, which consisted of nineteen eminent liturgists, dealt with the Canon of the Mass.

5 Dom Cipriano Vagaggini OSB, member of Coetus X and author of *The Canon of the Mass and Liturgical Reform* (London: Geoffrey Chapman, 1967).

12

The Sacrament of the Holy Eucharist and Eucharistic Worship

The Sacrament of the Holy Eucharist

The eucharist is the greatest of the sacraments of the Church. In it, Christ is truly present under the forms of bread and wine. With his body and blood he once offered himself on the cross. In this sacrament he offers himself in an unbloody manner to his heavenly Father and gives himself to his people as nourishment for their souls.

During the Liturgy of the Eucharist, when the priest repeats the words of Christ, the bread and wine are consecrated by the power of the Holy Spirit. They cease to be bread and wine, and become the body and blood of Christ really present to us. We receive the whole Christ, body, blood, soul and divinity, in the eucharist, and in either of the species. When either consecrated species is divided, the whole Christ is present in each part of the species.

The outward signs of the sacrament of the eucharist are bread and wine (the matter) and the words of institution (the form). All the sacraments confer sanctifying grace. In addition each sacrament confers a specific grace, which in the case of the eucharist is an intrinsic union with Christ (I Corinthians 10:16-18). The eucharist is also food for the soul, preserving and increasing its supernatural life. Through it we offer satisfaction to God for our sins and obtain the grace of repentance. Finally, the eucharist is a pledge of the happiness of heaven and of the future resurrection of the body. The reception of the eucharist is necessary for salvation insofar as Christ has made salvation dependent on the partaking of his body and blood (John 6:53-54).

The tabernacle and reservation

What is the liturgical significance of the tabernacle in the church and of the practice of reservation of the Blessed Sacrament? The origins of reservation were purely practical, namely the availability of consecrated hosts for viaticum and for the communion of the sick. Only much later, and gradually, did the principle of venerating the reserved sacrament develop as a rite separate from the Mass. It was only after the Council of Trent that a fixed tabernacle came into widespread use for reservation, and it was even later that the practice of installing the tabernacle on the principal altar in the church became common. Even so, cathedrals and greater churches retained a separate Blessed Sacrament Chapel for reservation.

Since the Second Vatican Council, certain norms have been established concerning the tabernacle [GIRM 276, 277; Sacred Congregation of Rites, Instruction *Eucharisticum mysterium* (1967), 53-55; GIWE (*General Introduction to Holy Communion and Worship of the Eucharist Outside Mass*) 5-11; Code of Canon Law (1983), canons 934-944]. It should be situated in a separate chapel, rather than in the sanctuary. It is not appropriate for the sacrament to be reserved in close proximity to the altar on which Mass is celebrated. Christ's presence in the celebration of the eucharist is to be perceived differently from his presence for private adoration and prayer in the reserved sacrament:

> 'To express the sign of the eucharist, it is more in harmony with the nature of the celebration that, at the altar where Mass is celebrated, there should if possible be no reservation of the sacrament in the tabernacle from the beginning of Mass. The eucharistic presence of Christ is the fruit of the consecration and should appear to be such' [GIWE 6].

The separate chapel should be suitably designed, with regard to space and atmosphere, for people to be able to make their private devotions. It should be in a reasonably prominent and dignified position.

If the positioning of the tabernacle in the sanctuary is unavoidable, it should not be placed in a central position behind the altar, but to one side. The placing of the presidential chair in front of the tabernacle is to be avoided. Holy communion may for good reasons be given to the faithful outside Mass, in which case the hosts are taken from the tabernacle. But at Mass the faithful should receive hosts consecrated at the same Mass.

Holy Communion under both kinds

Christ instituted the eucharist under two kinds, bread and wine, and it was clearly intended that reception should be of both kinds. Sadly, by the twelfth century, the laity had largely withdrawn from receiving the chalice, and indeed from receiving communion at all except infrequently. As we have seen, the Council of Trent decided it would not be appropriate to restore the chalice to the laity. However, the Second Vatican Council opened the way to this. In England and Wales permission has been given by the Holy See for the laity to receive the chalice at both Sunday and weekday Masses.

Not all parishes have availed themselves of this permission, unfortunately, despite the strong encouragement of the Church's teaching:

> 'It is most desirable that the faithful should receive the body of the Lord in hosts consecrated at the same Mass and should share the cup when it is permitted. Communion is thus a clearer sign of sharing in the sacrifice that is actually being celebrated' [GIRM 56(h)].

> 'The sign of communion is more complete when given under both kinds, since in that form the sign of the eucharistic meal appears more clearly. The intention of Christ that the new and eternal covenant be ratified in his blood is better expressed, as is the relation of the eucharistic banquet to the heavenly banquet. ... the faithful should be urged to take part in the rite which brings out the sign of the eucharistic meal more fully' [GIRM 240-1].[1]

Ministers of Communion

The ordinary minister of communion is a bishop, priest or deacon: the term 'ordinary' relates to their orders. Whenever priests or deacons are present in the sanctuary at Mass, they should distribute holy communion, unless for some good reason they are prevented from doing so.

In many churches, 'extraordinary ministers', i.e. lay ministers, are now (with the priest) distributing holy communion at Mass. It can be said that this new ministry is both important and valuable, and has been welcomed and accepted by most of the faithful. It is not a makeshift expedient, and the ministers are not simply 'helping out the priest'. It is an authentic ministry enjoying the full authority of the Church.

This ministry is both a lay ministry and a liturgical ministry. It was first established by Pope Paul VI in the Instruction *Immensae Caritatis* issued on 25 January 1973. In this the Pope wrote:

> 'Christ has left to the Church the wonderful gift of the Eucharist ... Provision must be made lest reception of communion become difficult because of insufficient ministers ... So that the faithful may not be deprived of this sacramental help and consolation, it has seemed appropriate to the Pope to establish special extra-ordinary ministers, who may give holy communion to the faithful.'

Subsequently the ministry was given specific authority in the new *Code of Canon Law* (1983), canons 230, 910, 911 and 943. [cf. also GIWE 17, 60.]

Ministers have to be carefully chosen and trained. They are commissioned by the bishop, and the commission is renewed annually. Their first duty is to help the priest give the hosts and the chalice at Mass. This help is even more needed when congregations receive the chalice. Ministers also take communion to the sick, the elderly, the housebound, and the dying. They can help the priest when communion is given outside Mass. In the absence of a priest, a minister can hold a communion service and also a service in honour of the Blessed Sacrament with exposition, but without giving the blessing.[2]

Worship of the Eucharist outside Mass

Following the revision of the rite of Mass, the Instruction *Eucharisticum Mysterium* was published on 25 May 1967. This regulated the practical arrangements for the worship of the eucharist outside Mass. It also clarified the relationship between this worship and the Mass in accordance with the teaching of the Second Vatican Council and of other documents.

This was subsequently revised, and The Roman Ritual *De Sacra Communione et de Cultu Mysterii Eucharistici extra Missam* was published in the Latin form in 1973. The adapted English version, *Holy Communion and Worship of the Eucharist Outside Mass*, approved for use in England, Wales, Scotland and Ireland, was published in 1978.

Before the Second Vatican Council, reception of holy communion outside Mass and the service of Exposition of the Blessed Sacrament and Benediction tended to be seen as rites on their own, separate from the Mass. The General Introduction to the rite repeated and amplified the teaching of *Eucharisticum Mysterium* on the validity of eucharistic worship of this sort and its link with the Mass. The *Decree of the Sacred Congregation for Divine Worship* which accompanied the rite spelt out this teaching succinctly:

> 'The celebration of the eucharist in the sacrifice of the Mass is the true origin and purpose of the worship shown to the eucharist outside Mass. The principal reason for reserving the sacrament after Mass is to unite, through sacramental communion, the faithful unable to participate in the Mass, especially the sick and aged, with Christ and the offering of his sacrifice.
>
> In turn, eucharistic reservation, which became customary in order to permit the reception of communion, led to the practice of adoring this sacrament and offering to it the worship which is due to God. This cult of adoration is based upon valid and solid principles.'

(a) Holy Communion outside Mass

The rite of distributing holy communion outside Mass has the following structure:

Introductory rites:
    Greeting
    Penitential rite

Celebration of the Word of God:
    Reading(s)
    General Intercessions

Holy Communion:
    The Lord's Prayer
    The sign of peace
    Communion
    Silent prayer or psalm/song of praise
    Concluding prayer

Concluding rite:
    Blessing
    Dismissal

In several important respects this rite reflects the structure of the Mass. As with most rites today, there is a celebration of the word so that, as in the Mass, the people might be nourished by the word and 'by hearing it they learn that the marvels it proclaims reach their climax in the paschal mystery of which the Mass is a sacramental memorial and in which they share by communion' [rite #26]. There is considerable choice of readings and prayers. There is also a shorter rite of distributing holy communion outside Mass for use when the longer form is unsuitable or when there are only one or two communicants.

The Sacrament of the Holy Eucharist

(b) Exposition and Benediction
The Rite of Eucharistic Exposition and Benediction is as follows:

Exposition:
  Song
  Exposition

Adoration:
  Readings, homily, prayers, songs *ad libitum*
  OR Liturgy of the Hours

Benediction:
  Eucharistic Song
  Prayer
  Blessing

Reposition:
  Reposition
  Acclamation

This rite has considerable flexibility built into it, especially during the period of adoration. The latter is to consist of prayers, songs and readings, and periods of silent prayer. Not all the readings have to be scriptural. The Introduction stresses that:

> '... exposition invites us to the spiritual union with Christ that culminates in sacramental communion. ...This kind of exposition must clearly express the cult of the blessed sacrament in its relationship to the Mass. The plan of the exposition should carefully avoid anything which might somehow obscure the principal desire of Christ in instituting the eucharist, namely, to be with us as food, medicine and comfort' [rite # 51].

Provision is also made for eucharistic processions and eucharistic congresses.

Music and singing in these rites

These rites lend themselves very readily to singing and music. This is particularly the case with the rite of exposition, where there are specific instructions on this point. The English version of this rite approved for use in England, Wales, Scotland and Ireland gives many resources, especially for singing, in an appendix.

The rite for the distribution of communion outside Mass allows for a psalm or chant after the first reading, a hymn during the distribution, and a psalm or song of praise after the distribution. It is possible to have singing at other points in this rite. All the songs or chants should reflect the theme of the rite or of the current liturgical season.

The rite of exposition and benediction allows for an opening song, songs and responses to readings during the period of adoration, a hymn or other eucharistic song at the end of this period, and a sung acclamation during the reposition. The custom of afterwards processing to a chapel or statue of Our Lady and singing a hymn or antiphon in her honour is commended. In all this rite there is considerable scope for imaginative choice of relevant material for singing or chanting, and perhaps also for quiet meditative music at appropriate times. It is of great importance that there should be adequate periods of silence.

Lay led services

It has already been noted that lay ministers can, in the absence of a priest and with permission, hold services of holy communion and services of exposition of the Blessed Sacrament. In addition, lay ministers are authorised by the new Code of Canon Law (1983) [canon 230 # 3] to exercise the ministry of the word and to preside over liturgical prayers in the absence of a priest.

So far in the UK such services are mainly held on weekdays, usually when a priest is on an extended absence and no supply priest is available. In some missionary countries and in some countries with a severe shortage of priests it is necessary for services to be led by lay persons on a Sunday. It is conceivable that we shall be in this position within a few years.

This situation is already catered for in Canon Law, where canon 1248 # 2 enjoins:

> 'If it is impossible to assist at a eucharistic celebration, either because no sacred minister is available or for some other grave reason, the faithful are strongly recommended to take part in a liturgy of the Word, if there be such in the parish church or some other sacred place, which is celebrated in accordance with the provisions laid down by the diocesan bishop.'

Further attention has been paid to this problem and on 2 June 1988 the Congregation for Divine Worship issued a *Directory on Sunday Celebrations in the absence of a priest*.[3] This Directory contains a detailed review of the nature of Sunday and gives detailed guidance on the organisation of services presided over by a lay person. If Mass is not possible, then first place is to be given to a Liturgy of the Word. This may be followed by communion. It is anticipated that most congregations will desire to receive communion on these occasions. This is understandable, but perhaps further catechesis is needed on the significance of the ministry and celebration of the word.

We have, in effect, been warned by this Directory to be prepared for Sunday celebrations without a priest. In our case we have plenty of advance warning to begin planning, training and providing resources well before the crisis occurs. These services will call for careful organisation and planning, with co-ordination between those responsible for reading, music and singing, leading the prayers, and distributing holy communion. It is not suggested that there should be a 'team ministry' at these services, and it may be that a different type of lay minister will be needed in some cases, namely a person with skills at presiding. There is a welcome flexibility envisaged for these services, which we hope will be retained, and the musical arrangements and choice of sung material will be of great importance in making these services spiritually and liturgically effective.

Notes

1 For a fuller account of communion under both kinds, see my book *Why Receive the Chalice?* (Kevin Mayhew, 1990).

2 I have given a detailed account of this ministry in my book *Preparing to be a Minister of Communion* (St Thomas More Centre, 1990).

3 English translation in *Liturgy* 13:1 (October–November 1988).

13

The Liturgy of the Hours

Origins

The Divine Office is the official public prayer of the Church. It complements the celebration of the eucharist in the offering to God of praise and prayer for the needs of the world. The Church has always taken seriously the duty of ceaseless prayer (1 Thessalonians 5:17; Colossians 4:2). This was observed from earliest times by the practice of praying regularly every day at fixed times. At first this tended to be an observance by individuals or small groups. In time, and especially after the separation of church from synagogue, these devotions were systematised and developed into public communal services.[1]

After the 'Peace' of 313, these devotions became church services, at least in cathedrals and greater churches. It is not until the fourth century, therefore, that we can discern a distinctive daily office. But only in its broadest structure does the fourth century office resemble what we are familiar with as the office today. We could take as an example the office as celebrated at the cathedral in Milan in the time of Ambrose (bishop 374-397).[2] The main offices were those of Morning and Evening Prayer.

Morning Prayer was a celebration of Christ's resurrection, symbolised by the light of morning and the new day. There would have been psalms, probably the same ones on most days, and very likely including Psalm 50 and the 'laudal' Psalms 148-150; canticles, such as the *Gloria in excelsis Deo*; a hymn, especially one composed by Ambrose such as *Aeterne rerum conditor/noctem*; a reading (perhaps); and prayers.

Evening Prayer probably included the *lucernarium*, the lighting of lamps ceremony. Evening with the approach of darkness symbolised sin and evil, and the lamp symbolised the light of Christ overcoming the powers of darkness. There would have been psalms, probably including Psalm 141 (cf. verse 2); canticles; hymns such as Ambrose's *Deus creator omnium*; a reading (perhaps); and prayers.

There were two lesser offices, probably attended by fewer of the faithful. At midday there was a simple office, probably consisting of all or part of Psalm 118. At cockcrow there was the night office, that is, a short vigil service of readings and prayers. On greater feasts the latter was replaced by an all-night vigil, which would surely have included some of Ambrose's hymns, for he wrote his first 'office' hymns for use at such a vigil in a time of danger.[3] With some qualification,[4] one can regard this as typical of the fourth century office in the west.

The 'cathedral' office

The type of office just described is classified by many liturgists as the 'cathedral' type of office. Its characteristics were as follows. The daytime offices were essentially services of praise and prayer. They were popular services in both senses: they were designed for the people and were attended by the people. Only a limited number of psalms were used, and there was little variation in the psalms chosen from day to day. Scriptural readings, if any, were brief. There was no continuous recitation of psalms and no continuous reading of scripture. These offices were services of the local worshipping community, and they were performed by clerics and laity together, presided over by the bishop in the case of cathedral offices.

The 'monastic' office

In contrast to this, another type of office developed, called by liturgists the 'monastic' type of office. This was the form of office developed by monks as part of their ascetic life. Although there were similarities to the 'cathedral' office, the 'monastic' office was fundamentally private worship, albeit in a public form, carried out basically for the edification of the monk. There were more offices in the daily cycle than in the 'cathedral' office. In addition to morning and evening prayer, there were the daytime offices of terce, sext and none, and the long night office of vigils. Eventually two other offices were added, prime and compline. Much more use was made of psalmody and scriptural reading than in the 'cathedral' office: in fact the 'monastic' office was largely based on two principles, namely the recitation of all the psalms every week and the reading of the whole Bible every year.

A monasticised office

Unfortunately perhaps, these two types of office interacted on each other. In some places monks attended the public office, prefixing their psalmody to the 'cathedral' office. In other places, the two types became fused. From the sixth century the 'cathedral' office was gradually replaced by the 'monastic' office. As a result, the office became increasingly monasticised in structure and length. It ceased to be the prayer of the people, and instead became thoroughly clericalised in the sense that it was complex in form and remained in the Latin language when that language had ceased to be generally spoken.

The reform of Pius V
The reformed Roman Breviary issued by Pius V in 1568 was pre-eminently a prayer book for clerics. Although it was formally a choral office, many clerics could not or did not attend communal celebrations of the office, and yet were required to recite the entire office as a personal obligation. Although there were certain subsequent reforms of the Roman Breviary, notably by Urban VIII in the seventeenth century and by Pius X who issued a new psalter in 1911, it still remained a burdensome obligation on clerics. The principle of the weekly recitation of the psalms and the yearly reading of the whole Bible remained, and persisted as an unalterable norm throughout all attempts to reform and shorten the office until the Second Vatican Council. Even then, it was still assumed that all (or nearly all) the psalms should be used and repeated at fixed intervals, and most of the scriptures should be read in the course of the year. We shall return to this criticism shortly.

The Second Vatican Council
Despite some simplification of rubrics in 1955 and 1960, the office as set out in the Roman Breviary was still rather complicated, and an *ordo* was usually needed to ensure that the correct office was being recited. The office was in many ways beautiful and dignified. It had greatly impressed John Henry Newman when he first used it as an Anglican in 1836, and he wrote Tract 75: 'On the Roman Breviary as embodying the substance of the devotional services of the Church Catholic', which begins as follows:

The Liturgy of the Hours

'There is so much of excellence and beauty in the services of the Breviary, that were it skilfully set before the Protestant by Roman controversialists as the book of devotions received in their communion, it would undoubtedly raise a prejudice in their favour . . .'

However, in the twentieth century, for the average (especially the non-monastic) cleric the number of psalms to be recited in the course of the day was excessive. Because of the length of the divine office, it was not surprising that some priests recited it rapidly and tried to complete the recitation as early as possible in the day, irrespective of the times at which the individual offices were intended to be said, lest time should run out and the obligation remain unfulfilled. There was a need for the office to be shorter so that it could be recited with less haste and more meaningfully.

The Constitution on the Sacred Liturgy

Chapter IV of the Constitution laid down norms for the revision and simplification of the office. Morning Prayer and Evening Prayer were to be considered the chief hours and celebrated as such. The hours should as far as possible be recited at the time of day for which they were intended. Compline should be a prayer suitable for the end of the day. Prime was to be suppressed, and, in private recitation, only one of the little hours (terce, sext or none) had to be said. The Constitution also laid down that the psalms were to be distributed over a longer period than one week. Matins was to be made up of fewer psalms and longer readings, and adapted so that it could be recited at any hour of the day.

Whilst giving much attention to priests and religious reciting the office, the Constitution recognised the need to restore the office to the people:

'Pastors of souls should see to it that the chief hours,

especially Vespers, are celebrated in common in church on Sundays and the more solemn feasts. And the laity, too, are encouraged to recite the divine office, either with the priests, or among themselves, or even individually' [CL 100].

Unfortunately, the first part of this section has not been generally implemented. While there are difficulties in doing this, it seems that in most parishes the question of celebrating even this one office a week has not been considered. There is, unfortunately, a widespread misunderstanding of the liturgical significance of the office.

On the other hand, the second part of this section has not remained entirely unfulfilled. The office has been simplified, shortened and translated; and a surprising number of lay people have taken to praying it, either privately, or with spouses, or in small groups. In some parish churches weekday Masses are preceded by Morning or Evening Prayer.

Chapter IV of the Constitution has a very powerful statement about the importance and significance of the divine office in the life of the Church:

> 'Jesus Christ continues his priestly work through the agency of his Church, which is ceaselessly engaged in praising the Lord and interceding for the salvation of the whole world. This she does not only by celebrating the eucharist, but also in other ways, especially by praying the divine office ... When this wonderful song of praise is rendered by priests ... or by the faithful praying together with the priest in an approved form, then it is truly the voice of the bride addressing her bridegroom; it is the very prayer which Christ himself, together with his body, addresses to the Father ... Hence all who perform this service are not only fulfilling a duty of the

Church, but are also sharing in the greatest honour accorded to Christ's spouse, for by offering these praises to God they are standing before God's throne in the name of the Church their Mother' [CL 83-85].

The Constitution repeatedly stresses that the office is the public prayer of the Church. It is distinct from but related to personal prayer. Those who pray the office should 'improve their understanding of the liturgy and of the Bible, especially the psalms'. 'In the revision of the Roman Office, its ancient and venerable treasures are to be adapted so that all those to whom they are bequeathed may more extensively and easily draw riches from them' [CL 90].

This last quotation gives the clue, perhaps, to the nature of the revision of the office which was made, namely that it is a radical but conservative reform. The new office has retained, albeit in a less complex and burdensome way, much of the clerical and monasticised character it had borne for centuries. The Liturgy of the Hours is still predominantly a 'monastic' office and there is great scope for introducing more elements of a 'cathedral' type into it. For example, the use of selected psalms only, not of all the psalms, with the addition of other elements of praise and prayer, would make it an authentic people's office as against a clerical office.

Without abandoning the essential characteristics of the divine office, there needs to be more variety, flexibility, imaginativeness and relevance built in to this part of the liturgy if it is to fulfil its function as the prayer of the whole People of God and if it is to be restored to the mainstream worship of our parish churches.

The Liturgy of the Hours

The task of revising the divine office was entrusted to Group 9 of the *Consilium ad exsequendam Constitutionem de Sacra Liturgia* (the 'Liturgy Consilium'). Under its *Relator generalis*, Aimé Georges Martimort, this group took six years to complete its work, a task involving over one hundred specialists in various fields. The Group was sub-divided into nine study groups (*coetus*), each of which worked on a specific part of the office.

After widespread consultation, the revised office was issued. The title 'Roman Breviary' was not used; instead the new divine office was entitled 'The Liturgy of the Hours', a name which suggests very appropriately the sanctification of time throughout each day. It came into use in 1971, when the Latin version in four volumes was published. The English version approved for use in England and Wales, Scotland, Ireland, Australia and thirteen other countries was published in three volumes in 1974. It was compiled by a committee under the chairmanship of Dom Placid Murray OSB of Glenstal Abbey. Subsequently, selective editions of the office have been published, the most popular and practical of which is *Morning and Evening Prayer from the Divine Office*.[5] The latter, with its useful introduction, is strongly recommended for an initial study of the office.

General Instruction on the Liturgy of the Hours

This document can be described as an outstanding liturgical statement on the nature and significance of the divine office. It is also a comprehensive guide to the *Liturgy of the Hours*, giving a description of each part of the office, pastoral notes, and directions concerning the celebration and recitation of the office. It is essential reading for a study of the daily prayer of the Church.[6]

Structure of the Liturgy of the Hours

There are now five offices making up the Liturgy of the Hours:

Morning Prayer (Lauds)
The Middle Hour (Terce or Sext or None)
Evening Prayer (Vespers)
Office of Readings (said at any convenient time)
Night Prayer (Compline)

The Liturgy of the Hours

At each of the offices there are the following elements:

Hymn
Psalms
The Word
Prayer

(a) Morning and Evening Prayer
These are the chief offices on which the others hinge, so to speak, and they have a similar plan:

Introduction ('O God come to my aid . . .')
Hymn
Psalmody:
   Morning   *Evening*
   1st psalm   1st psalm
   OT canticle   2nd psalm
   2nd psalm   NT canticle
The Ministry of the Word:
   Scripture reading
   (A period of silence)(optional)
   Short responsory
   (A homily may be given)
Gospel canticle:
   Morning: The Benedictus
   Evening: The Magnificat
Prayer:
   Petitions
   (A period of silent prayer)(optional)
   The Lord's Prayer
   Concluding prayer
Blessing
Dismissal

(b) Office of Readings

The structure of this office is much simpler than that of the former matins:

> Introduction
> Hymn
> 3 psalms (or sections of psalms)
> Versicle and response
> Scriptural reading + responsory
> Patristic or hagiographical reading + responsory
> (*Te Deum* on Sundays outside Lent, feasts and solemnities)
> Concluding prayer
> 'Let us praise the Lord ...'

(c) The Middle Hour

Consists of the following elements:

> Introduction
> Hymn
> 3 psalms (or sections of psalms)
> Short lesson
> Versicle and response
> Concluding prayer
> 'Let us praise the Lord ...'

Additional texts are provided for saying all three hours (terce, sext, none) if desired. If more than one hour is said, the additional psalms are normally taken from the so-called 'complementary psalms'.

(d) Night Prayer

This is intended to be said before retiring for the night. The arrangement is as follows:

> Introduction
> Examination of conscience (optional)

Hymn
Psalm(s)
Scripture reading
Responsory
Nunc dimittis
Concluding prayer
Blessing
Anthem to the Blessed Virgin

Elements of the office

(a) *Office Hymns*

The office hymns have an important liturgical function. They indicate, often more specifically than other parts of the office, the characteristics of the time of day or the liturgical season or the feast being celebrated. They are therefore now placed at the beginning of each office so as to set the theme for that office. They are intended to be sung, not by a specialist choir, but by the whole assembly. 'They help to move the people taking part and draw them into the celebration' [GILH 173].

From this the primary characteristics of the office hymn may be summarised as follows. The hymn should be laudal in character, proclaiming, rejoicing, making remembrance of a mystery or occasion or time. It is not a theological treatise. It should be simple and not complicated; scriptural and sound in doctrine, but not heavy with allegory or metaphor; dignified and solemn, but not ponderous or triumphalist. It should, of course, be lyrical and poetical.

The Latin office hymns have a long and interesting history. For the *Liturgia Horarum*, the Latin edition of the new office, the hymnary was thoroughly revised by *coetus* 7 of Group 9 (of the Liturgy Consilium), under their *Relator*, the distinguished classicist and hymnologist Dom Anselmo Lentini of Monte Cassino Abbey. The new Latin hymnary contained 291 hymns, in contrast to the 171 hymns of the Roman Breviary. The best hymns were retained and restored to their original version (having been 'classicised' by Urban VIII). Many other Latin hymns not previously in use were included. Seven twentieth century hymn writers are represented in the new hymnary. Forty-two completely new Latin hymns were composed for the *Liturgia Horarum*, all of them by Dom Anselmo Lentini. There is now a much richer variety of hymns, and the hymns are all suitable and relevant to the office in which they occur.[7] The tunes for these hymns are now available in the *Liber Hymnarius* (Solesmes, 1983).

It is a matter of some regret, although understandable, that with the widespread use of vernacular translations of the office, this fine body of Latin hymns is not used very much and that many of those who pray the office regularly do not know them. It has to be admitted also that these Latin hymns, admirable in themselves, are suited more to 'specialist' singers with an understanding of Latin and an ability to sing the tunes to which they are set than to popular use in the parish church.

Hymns had to be provided for the English version of the Divine Office by the committee under Dom Placid Murray. After much investigation and consultation, the final selection of English hymns was made by Monsignor John Humphreys and Mrs Susan Chapman. The aim was to provide, especially for Morning, Evening and Night Prayer, hymns which could be readily sung by congregations and religious communities. An index of hymn tunes and metres was compiled by Father Laurence Hollis. It was decided to include (after the model of the German interim breviary) a selection of religious poetry for alternative use in private recitation, especially in the Office of Readings and the Middle Hour. These texts were selected by Father (now Monsignor) Peter Coughlan, with help from a group in Rome. Some of the hymns were taken from the *Stanbrook Abbey Hymnal* and these are excellent office hymns.

The committee had a difficult task, being limited to hymns already available, and not being able to commission new hymns. They have provided an interesting selection of hymns, and it is to be hoped that other office hymns will eventually be composed, especially in areas not well covered by the existing hymnody. A commendable collection of English hymns for the office, compiled by the Panel of Monastic Musicians, was published in 1976 entitled *A Song in Season* (Collins). It should, of course, be borne in mind that any suitable hymn may be used in the office.[8]

(b) *Psalms*

From its very beginnings the Christian Church has used the psalms in the same way as the Jews did, that is as a liturgical book. The Jewish rubrics to the psalms are given in some translations of the Bible, especially those derived from the Septuagint, and these indicate clearly their liturgical use among the Jews. The Book of Psalms has often been described as 'the hymnal of the Second Temple'.

The Hebrew name for the psalms is 'songs of praise', while the Greek word *psalmoi* means 'songs accompanied by string music'. These sacred songs cover various aspects of man's relationship with God and of the different situations in which he finds himself. The psalms can be classified under certain headings, e.g. praise, thanksgiving, laments, entrance hymns, blessings, and so on. It is hardly necessary to say that the psalms should be sung whenever possible. They 'are not readings nor were they composed as prayers, but as poems of praise' [GILH (*General Instruction on the Liturgy of the Hours*) 103].

St Benedict insisted in his Rule that the monks should sing all 150 psalms each week in the office. Some psalms were assigned to particular hours, the rest were used consecutively, not selectively, e.g. Psalms 109-147 were mostly assigned to vespers. The original 'cathedral' office only used a few psalms, and these were selected because of their suitability for Morning or Evening Prayer. However, under the influence of the monastic office, the Roman office adopted the principle of reciting the entire psalter during the course of the week. Although the distribution of the psalms was improved in the new Roman psalter of 1911, this principle was observed until after the Second Vatican Council.

The Liturgy of the Hours, however, has a four week psalter. Each office, except Night Prayer, has only three psalms (or equivalent), and these have been allocated selectively throughout. This has lightened the burden and it has also provided a more meaningful use of the psalms. A brief silence after each psalm is valuable, and it is to be hoped that the 'psalm collects' for recitation after each psalm will soon be widely available. But it is still taken for granted that all the psalms (except 57, 82 and 108 which have been omitted because they contain imprecatory verses) must be repeated regularly in the course of the office.

The tradition of including an Old Testament canticle among the psalms at Morning Prayer has been retained, and there are now New Testament canticles at Evening Prayer. This is a commendable addition to the office, and amounts to a restoration of these liturgical canticles to use in Christian worship.

(c) *The Word*

The ministry of the word now enjoys a significant place in almost every rite of the Church. In the office there has traditionally been a Liturgy of the Word at each of the hours. In some cases the readings had become so abbreviated that the short passages which resulted were of little significance. In the Liturgy of the Hours the prayerful reading of scripture has a place of importance. Care was taken in the revision of the office to arrange the readings so that they were varied and meaningful.

The Liturgy of the Hours

(i) *Short readings*
These are provided for all the hours except the Office of Readings. 'They are selected to express briefly and succinctly a biblical phrase, theme or exhortation' [GILH 156], and during the ordinary time of the year they vary on each day of the four week cycle.

(ii) *Morning and Evening Prayer*
At these offices, a short reading is provided according to the day, season or feast, and there is much variety. The short reading 'is to be read and heard as the true proclamation of the word of God; it emphasises certain short passages which may receive less attention in the continuous reading of the scriptures' [GILH 45].

Alternatively, a longer scripture reading, chosen for the occasion, may be used at Morning or Evening Prayer, especially in celebrations with the people [GILH 45].

(iii) *The Office of Readings*
[GILH 64-67; 143-155; 159-168]
'The purpose of the Office of Readings is to present ... a more extensive meditation on sacred scripture and on the best writings of spiritual authors ... Prayer should accompany the reading of sacred scripture to make it a conversation between God and man ...' [GILH 55-56]. There are two readings:

(A) the first is from the scriptures, chosen either from a one-year cycle of readings, which is given in full in the Liturgy of the Hours, or from a two-year cycle of readings;[9]

(B) the second is from the Fathers or Church writers, taken either from the text given in the Liturgy of the Hours or from the optional lectionary;[10] or on saints' days it is a hagiographical reading as given in the Liturgy of the Hours. In addition to these readings, Bishops' Conferences may prepare collections of other suitable readings to form a supplement to the optional lectionary.

The lectionaries for the Office of Readings were the result of several years of intensive investigation and work. In the Apostolic Constitution promulgating the revised Divine Office [*Canticum Laudis*], Paul VI had this to say concerning the rationale of the new scriptural lectionary:

> 'In the new series of readings from Sacred Scripture there is a wider treasury of the Word of God. The readings have been chosen to harmonize with the readings at Mass. The passages in themselves show a unity of argument, and during the course of the year they try to present the principal chapters in the history of salvation' [5].

He then noted the 'better selection' of passages available for the second reading and the new style of hagiographical lessons which present 'the spiritual significance of the saints in the life of the Church' rather than a detailed biography [6, 7].

(d) Prayer

The entire office is an act of prayer: 'enriched with readings, it is principally a prayer of praise and supplication, indeed it is the prayer of the Church with Christ and to Christ' [GILH 2]. In addition each office has a specific section devoted to supplicatory prayer. Morning and Evening Prayer have, appropriately, the longest provision for this prayer. 'At Lauds intercessions have been added to consecrate the day in order to prepare for the work of the day; while at Vespers supplications have been added following the pattern of the Prayer of the Faithful (at Mass)' [*Canticum Laudis* 8]. Special intentions can be added to these, and Bishops' Conferences may draw up new intercessions. Following the intercessions at Morning and Evening Prayer, the Lord's Prayer is said, and then a final collect. As the Lord's Prayer is also recited at Mass, it is now recited officially three times each day, which is an ancient Christian custom. All the hours end with a collect [cf. GILH 179-200].

The significance of the Liturgy of the Hours

The Liturgy of the Hours or Divine Office is often referred to as the Prayer of the Church: this is an apt name because it is the official communal prayer of the people of God assembled as Christ's followers in the Church. It has a dignity and importance of its own which distinguishes it from private personal prayer. The description of the office in the *General Instruction on the Liturgy of the Hours* has already been quoted above. It ascribes to the divine office the highest dignity of any form of prayer except for the eucharist. It is the constant round of praise and prayer offered to the Father by the Son, our High Priest, and by his people. The priesthood of Jesus Christ is exercised in this Prayer of the Church as is that of each baptised person. We are a 'priestly people' and one of our noblest tasks, after the celebration of the eucharist, is to celebrate the office as the whole Body of Christ.

Although the Liturgy of the Hours is now recited by a growing number of the laity, the majority of Catholics have no contact with the Prayer of the Church. This is in contrast to the Orthodox Churches where the pattern of daily prayer in the home, in front of the icons, is linked to the divine office. Even though only a few prayers may be recited in the home, the manual of prayer contains liturgical texts taken from the office books. For most Catholics there is no such link between their personal prayer life and the public Prayer of the Church. The office functions chiefly as a form of clerical prayer, with an implication that clerics and religious (and a few lay people) say it on behalf of the whole Church. This 'substitutionary' or 'representative' celebration of the office is surely against the mind of the Church as expressed in the *Constitution on the Sacred Liturgy* and in the *General Instruction on the Liturgy of the Hours*. It is also contrary to the main principles of the liturgy. There is some hope that this situation will improve as moves are being made by some diocesan commissions to promote the celebration of some of the hours in the parish church.

Unlike the eucharist, the office has to be celebrated every day. Through it each day is filled by semi-continuous public prayer, and each day and night are thus sanctified in God's presence. Each part of the day, and especially morning and evening, is sanctified and marked out in its own distinctive way. Seasons and festivals are also observed in the office. The Church's liturgy is thus 'filled out' and extended in time. There is no tension between the timeless divine mysteries and time-bound human life. Christ entered the sphere of time at his birth and his saving acts were historical events. The liturgy is, in a sense, incarnational: it effects a harmony between the infinity of God and the finite time in which our salvation is actualised.

It could be said that the Church is being itself most authentically in praying the Liturgy of the Hours. There is an anamnetic quality about the office, an assurance of Christ's presence in the Church as we continually discern the present reality of our salvation. Perhaps there is wisdom in the definition of the Liturgy of the Hours given in Canon Law, despite the apparent assumption that the ministry of the word is the main element in the office:

> 'In fulfilment of the priestly office of Christ, the Church celebrates the liturgy of the hours wherein it listens to God speaking to his people and recalls the mystery of salvation. In this way, the Church praises God without ceasing, in song and prayer, and it intercedes with him for the salvation of the whole world' [canon 1173].

The divine office enables Christians, both collectively and individually, to locate themselves in time, God-filled time, so to speak. By orientating themselves liturgically through the observance of the hours, they are able to locate their prayer in that of the Church. In this way their prayer life becomes more fulfilling and authentic. As Pope Paul VI expressed it in the Apostolic Constitution *Canticum Laudis*:

> 'Since the life of Christ in his Mystical Body perfects and elevates the personal life of each of the faithful, there can be no opposition between the prayer of Christ and the personal prayer of the individual, but instead the relationship between them is strengthened by the Divine Office.
>
> ...The prayer of the Office as it becomes truly personal prayer forms a clear link between the liturgy and the whole life of the Christian, since every hour of the day and night is itself a kind of *leitourgia* wherein they give themselves to the ministry of the love of God and their fellowmen, and are joined to the actions of Christ who by his life among men and by his sacrifice sanctified the life of men. This deepest truth of the Christian life is shown forth and at the same time brought about by the Liturgy of the Hours, and so it is offered to all the faithful ...' [8].

Singing the divine office

Since the office is essentially a liturgical form of prayer, communal celebration (even of two or three persons) is always to be preferred to individual recitation. In communal celebrations, and especially in the parish church with the people on Sunday and feast days, the laudal parts should whenever possible be sung, i.e. the hymn and the psalms. The hymn should be sung by the entire assembly, and the tune selected should therefore be suited to congregational singing. It should be easy to 'pick up' and in keeping with the theme of the hymn (e.g. morning praise, evening thanksgiving, celebration of a feast).

Psalms usually present difficulties, but need not do so. In a parish celebration, psalmody could be limited to a single psalm; or until the congregation become experienced in psalmody, one psalm could be sung and the rest recited. There are other alternatives. The psalm verses can be sung by a cantor or choir, and the people sing a simple refrain (antiphon) after each verse. A psalm can be sung by a cantor while the people listen. All these modes have historical precedent, and they could all be employed in turn. There is no need to impose upon the people right from the start the rendering of the whole two psalms and a canticle by two 'sides' or 'choirs' singing alternate verses. It may be preferable to begin with learning only one or two psalms at a time and to repeat them every Sunday until the people are ready to learn further psalms.

It may be best to postpone the singing of the antiphons by the congregation as they usually present an additional complication in what already seems to the newcomer a complicated form of prayer. Instead the antiphons can be recited by all, or sung by a cantor only.

It is more effective for the responsory after the scriptural reading to be sung, preferably by cantor and people. A short practice before the office begins is advisable.

The *Magnificat* should be sung, either by the people or by the choir. There seems no overriding reason why this has to be sung by the congregation, and it may be appropriate for the choir to sing an elaborate version of this canticle while the altar is being incensed.

There is provision for conflating Evening Prayer with the Service of Exposition and Benediction, and this gives obvious scope for congregational singing.

The growth of congregational participation in the office will be promoted or retarded by the quality of the musical arrangements. Tunes must be carefully chosen and must be within the capacity of the average congregation. It is essential to have a cantor: he or she will play a leading role in the celebration. Practice and instruction are important, and flexibility and imaginativeness are needed. [There are some notes on singing in GILH 267-284].

Notes

1. The history of the daily office, though interesting, is rather complicated. The following are recommended as an introduction to this subject: J.D. Crichton, *Christian Celebration* (Geoffrey Chapman, 1981), 'The Prayer of the Church', ch. 3; Robert Taft, *The Liturgy of the Hours in East and West* (Collegeville: The Liturgical Press, 1986); George Guiver, *Company of Voices: Daily Prayer and the People of God* (London: SPCK, 1988).

2. Taken with modifications from F. Homes Dudden, *The Life and Times of St Ambrose* (Oxford: Clarendon Press, 1935), vol. II, pp. 442, 466.

3. At the time of the Donatist heresy, and during the persecution by the Donatists of the orthodox faithful at Milan by Justina, mother of the Emperor Valentinian, 'the custom arose of singing hymns and psalms, after the use of the eastern provinces, to save the people from being utterly worn out by their long and sorrowful vigils' (Augustine, *Confessions*, 9:7).

4. This was a typical office up to a point, but Milan can be considered to have been more advanced in these matters than many other places. Milan was also a

pioneer in the use of office hymns, thanks to Ambrose. Hymns were taken up in the monastic office (cf. the rules of Caesarius, Benedict and Aurelian), but were not universally used in the Roman office until the twelfth century. Finally, it must be emphasised that there was much variation from place to place in the development and form of the office, and the observance and development of the office was intermittent in many places.

5   Published jointly by Collins, Dwyer and Talbot, 1976.

6   The *General Instruction* is given in full at the beginning of the first volume of *The Divine Office*; and also in *The Liturgy of the Hours: The General Instruction on the Liturgy of the Hours* with a commentary by A.M. Roguet (E.J. Dwyer and Geoffrey Chapman, 1971). There are selections from the GILH in *Morning and Evening Prayer, op. cit.*

7   For a critical edition of the Latin office hymns of the *Liturgia Horarum*, see Anselmo Lentini (ed.), *Te Decet Hymnus: L'Innario della 'Liturgia Horarum'* (Vatican Press, 1984). Cf. also forthcoming work by the present author *The Office Hymn in the West: Its Nature and Function*.

8   *Hymns Old and New* (Kevin Mayhew, various editions) makes considerable provision for the Liturgy of the Hours in the parish church with a selection of psalms and of hymns for seasons, feasts and times.

9   The two-year cycle of scriptural readings is summarised in GILH 146-152 and listed in detail in *Notitiae* vol. 12 (1976), pp.238-248; 324-333; 378-388.

The Liturgy of the Hours

10 An alphabetical index of the one-year cycle of patristic readings which are provided in the Liturgy of the Hours is given in *Notitiae* 10 (1974), pp. 253-276: the references are to the volume and page number of the Latin *Liturgia Horarum* (first edition; this index is included in the second edition). No definitive and complete edition of the optional patristic lectionary has been published. But there have been initiatives such as the *Word in Season* series published by Talbot.

14

The Sacraments of Initiation

Baptism

Christian initiation is begun in baptism, brought to perfection in confirmation, and completed in the eucharist, although few Catholics today receive the sacraments in that order.

We believe that God created the world out of love. Creation was the starting point in the history of salvation. It reached its focal point with the Incarnation, which can be regarded as 're-creation'. Through baptism, men and women become part of salvation history and members of the Kingdom, waiting in joyful hope for Christ's coming.

Baptism is the sacrament of redemption. It makes us part of redemption history and sets us on the road to final redemption. It is the gateway to the other sacraments. In baptism we submit ourselves to God's love, renounce evil, and choose the life of the Kingdom of God. Accordingly,

The Sacraments of Initiation

baptism is a response to the new and final covenant offered to mankind, and a response of faith to the gospel message.

Through baptism we are redeemed, re-created, and incorporated in Christ. We die to sin, rise again to newness of life: our baptism parallels the death and resurrection of Christ (Romans 6:3-4; Colossians 2:12). We share in the paschal mystery and enter into the life of the risen Christ. Having turned away from sin (the old life) we turn to God and receive the gift of the Holy Spirit (Acts 2:38; 1 Corinthians 12:13).

In baptism we are incorporated into the Church, the Spirit-filled Church which is the Body of Christ. We become members of the new People of God, a holy nation and a royal priesthood (1 Peter 2:9). We exercise our baptismal priesthood by worshipping God and by mission: at our baptism we are commissioned to evangelise and to share in Christ's redeeming work in the world.

Baptism is entry into life. It is regeneration: we are born again into everlasting life, becoming the adopted children of God, and sharing the life of the Trinity: hence the Trinitarian formula used at baptism.

To sum up, baptism is re-birth through water and the use of words, in which we are freed from slavery to sin, our sins are forgiven, punishments due for sin are remitted, we receive new life in Christ and the Holy Spirit, and we are initiated into the Church and enabled to encounter God in love in the other sacraments.

The requirements for baptism are:

1 in the case of adults, faith, repentance and intention; in the case of infants, faith on the part of the community, and especially the parents;

2 the threefold pouring of water (or immersion): this is the *matter* of the sacrament;

3 the Trinitarian formula ('I baptize you in the name of the Father, and of the Son and of the Holy Spirit'): this is the *form* of the sacrament of baptism.

The Second Vatican Council

We saw in Chapter Five that the early pattern of initiation in the west underwent considerable alteration. The anointing with chrism by the bishop was detached and eventually became a completely separate rite and a separate sacrament. When the rite of baptism was no longer followed by a celebration of the eucharist, the reception of holy communion for the first time ceased to have an initiatory significance, at least in practice and in popular perception. As for the rite of baptism, the progressive staged rite, designed for groups of adults, comprising a lengthy catechumenate and then a period of purification before baptism at the Easter Vigil, was telescoped into a single rite performed on one day in a brief space of time. This rite, designed for adults, was used equally for children.

The Council of Trent ordered the revision of liturgical books. The last volume to appear was the *Rituale Romanum* in 1614. This contained the rite of baptism, which was not greatly changed from the late medieval rite. The gift of salt, the exorcisms, the anointings, the delivery and return of the creed, the *effeta* and other relics of the catechumenate were retained. Two versions of the rite were printed in the Roman Ritual. The first was the rite for adults. The second was in reality the same rite abbreviated for children. This remained almost unaltered until the Second Vatican Council. In England and Wales an indult permitted the use of the shorter version with adults.

The *Constitution on the Sacred Liturgy* [chapter III] ordered the revision of the sacramental rites. They could be administered in the vernacular and adapted rites could be drawn up to meet linguistic and other needs in particular regions. The rite of baptism of adults was to be revised and the catechumenate was to be restored. A new and separate rite of baptism of chilcen was to be drawn up. As a result, the new rites were issued, firstly in Latin, starting with the Rite for the Baptism of Children in 1969, followed by the Rite of Confirmation in 1971 and the Rite of Christian Initiation of Adults in 1972. Translations were made by the International Commission on English in the Liturgy (ICEL), and editions for use in England and Wales were published as follows: Rite of Baptism of Children 1970, Rite of Confirmation 1975, and the Rite of Christian Initiation of Adults (RCIA) 1974, revised edition 1988.

For a full understanding of the rites of initiation, readers are strongly recommended not only to study the new rites themselves, but also to read the very informative introductions and pastoral notes which accompany the RCIA, The Rite of Baptism for Children, and the Rite of Confirmation.

The Rite of Christian Initiation of Adults

In restoring the catechumenate, the Second Vatican Council said that this should be the preferred way in which adults joining the Catholic Church prepare for baptism. This means that initiation into the Church is spread over a period of time so that there is a gradual process of growth and development in faith and understanding, with a corresponding growth in commitment. The soundness of this approach in terms of personal development, cognitive growth, and spiritual formation is clear. The candidate is encouraged to reach maturity in the faith at his or her own pace. 'Readiness', a concept much used by teachers today, is an important criterion for moving on to each successive stage.

This is a sound approach not only in personal terms but also in the social dimension. 'Initiation' implies not merely *becoming* a Catholic but *being initiated into* (or 'getting on the inside of') the Christian community and its beliefs and practices. The candidate needs to feel he or she is growing into the community, being increasingly accepted by it, and progressively identifying with its norms. This aspect has often been overlooked in the past. A brief formal ceremony, carried out in an almost empty church, hardly suggests that initiation in a meaningful way is taking place.

In the RCIA process ('not a programme but a process') this acceptance by the community is an important feature. But it goes further than this. RCIA operates *within* the community of the local church. The whole parish brings about and takes responsibility for the initiation of its new members. It is an activity of the parish as a community and all parishioners are involved in it. Some parishioners will be involved as members of the RCIA Team, others will be sponsors, prayer companions, ministers of hospitality, and so on. RCIA is based on lay initiative. All parishioners are asked to support candidates by prayer, by being welcoming, by taking an interest in their development, and by taking part in the various liturgical rites which mark the candidates' progress towards full membership of the Church.

The steps and stages of the RCIA as are follows:[1]

1 PERIOD OF ENQUIRY
  [Period of evangelization and pre-catechumenate]

   A time for inquiry, faith-sharing, and an introduction to gospel values. A time for the beginnings of faith. Friendly and informal meetings are held, and these are usually open to all who wish to learn more about the Catholic faith, whether or not they feel committed to go further. Some parishes throw these meetings open to all parishioners wishing to deepen their faith. This practice is not recommended. Other provisions should be made, possibly under the RCIA 'umbrella', for parish catechesis. It is not desirable to 'mix' enquirers with parishioners engaged in 'in-service training', especially as their needs are different. Catholics attend these meetings either because they are part of the Team or because they are engaged in 'faith-sharing'.

Enquirers who are able to commit themselves further and are considered ready for this step are then accepted by the Church as catechumens.

FIRST STEP
Acceptance into the order of catechumens.
    This is the liturgical rite which marks the beginning of the catechumenate proper. The candidates express and the Church accepts their intention to respond to God's call to follow the way of Christ.

2 PERIOD OF THE CATECHUMENATE

During this time, the catechumen's faith and conversion to God are nurtured and helped to grow.
    Instruction is given by the catechists, based on the needs of the individual.
    During the catechumenate, there are liturgical rites to assist the process of growth: namely, celebrations of the word, prayers of exorcism, and blessings.
    When the catechumens are ready for the sacraments of initiation, they take part in the Rite of Election.

SECOND STEP
Election or enrolment of names.
    This liturgical rite usually takes place on the First Sunday of Lent.[2] It is preferable for it to be carried out by the bishop in his cathedral.[3]
    In this rite, the Church formally ratifies the catechumens' readiness for the sacraments of initiation, and the catechumens (now the elect) express the will to receive them.

3 PERIOD OF PURIFICATION AND ENLIGHTENMENT

A time of reflection, conversion and spiritual preparation for initiation. This period normally occupies the Lenten season.

It is marked by liturgical rites, namely the scrutinies, presentations of the creed and the Lord's Prayer, and preparation rites on Holy Saturday.

THIRD STEP
Celebration of the sacraments of initiation.

This is the liturgical rite, usually integrated into the Easter Vigil, by which the elect are initiated through baptism, confirmation, and the eucharist.

4 THE PERIOD AFTER BAPTISM
[Period of post-baptismal catechesis or mystagogy]

The newly initiated now experience being fully part of the Christian community by means of suitable catechesis and particularly by participation with all the faithful in the Sunday eucharistic celebration.

It is interesting to note that at the Easter Vigil and in the reception of baptised Christians into Full Communion (see below), confirmation is usually administered by a priest. It is also interesting to note that at the Easter Vigil unbaptised adults receive the threefold unitary rite of initiation (baptism, confirmation and eucharist, and in that order) as in the early Church.

Reception into the full communion of the Church

Strictly speaking, the catechumenate is for the unbaptised. For those seeking admission into the Church who have already been baptised there is a Rite of Reception of Baptised

The Sacraments of Initiation

Christians into the Full Communion of the Catholic Church.[4] Two versions are given, one for reception within Mass, the other for reception outside Mass. Within Mass, the celebration takes place after the homily. There is an invitation, a simple profession of faith, and the act of reception. If the person being received has not received the sacrament of confirmation, the celebrant then administers it. Then follows the celebrant's sign of welcome, general intercessions, and a sign of peace. After this the Liturgy of the Eucharist is celebrated. Outside Mass, there is a Liturgy of the Word, then the reception as noted above, and the rite concludes with the Lord's Prayer.

In England, Wales and Scotland, as most adults joining the Catholic Church have already been baptised, the Holy See has granted permission for the Rite of Reception of Baptised Christians into the Full Communion of the Catholic Church to be carried out at the Easter Vigil. The adapted form for this is given as Appendix 1 in the Rite of Christian Initiation of Adults as approved for use in England, Wales and Scotland (1988 edition). The reception at the Easter Vigil is broadly similar to the rite described above. After baptisms (if there are any) have taken place, the candidates for reception join in the profession of faith and are then received. Together with any newly baptised adults, they are confirmed and then participate in the Liturgy of the Eucharist and receive their first holy communion.

In practice, candidates for reception undertake a modified version of the programme for catechumens, with some of the liturgical rites as appropriate, e.g. the presentation of the creed and the Lord's Prayer.[5] It is held to be important that these candidates should undergo a progressive preparation and reception into the community in a comparable way to catechumens. They are not catechumens, however, and nothing should be done to confuse them with catechumens, either in catechesis or in liturgical rites.

The Rite of Adult Baptism

The norm is for the baptism of adults to take place at the Easter Vigil. After the homily, the candidates are presented to the celebrant, the assembly is invited to pray for the candidates, the Litany of the Saints is sung, and the baptismal water is blessed. The candidates then make a renunciation of sin, they are anointed with the Oil of Catechumens, and they make a simple profession of faith (a traditional threefold credal questioning). The baptism then takes place, followed by the 'explanatory rites', the clothing with a baptismal garment and the presentation of a lighted candle. The celebrant then proceeds to the sacrament of confirmation.

In exceptional circumstances, the bishop can allow, in individual cases, the use of a form of Christian initiation that is simpler than the usual, complete rite, and it can be administered outside the Easter Vigil [RCIA 307f]. There is a certain flexibility in the rite, but the basic structure and sequence is similar to that observed at the Easter Vigil.

The Rite of Baptism of Children

It may seem strange that although the majority of candidates for baptism have for centuries been children, and usually very young babies, we have had to wait until the second half of the twentieth century for a rite of baptism specifically designed for young children. The *Constitution on the Sacred Liturgy* laid down that the revised rite for the baptism of children was to take full account, firstly, of the fact that the candidates were infants and not adults, and, secondly, of the responsibilities and duties of parents and godparents.

The latter point is of particular importance regarding the faith that is a requirement of the sacrament. As an infant or young child is unable to make the response of faith, he or she is baptised in the faith of the Church in a rather different sense from adults. In the case of the child, the local community declares the faith of the Church and undertakes responsibility for providing the environment in which the child will be able to grow in personal faith. This is one reason why the Church now prefers to baptise children in groups and in the presence of the parish, and pre-eminently at a Sunday Mass.

Since parish structures are not always sufficiently developed to provide an adequate faith environment for the newly baptised child, a serious responsibility falls on parents and godparents. Not only should godparents be practising and committed Catholics and capable of seeing that the child grows up in the faith, but parents, and preferably godparents also, must undergo suitable training and preparation. In many parishes today, there are programmes of preparation which have borrowed certain features from the RCIA, such as working through progressive stages with a series of liturgical celebrations, and a programme which involves both parents and the parish.

The rite is as follows:

1 RECEPTION OF THE CHILDREN

This takes place at the church door. The celebrant greets everyone and especially the parents and godparents, and speaks briefly about the occasion.

The celebrant then questions first the parents, and then the godparents.

The celebrant welcomes the children in the name of the Christian community and claims them for Christ by the sign of the cross. He signs each child on the forehead and invites the parents and godparents to do the same.

2 CELEBRATION OF GOD'S WORD

Gospel reading (either one or two readings).

Homily. The homily is intended for the parents in particular, and the children can be taken out and looked after by friends so that parents can listen to it.

Intercessions.

3 PRAYER OF EXORCISM AND ANOINTING BEFORE BAPTISM

The prayer of exorcism asks God to set the child free from original sin, to make him (her) a temple of God's glory, and to send the Holy Spirit to dwell with him (her).

The anointing on the breast with the Oil of Catechumens in the name of Christ our Saviour is for strengthening the child with his power.

4 CELEBRATION OF THE SACRAMENT

Brief introduction by celebrant.

Blessing and invocation of God over the baptismal water.

Renunciation of sin and profession of faith by the parents and godparents. This is not done on behalf of the child, but by the parents and godparents in their own name. They are asked to renew the vows of their own baptism, to reject sin, and to profess their faith. They are presenting the child for baptism 'in the faith of the Church' and will be responsible for bringing up the child in the practice of the faith and free from the poison of sin. Finally, the celebrant and congregation together give their assent to

The Sacraments of Initiation

this profession of faith.

The children are then baptised.

Anointing with chrism. The child has been freed from sin, given a new birth by water and the Holy Spirit, and welcomed into God's holy people. He (she) is now anointed 'with the chrism of salvation': 'As Christ was anointed Priest, Prophet, and King, so may you always live as members of his body, sharing everlasting life'.

Clothing with the white garment, signifying that the newly baptised children have been clothed in Christ and that the white garment is the outward sign of their Christian dignity: 'With your family and friends to help you by word and example, bring that dignity unstained into the everlasting life of heaven.'

The lighted candle. The celebrant takes the Easter candle and says 'Receive the light of Christ'. The child's candle is lit from it and the celebrant declares; 'Parents and godparents, this light is entrusted to you to be kept burning brightly. These children of yours have been enlightened by Christ. They are to walk always as children of the light. May they keep the flame of faith alive in their hearts.'

The *effeta* or prayer over ears and mouth. The celebrant touches the ears and mouth of each child with his thumb, saying 'May (the Lord Jesus) touch your ears to receive his word and your mouth to proclaim his faith.'

5 CONCLUSION OF THE RITE

Lord's Prayer.

Blessing. The celebrant blesses first the mothers, who hold the children in their arms, then the fathers, and lastly the entire assembly.

It is now the intention of the baptismal rite that the relationship between baptism and the resurrection of Christ should be made clear. The Church therefore prefers baptisms to take place on Sundays, the day on which the paschal mystery is celebrated. The paschal candle, which is to be kept in the baptistry outside the Easter season, is used during the rite. Children who are ready for baptism about Easter time should be baptised at the Easter Vigil, which is the normative time for baptism, and there is an adapted form of the rite for this.

The rite is to be seen as a journey in faith. It commences at the door, to signify a seeking of admission. Then there is a procession to the lectern to hear the word, and a procession to the font for baptism. Finally there is a procession to the sanctuary to symbolise the completion of the rite by going to the altar for the Our Father and blessing, the altar being the place where the eucharist, the fulfilment of initiation, is celebrated.

The Introduction to *The Rite of Baptism for Children* [9] has the following instruction regarding baptism during Mass: 'On Sunday, baptism may be celebrated even during Mass, so that the entire community may be present and the necessary relationship between baptism and eucharist may be clearly seen, but this should not be done too often.' Baptism may also be celebrated during Mass on weekdays, and the necessary adaptations for baptisms within Mass are given in the rite.

The Sacraments of Initiation

Confirmation

We have seen that in the western Church confirmation became a separate sacrament during the middle ages. The Second Vatican Council ordered the revision of the rite and insisted that the intimate connection of confirmation with the whole of Christian initiation should be 'more lucidly set forth; for this reason it will be fitting for candidates to renew their baptismal promises just before they are confirmed' [CL 71]. The connection of confirmation with baptism is also emphasised in the encouragement given for the godparent at the candidate's baptism to be also the sponsor at his or her confirmation.

Confirmation is a completion of baptism: in the sacrament the bishop ratifies or completes what was begun at baptism. Confirmation is a conferring of the gift of the Holy Spirit. In baptism the Holy Spirit is bestowed for the forgiveness of sin and for rebirth. The Holy Spirit comes down upon the water so that it is effective in remitting sin. In confirmation the Holy Spirit is given for the fullness of grace, for spiritual strength, and for strength to preach the gospel and to bear witness in one's Christian life to the word of God. The name 'confirmation' refers to this strengthening.

In the sacrament of baptism, the candidate shares in the mystery of Easter. It is because of Christ's death and resurrection that he or she is able to have new life at baptism. In the sacrament of confirmation, the candidate shares in the mystery of Pentecost, for he or she is now strengthened to preach the gospel and participate in the mission of the Church. 'Ordinarily the sacrament is administered by the bishop so that there will be a more evident relationship to the first pouring forth of the Holy Spirit on Pentecost ... Thus the reception of the Spirit through the ministry of the bishop shows the close bond which joins the confirmed to the Church and the mandate to be witnesses of Christ among men and women' [IRC (Introduction to the Rite of Confirmation) 7].

In baptism we become a priestly people, and we share in the priesthood of Christ because of our permanent consecration to the worship of God. In confirmation we share in Christ's priesthood by our permanent consecration to the mission of Christian witness. 'This giving of the Holy Spirit conforms believers more perfectly to Christ and strengthens them so that they may bear witness to Christ for the building up of his body in faith and love. They are so marked with the character or seal of the Lord that the sacrament of confirmation cannot be repeated' [IRC 2].

In the *Apostolic Constitution on the Sacrament of Confirmation*, Pope Paul VI dealt with the question of the form of the sacrament. He decreed firstly that the laying on of hands before the anointing was to be retained, and secondly that the anointing was the essential form of the sacrament. This was an important declaration in view of past controversy about the place of the two actions in the rite. He wrote as follows:

> 'In order that the revision of the rite of confirmation may fittingly embrace also the essence of the sacramental rite, by our supreme apostolic authority we decree and lay down that in the Latin Church the following should be observed for the future:
>
>> The sacrament of confirmation is conferred through the anointing with chrism on the forehead, which is done by the laying on of the hand, and through the words: *Accipe signaculum doni Spiritus Sancti*.
>
> Although the laying on of hands on the candidates, which is done with the prescribed prayer before the anointing, does not belong to the essence of the sacramental rite, it is nevertheless to be held in high esteem in that it contributes to the integral perfection of that rite and to a clearer understanding of the sacrament. It is evident that

The Sacraments of Initiation

this preceding laying on of hands differs from the laying on of the hand by which the anointing is done on the forehead.'

It should be noted, then, that there is a twofold action. Firstly, the laying on of hands (i.e. extending the hands over the candidates) by the bishop and the concelebrating priests. This is not an essential element for the validity of the rite, but has been retained to keep the integrity of the rite. It is the biblical gesture by which the Holy Spirit is invoked [IRC 9]. At this point the bishop says 'Send your Holy Spirit upon them . . . Give them the spirit of wisdom and understanding . . . (etc).' Secondly, there is the anointing on the forehead, which also consists of a laying on of the hand. The anointing with chrism represents the spiritual anointing of the Holy Spirit: 'Signed with the perfumed oil, the baptized person receives the indelible character, the seal of the Lord, together with the gift of the Spirit, which conforms him more closely to Christ and gives him the grace of spreading the Lord's presence among men and women' [IRC 9].

The Pope also decreed that the formula was to be changed from the traditional one, 'I sign you with the sign of the cross and confirm you with the chrism of salvation. In the name of the Father and of the Son and of the Holy Spirit', to the ancient formula belonging to the Byzantine rite 'N. be sealed with the Gift of the Holy Spirit'.

Ordinarily confirmation should take place within Mass in order to express the initiatory character of the eucharist, and the newly confirmed should receive holy communion. Children being confirmed who have not made their first communion should either make it at this Mass, or else the rite of confirmation should be celebrated outside Mass, in which case it should be preceded by a Liturgy of the Word.

Music and singing at the rites of initiation

(a) At the Easter Vigil

When the rites are performed at the Easter Vigil, the Litany of the Saints should be sung by cantors with the assembly singing the responses. It is more suitable for the Blessing of the Water to be sung rather than said by the celebrant, and the music for this is provided in the rite. If the Easter candle has been held in the water, the people sing an acclamation as the celebrant lifts it out of the water. If the baptisms take place at the font, the Litany of the Saints should be sung during the procession to the font, and a suitable song may be sung during the procession from the font to the sanctuary. A song is to be sung during the sprinkling with baptismal water. A suitable song may be sung before the celebration of confirmation begins and during the conferral of the sacrament.

It is important not to introduce singing or background music at any other point in the rites of initiation because this would be inappropriate. Music would also be distracting during important actions such as baptismal promises and profession of faith which ought to be heard by the people. Apart from the provisions noted above, the main emphasis in the musical arrangements will be to make the whole Easter Vigil as meaningful as possible.

(b) Baptism and confirmation celebrated during Mass

The main emphasis in these cases will be on the musical arrangements for the Mass, rather than for the rites, which do not call for any music or singing. In the choice of opening and final hymns, for example, the baptism or confirmation could be marked with hymns with a paschal or pentecost theme. Modern hymn books contain numerous hymns suited to baptism and confirmation.

(c) Baptism and confirmation outside Mass
There is definite scope here for songs and chants suited to these occasions: opening and final hymns, responsorial psalm, and so on.

(d) RCIA liturgies
Most of these take place during a Mass, and once again it is at appropriate points in the Mass that suitable songs should be sung rather than during the actual RCIA rite which is usually short and does not call for singing. The 1988 edition of the RCIA gives a short selection of acclamations, hymns and songs. It is to be hoped that more hymns and chants specifically suited to RCIA liturgies will be composed.

Notes

1 I have made considerable use here of the actual wording of the pastoral notes and instructions accompanying the rite in *Rite of Christian Initiation of Adults* (London: Geoffrey Chapman, 1988), p. 14 and elsewhere. It does not seem necessary to place all such phrases within quotation marks.

2 The season of Lent developed largely as the period of purification and enlightenment of the catechumens preparing for baptism at Easter.

3 This restores to the bishop of the diocese a role in the earlier stages of initiation.

4 The rite previously in use for a baptised person joining the Catholic Church, The Form of Reconciling a Convert and of Absolving Him from Excommunication, has been abolished. It should be noted that in the case of eastern Christians, no liturgical rite is required, but simply a profession of Catholic faith [RCIA 388].

5 It will be said in criticism that one cannot present the creed and the Lord's Prayer to someone who is already, at least technically, a Christian through baptism. In the experience of the present author such rites are greatly welcomed and considered to be meaningful and pastorally helpful. On the other hand, exorcisms and scrutinies would be quite inappropriate in the circumstances.

15

Other Sacraments and Rites

The Sacrament of Matrimony
The sacrament of matrimony bestows sanctifying grace on the husband and wife as well as the specific grace to help them in their marriage. The essence of the sacrament lies exclusively in the contract of marriage, and so the bride and groom minister the sacrament to each other. The Church requires, under normal circumstances, a priest or deacon to preside at the celebration, to be an official witness to the making of the contract, to give a blessing (which is not part of the sacrament but is a sacramental) and to be the minister of the accompanying ceremonies. The matter of the sacrament, then, is the contract, and the form is the mutual declaration of consent to the contract.

This sacramental rite is, therefore, somewhat different in outward appearance from other sacramental rites in that the outward sign is operated by two lay persons, not by the minister, and that the contractual declaration is necessarily legalistic in form. It is important, then, that the accompanying ceremonies, as well as the prayers, readings and homily, convey as effectively as possible the rich significance, both spiritual and human, of the permanent loving relationship and mutual commitment into which the couple are entering.

The Rite of Marriage

The Roman Ritual of 1614, which brought to completion the liturgical revision set in motion by the Council of Trent, provided a rite of marriage which was derived basically from the medieval rite. But it was a brief and bald rite, because there was a variety of local customs in Europe and these continued to be permitted in the celebration of marriage. In England the rite used from the Reformation until 1970 was not the Roman rite but a version of the Sarum rite.

As part of the Second Vatican Council's revision of the liturgical rites the *Ordo Celebrandi Matrimonium* was issued in 1969. The Council's legislation allowed for local adaptations in sacramental rites. In 1970 a rite for England and Wales was approved which made use of the ICEL translation of the Latin rite, and made certain adaptations. Unfortunately many of the rich and distinctive features of the previous rite derived from Sarum were not retained. This was regrettable in itself and it also meant that Catholics in England and Wales were no longer using a rite which has much in common with the Anglican and Free Church rites.

There are two versions of the marriage rite. The preferred form takes place within a nuptial Mass, and this uses the texts given in the 1970 Roman Missal. Both versions use readings given in the Lectionary for Mass. The main features are as follows, with the parts proper to the nuptial Mass in square brackets:

Other Sacraments and Rites

1 INTRODUCTORY RITES

    Greeting
    [Penitential rite]
    [Glory to God in the highest]
    Opening Prayer
    Liturgy of the Word
    Homily

2 THE MARRIAGE RITE

    Address
    Preliminary questions
    Declaration of consent
    Blessing and exchange of rings
    Prayer of the Faithful
    Nuptial blessing (when the nuptial Mass is not celebrated)

3 LITURGY OF THE EUCHARIST

    [with nuptial blessing after the Lord's Prayer]

4 CONCLUDING RITE

    Lord's Prayer (when the nuptial Mass is not celebrated)
    Blessing
    Dismissal

5 SIGNING OF THE CIVIL REGISTER
   (if not already done)

Revision of the Marriage Rite

Work has been proceeding since 1984 on a proposed revision of the marriage rite for England and Wales. The intention of the revision is to provide a rite which is more traditional, more flexible, and phased. Various traditional features would be included, including some which were abandoned in 1970. The new rite would be constructed more flexibly, so that in addition to a standard rite there would be some much needed adaptations to meet the pastoral reality of other situations, such as inter-church and inter-faith marriages, marriages of non-practising or uncatechized Catholics, catechumens, elderly or previously married partners, and regularizations. Experience gained from the RCIA, the funeral rite, and the pastoral care of the sick has shown the great pastoral value of staged rites, and the projected revision of the marriage rite will contain a sequence of rites for use at choice at engagement, during marriage preparation, at the wedding itself, at the reception, in the new home, at reconciliations, and at anniversaries.

The proposed rites will be enriched in various ways and there will be a wider choice of prayers, blessings, acclamations, and other elements of the rite. Widespread consultation has taken place, all available sources both historical and contemporary have been studied, and some original euchological material has been commissioned. This revision, which is being carried out by a sub-committee of the Committee for Pastoral Liturgy of the Bishops' Conference of England and Wales, is still in progress.[1]

Music and singing at weddings

Care and discrimination are needed in arranging the music for a wedding. It would be easy to overload the occasion with too much music and worse still with unsuitable music. Folk lore still seems to dominate much of what we do at weddings, and there is a tendency to see the occasion as 'the bride's day'. This often means that liturgical considerations have a low priority. One hopeful factor, however, is the increasing tendency for the rite to be fully discussed in advance with the priest and other persons involved, such as the organist. The couple are helped to select readings and other variants,

Other Sacraments and Rites

to compose petitions for the Prayer of the Faithful, and to choose hymns. This may help to avoid hackneyed and conventional hymns and musical arrangements.

During the bride's procession, some calm organ music or a meditative chant might be preferable to grand triumphal marches. An opening hymn or song suited to the occasion is desirable and would involve the whole assembly. The *Lord have mercy, Glory to God, Holy, holy,* and *Lamb of God* can be sung if the congregation consists mainly of practising Catholics, but here and elsewhere consideration must be given to the presence of non-Catholics and non-practising Catholics. Also the overall length of the ceremony needs to be kept in mind. If a cantor is available, the responsorial psalm might well be sung (and perhaps there could be a very brief rehearsal before the Mass starts): this will emphasise the importance of the Liturgy of the Word. There is no place for singing during the marriage rite itself, except during the signing of the register. Offertory and communion hymns are usually popular with brides and bridegrooms, but they should be relevant hymns, and not just 'favourite' hymns. Some silence during communion is important. When there is no nuptial Mass, the careful choice of entry music, opening and other hymns, and recessional music is even more important.

The Sacrament of Order

The revised *Rite of Ordination of Deacons, Presbyters and Bishops* was published in 1968. Some simplification has taken place and there is a similar pattern for the conferring of each order (during Mass, after the gospel and homily):

    Questions
    Litany of the Saints
    Laying on of hands (in silence)
    Prayer of ordination
    Delivery of the symbols of office

In the *Apostolic Constitution on the Rite of Ordination* (18 June 1968), Pope Paul VI decreed, 'to avoid all controversy', that the matter and form of the conferring of each order should be as follows: the matter consists of the laying of the bishop's hands upon the candidates for the diaconate and presbyterate, and the laying of hands on the head of the bishop elect by the consecrating bishops (or at least the principal consecrator). This is done in silence. The form consists of the consecratory prayer, of which the following words are of the nature of the rite and essential for validity:

Deacons: Lord,
send forth upon them the Holy Spirit,
that they may be strengthened
by the gift of your sevenfold grace
to carry out faithfully the work of the ministry.

Priests: Almighty Father,
grant to these servants of yours
the dignity of the priesthood.
Renew within them the Spirit of holiness.
As co-workers with the order of bishops
may they be faithful to the ministry
that they receive from you, Lord God,
and be to others a model of right conduct.

Bishops: So now pour out upon this chosen one
that power which is from you,
the governing Spirit
whom you gave to your beloved Son, Jesus Christ,
the Spirit given by him to the holy apostles,
who founded the Church in every place
to be your temple
for the unceasing glory and praise of your name.

These rites should be carried out in the presence of the Christian assembly whenever possible.

Other Sacraments and Rites

The Sacrament of Reconciliation (Penance)

We were liberated from sin in baptism. In the sacrament of reconciliation our post-baptismal sins are forgiven and we are reconciled to God. We are also reconciled with our fellow-Christians and our baptismal priesthood is restored to us. The Second Vatican Council decreed:

> 'The rite and formulas for the sacrament of penance are to be revised so that they give more luminous expression to both the nature and effect of the sacrament' [CL 72].

The new *Rite of Penance* was published on 2 December 1973. The Introduction accompanying it can be recommended for its account of the mystery of reconciliation in the history of salvation and the place of reconciliation in the life of the Church. 'Going to confession' used to be considered a private and personal affair. Now the social and communitarian aspects of sin and reconciliation are emphasised, and encouragement is given to the holding of penitential services in church, especially during Advent and Lent.

Three rites for reconciliation are provided:

(a) of individual penitents,
(b) of several penitents with individual confession and absolution,
(c) of penitents with general confession and absolution.

Two leading themes of the revised sacramental rites are conversion and reconciliation. The penitent is urged not merely to express his sorrow and receive forgiveness, but to turn away from sin back towards God: the Pope stresses the Greek term for repentance, *metanoia*, literally 'a change of mind', which in the New Testament has the implication of 'turning away', hence conversion. From the notion of reconciliation, another theme can be stressed, that of 'healing'. The penitent is restored to grace, to wholeness, and the sacrament will strengthen his whole life, not simply the areas of sin which he has confessed. For this reason, penitents are encouraged as part of their preparation to make a general review of the way they conduct their lives, not simply to identify the sins which they are to confess.

(a) Reconciliation of individual penitents

In general there is a more positive and constructive approach to the reconciliation of the individual penitent. There is to be a friendly welcome at the beginning and (optionally) a reading of a scriptural text by the priest or the penitent: 'Through the word of God the Christian receives light to recognise his sins and is called to conversion and to confidence in God's mercy [IRP (*Introduction to the Rite of Penance*) 17]. Then follows the confession of sins, the imposition of an act of penance, the penitent's prayer of contrition, and absolution by the priest. The penitent then praises the mercy of God and the priest tells him (her) to go in peace. [See detailed procedure in IRP 15-21.]

(b) Reconciliation of several penitents with individual confession

The second rite commences with a celebration of the word and a homily to assist the penitents to prepare for their individual confessions and absolution. The minister may assist the faithful by offering some brief considerations concerning what is to be confessed. A form of general confession, such as the *confiteor*, is recited by all present, followed by a song or litany to express sorrow. The Lord's Prayer is said. Individual confessions are then made. When all the individual confessions are finished, the assembly should sing a hymn of joy and thanksgiving. [Details in IRP 22-29.]

There are other places in this second rite where music would be appropriate: a hymn at the beginning on a relevant theme, such as God's goodness or praise to Christ our Saviour; a sung response to the readings; and perhaps quiet meditative music or a chant during the time for examination of conscience and while confessions are being heard.

(c) Reconciliation of penitents with general confession and absolution

The third rite would be conducted on similar lines, but without individual confessions and absolution. Time would specifically have to be allocated to private examination of conscience and act of contrition, and then the priest would pronounce the general absolution. At present the use of this form of the rite is severely restricted by the Holy See. [Details in IRP 31-35.]

The Anointing of the Sick

The *Rite of Anointing and Pastoral Care of the Sick* was issued in its Latin form on 7 December 1972. An interim English version was published by ICEL in 1973. This remained in use for a longer period than is usual for such interim versions, while a more adequate adaptation was in preparation. The definitive version proved to be worth waiting for. It appeared in 1983 and is regarded as one of the finest of the liturgical books.

The Second Vatican Council declared that 'extreme unction', the former name for this sacrament, might be more fittingly changed to 'the anointing of the sick', because it is not only for those on the point of death [CL 73]: it is a sacrament for anyone who is ill. The sick person is prayed for by the Church and anointed with oil as a sign of healing (cf. James 5:14-16). By this sacrament the sick are strengthened so that they are either restored to their work in the Church as a priestly people, or helped at the moment of death by associating their suffering with the passion and death of Christ their High Priest.

'This sacrament gives the grace of the Holy Spirit to those who are sick: by this grace the whole person is helped and saved ... Thus the sick person is able not only to bear suffering bravely, but also to fight against it ... If necessary the sacrament also provides the sick person with the forgiveness of sins and the completion of Christian penance' [GIPCS (*General Introduction, Pastoral Care of the Sick*) 6].

In the Apostolic Constitution accompanying the revised rite, Paul VI made certain changes in the rite. Previously, the dying person had been anointed on six senses (eyes, ears, nostrils, mouth, hands and feet). The Pope enacted that anointing was henceforth to be on the forehead and hands, and the priest was to say once only a revised formula:

'Through this holy anointing may the Lord in his love and mercy help you with the grace of the Holy Spirit. May the Lord who frees you from sin save you and raise you up.'

The Pope also laid down that in places where olive oil is unobtainable or difficult to obtain, another oil derived from plants may be used. The Oil of the Sick has to be blessed by the bishop, normally at the Chrism Mass on Holy Thursday.

The 1983 English edition of *Pastoral Care of the Sick* has been greatly amplified so as to cover conveniently (i.e. with adaptations and helpful layout of the texts) and adequately (with regard to pastoral care) all the various situations and circumstances in which the priest has to minister to the sick and the dying.

Other Sacraments and Rites

Rite of Funerals

In the early Church, the body of the dead person was prepared for the journey of hope. The dominant theme was paschal joy, a sense of triumph over death. The body was washed and anointed. There was a procession of the community dressed in white garments, singing psalms of hope and alleluias, carrying palm leaves and lights, and burning incense. A service of thanksgiving and praise, with readings and psalms, was held by the body. The eucharist was celebrated, and the kiss of peace was given to the body, which was then interred with the feet towards the east.

During the late middle ages, and in the Roman Ritual of 1614, the dominant keynote of funerals had become that of sin: black vestments became the norm, and there was great concern with forgiveness of sin, judgment, heaven and hell. The atmosphere of joy and thanksgiving had disappeared, and funerals were usually sorrowful affairs. This stress on fear of judgment and the burden of sin tended to overshadow the themes of welcome into paradise and the resurrection of the body which were still present in parts of the rite.

The Second Vatican Council decreed:

> 'The rite for the burial of the dead should evidence more clearly the paschal character of Christian death, and should correspond more closely to the circumstances and traditions found in various regions. This latter provision holds good also for the liturgical colour to be used. The rite for the burial of infants is to be revised, and a special Mass for the occasion provided' [CL 81-82].

It was clear from this that the Council Fathers wanted funerals to regain something of the joyful character which they had had in the early centuries when the connection between Christian death and the resurrection of Jesus Christ was uppermost in people's minds. The liturgical colour, intended to reflect this paschal character, is normally to be white. It is interesting to note that in the 1614 Ritual, white vestments were specified for the burial of a child.

The revised Funeral Rite (*Ordo Exsequiarum*) was published in the Latin form in 1969. Provision was made for adaptation by bishops' conferences. A translation was published by the National Liturgical Conference of England and Wales (edited for use in these countries by the St Thomas More Centre) in 1975. Provision was made for a vigil for the deceased: this was one of the major changes of the new rite. The funeral rite was arranged to take place in three stages: in the home, in the church and at the graveside. Another notable change in the rite was the replacement of the prayer 'Enter not into judgment . . .' and the responsory 'Deliver me, O Lord, from everlasting death in that dread day . . .' with the Final Commendation and Farewell, thus reverting to the spirit of funerals in the early centuries.

Like the other revised rites, the funeral rite was intended to be more flexible and more pastoral in practice: for example, provision was to be made for the needs of the mourners and for those attending the funeral who were non-Catholics and non-practising Catholics.

A new translation of the Latin version, with much amplification and adaptation, was published by ICEL in 1985.[2] An adaptation of this for use in England, Wales and Scotland has been prepared, and it is anticipated that this will come into use in Advent 1990.[3] The chief features of this projected new edition of the rite are as follows:

1 a revised translation of the notes, texts and rubrics of the Latin version;
2 a pastoral rearrangement and presentation of the contents of the book with some prayers taken from the Roman Missal;
3 the addition of supplementary texts to cover pastoral circumstances not provided for in the Latin text: e.g. interment of the ashes of a deceased person, service for

use in a crematorium chapel, funeral of a victim of accidental or violent death, prayers for a still-born child, neo-natal deaths, etc.;
4 Morning and Evening Prayer of the Office of the Dead from *The Liturgy of the Hours*;
5 new pastoral notes for each of the various rites;
6 a new General Introduction dealing with:
  (a) the theology of death in a pastoral context;
  (b) the various aspects of ministry to the deceased and to the mourners, and a ministry of reconciliation;
  (c) liturgical elements and practical guidance, including music.

Music at Funerals

The new *Order of Christian Funerals* will be the first of the revised and amplified liturgical books to give detailed and specific guidance on singing and music. The *General Introduction* has a section on music [# # 30-33]. It stresses that music is integral to the funeral rites: it allows the community to express convictions and feelings, it should support, console and uplift the participants, and create a spirit of hope in Christ's victory. The texts should express the paschal mystery of the Lord's triumph over death and should be related to the readings from scripture.

Guidance on music is given in the introductions to each of the constituent rites. Music is stated to be integral to the vigil service: preference should be given to the singing of the opening song and the responsorial psalm, while the litany, the Lord's Prayer, and a closing song may also be sung [# 68]. In the funeral liturgy, there should be an entrance song expressing belief in eternal life. The responsorial psalm should be sung if possible. When the gifts are brought to the altar, instrumental music or a song may accompany the procession: Psalm 18:1-6, Psalm 63, Psalm 66:13-20, and Psalm 138 are given as examples of suitable songs. The singing of the people's parts in the Liturgy of the Eucharist is recommended. During the rite of communion, the Lord's Prayer, the doxology, the *Lamb of God*, and a song for the communion procession (examples: Psalms 23, 27, 34, 63, 121) should be sung if possible. There is particular emphasis on the singing of the song of farewell. Singing is also encouraged during the procession to the place of committal. Wherever possible, the family should be involved in the choice of music. [# # 135, 139, 144, 147, 149]

When the funeral liturgy takes place outside Mass, preference should be given to singing the entrance song, the responsorial psalm, the gospel acclamation, and especially the song of farewell [# 181]. A song affirming hope in God's mercy and in the resurrection of the dead is desirable at the end of the rite of committal [# 214]. Comparable guidelines are offered for children's funerals.

Notes

1 Further information is given in *Liturgy* 10:5 (June 1986) and 11:4 (April 1987).

2 The original translation by ICEL (1970) was not adopted by the bishops of England and Wales.

3 Two issues of *Liturgy*, 14:1 (Oct.-Nov. 1989) and 14:2 (Dec. 1989-Jan. 1990), are devoted to the new Order of Christian Funerals.

16

People, Signs, and Sacraments

There is more to liturgy than rites and texts. To complete this survey of contemporary liturgy, the remaining chapters will be dealing with some important issues such as the meaning of liturgy and the significance of signs and sacraments, the design and decoration of churches and their contents, and the place of music, language and movement in worship. All these aspects have to be considered together and in their relationship to each other if we are to build up a 'total concept' of liturgy.

Worship, human life and the Church

To know God is to be caught up in a necessary relationship with him. We respond to the God who is almighty with adoration: but to the God revealed to us as a loving Father we respond in faith with praise, thanksgiving and love. For the man of faith, worship is an integral part of life, and at a different level worship is a human and social need.

Worship is also the constitutive activity of the Church founded by Jesus Christ. Worship makes the Church: we are being most authentically the 'Church' when we are engaged in liturgical worship. God has revealed to us his saving acts, and his people respond in faith in the Church's worship.

Liturgy, rite and ritual

Liturgy refers to the public, official worship of the Church, carried out by groups of Christians worshipping ecclesially, that is as the Church. The relationship between public and private prayer and its importance were discussed at the beginning of this book.

Because of its official public character, liturgical worship is formalised. This does not mean that it has to be perfunctory, dull and lifeless, or that there is no room for spontaneity, choice or change. A liturgy which has these characteristics is indeed poor liturgy. History suggests that liturgy, like other human concerns, needs revitalising and revising from time to time. Liturgy must be a living liturgy, seen as relevant to those who carry it out, and enjoying both stability and openness to revision. Change sometimes causes pain, but liturgy has to adapt at times to be able to function authentically as the worship of God's people. Tradition has an important place in liturgy and we look to its origins in the early centuries to discern the fundamental essentials, but not for slavish imitation. Liturgy is for people: it is not a sort of archaeology.

Liturgical worship is carried out according to prescribed forms, as distinct from the 'free worship' favoured in some churches. This means that there are certain unchangeable patterns and certain forms of words which have to be used. But there can still be areas of choice and the possibility of flexibility and adaptation, as in post-Vatican 2 liturgy.

The formal actions which constitute the liturgy are known

as *rites*. The correct meaning of the word *ritual* is the prescribed form of words used in a rite. However, these two words are often used interchangeably, and unfortunately the word 'ritual' is also used to mean 'ceremonial', especially in the terms 'ritualist', 'ritualistic' and 'ritualism'.

Religious rites are mostly related to basic human actions, such as washing (baptism), eating and drinking (the eucharist), and (in ancient times) the anointing of athletes or combatants for strength in a contest (anointing in baptism, confirmation, order, and sickness). Christianity provides a pre-eminent example of a religion with rites which have not been artificially constructed but are enrichments of natural institutions. Furthermore, Christian rites parallel human rites, replicating the human cycle from birth to death.

Unlike some religions, where rites serve the functions of controlling divine powers or protecting mankind from them, Christian rites are designed to develop a relationship between man and his creator.[1]

Rites have certain important functions in addition to embodying the form of liturgical observances.

(a) They have a symbolic character by means of which the human can share in the divine: for example, the eucharistic rite symbolises Christ the bread of life and at the same time it is the symbolic action by which we are linked to and receive that life.

(b) A rite is designed for regular use, and so the man-God relationship is constantly renewed and continued. A rite repeatedly puts before the worshipper the divine action which gave rise to the relationship.

(c) As with the eucharist, there is an anamnetic character to a rite insofar as the divine action is constantly made present once more and solemnly remembered.

(d) Rites, of course, strengthen a religious community by preserving its traditions, transmitting its beliefs and practices, and (in accordance with group dynamics) reinforcing its shared faith and *mores*.

Ritual, the form of words, is incorporated in official books such as missals, sacramentaries, rituals, office books and lectionaries. At least some of these books will be treated as holy objects. Books such as missals and lectionaries are usually bound in a dignified style, revered by being incensed, carried in processions, and set up conspicuously in places of honour.

Liturgical texts contain various types of euchological material, such as prayers, acclamations, performative rituals, songs, professions, and readings. Prayer texts will encompass various functions such as praise, adoration, love, repentance, expression of faith and hope, and petition. The material in the texts will also contain psalms, readings and creeds.

Ceremonial denotes the prescribed and formal actions carried out in worship. Some of these actions will be the essential matter of a sacrament, such as the pouring of water in baptism; others will be the 'illustrative rites', such as the exchange of rings and gifts at a wedding or the presentation of the paten and chalice at the ordination of a priest; others will have the function of lending dignity to an action, or object, or person: for example, leading a bishop in procession to his throne, placing lighted candles next to the book of gospels, and incensing the altar.

Liturgy, faith and doctrine

It is important to remember that Christians were worshipping Christ before they began to formulate beliefs about his person and nature. Worship comes before the formulation of doctrine. This is reflected in the old saying *lex orandi, lex credendi*, 'the law of praying establishes the law of believing'.[2] This priority of worship over doctrine was recognised at an early stage in the Church's history when the sacramental practice of the Church was cited to refute certain heretical claims. Liturgy is a norm of faith, so to speak. It is at the heart of the Church's mission, making the mystery of salvation present and active in the Church. In virtue of this it is a reliable witness to apostolic tradition. Here we can see the relationship between liturgy, faith and doctrine. By living out the mystery of salvation in liturgy, we foster a living faith.

Priest, people and participation

The Vatican Council has encouraged us to restore a more appropriate relationship between priest and people in the liturgy, and especially at Mass, which should be seen as offered by celebrant and people together, not by the priest alone and not by the priest as a substitute for the people. At the beginning of the present rite, the priest and people together prepare to celebrate worthily the 'sacred mysteries', and this 'togetherness' continues throughout, being particularly prominent in the first person plural of the eucharistic prayer. It is reinforced by the priest facing the people. There has been much re-ordering of worshipping space in our churches to reflect this change of relationship, especially in bringing priest and people nearer together into one community.

The notion of *participation* at Mass has been much misunderstood. It is not a matter of giving the people something to do, so that the priest does not do everything himself. It is not a matter of keeping people usefully occupied when they might otherwise be distracted or daydream. Participation is based on a correct understanding of the role of the people at Mass, and consists of the people carrying out their distinctive parts in the liturgy and associating themselves with the priest in the eucharistic action which he offers in the name of all present. Participation is not implemented by the singing of a few randomly chosen hymns. It requires an understanding of what is taking place and of the role of priest and people. Participation has to be understood in liturgical terms.

Silence and 'mystery'
Failure to understand the nature and importance of participation has led to another area of misunderstanding. In recent years there have been complaints from some who do not like the revised Mass, and especially the use of English and the eucharistic prayer said aloud, that the 'sense of mystery' has been lost.

This view arises from an unfortunate confusion. The eucharist is a 'mystery' in the traditional biblical and Christian sense of this word: it is part of God's eternal plan and is a means by which this plan is disclosed to us. Our knowledge of the mysteries of the Christian faith depends on revelation, and our understanding of them will necessarily be imperfect. One can spend a lifetime reflecting on the depths and riches of the eucharist without exhausting them.

But respecting the mystery of the eucharist, approaching it in awe and 'the fear of the Lord', is not the same as creating an atmosphere of mysteriousness. The use of Latin and the silent canon are quite irrelevant to reflection on the mystery of the eucharist, and indeed may well hinder and obscure it. Sometimes the critics complain that with the lack of silence, and the activities such as hand-shaking, they 'cannot get on with their prayers'. This reflects a lack of understanding of the nature of the eucharistic prayer and a failure to see that the people are involved in it. The proclamation of the eucharist prayer is emphatically not a time for silence and meditation divorced from participation and involvement in this action of the People of God. To think otherwise is to misunderstand the significance of the eucharistic prayer and to deny the most basic principles of the liturgy.

But there is a further underlying problem involved here,

namely a failure to identify the appropriate parts of the Mass when silence can be and should be observed for personal prayer and reflection. The importance of periods of silence at particular points in the Mass has been repeatedly stressed in this book. In some parish churches this principle is hardly recognised at all.

The Church and the Sacraments

It was noted at the beginning of this book that the sacraments are constitutive of the Church, an institution founded by Christ himself, of which he is the Head, in order to continue his work of redemption for all time. Through the faith of the Church, the salvation brought about by our High Priest Jesus Christ is applied to mankind.

Christ's saving work is accomplished in us by the sacraments, the sacred signs of God's love and grace. Not only is God's grace revealed to us in the sacraments: this grace is given to our souls by these sacred signs. Christ himself in his humanity is a sacrament of saving grace:

> *'He is the image of the unseen God*
> *and the first-born of all creation,*
> *... God wanted all perfection*
> *to be found in him*
> *and all things to be reconciled through him*
> *and for him ...*
> *when he made peace*
> *by his death on the cross.'*
> *(Colossians 1:15-20)*

Through his incarnation the world has been sanctified by the divine indwelling. Material things can be the vehicle or expression of God's grace. Water, oil, bread and wine have been made into sacramental signs. The world itself is in a sense sacramental: it is in the world and in the realm of the material that we receive God's saving grace.

Catholic Worship

The Second Vatican Council declared the Church to be a sacrament:

> 'By her relationship with Christ, the Church is a kind of sacrament or sign of intimate union with God, and of the unity of all mankind. She is also an instrument for the achievement of such union and unity' [CC 1].

The seven sacraments of the Church have been ordained by Christ for the enactment of his priestly work and for the gift of grace to our souls. Why do the sacraments occupy such a large place in a book on the liturgy of the Church? Firstly, because it is necessary for the Church to institute liturgical rites for the bestowal of the sacraments. Secondly, because a sacrament is also a sign by which we worship God. Thirdly, because the sacraments are prayers: in them we are united to Christ in his prayer to the Father. For these reasons, the sacramental rites and the sacrifice of the Mass are the main elements of the liturgy.

The teaching of the Second Vatican Council on this is worth quoting in full:

> 'The purpose of the sacraments is to sanctify men, to build up the body of Christ, and finally to give worship to God. Because they are signs they also instruct. They not only presuppose faith, but by words and objects they also nourish, strengthen and express it: that is why they are called 'sacraments of faith'. They do indeed impart grace, but, in addition, the very act of celebrating them disposes the faithful most effectively to receive this grace in a fruitful manner, to worship God duly, and to practise charity' [CL 59].

Signs and symbols

Signs and symbols play a leading part in our worship. These two terms are often used interchangeably, but to some extent they can be distinguished. *Signs* often arise in the natural order of things and indicate or suggest the presence (or impending presence) of something else. Clouds are a sign of rain, feverishness is a sign of illness, yawning is a sign of tiredness, tears are a sign of sorrow and laughter of joy, and crumbling walls are a sign of decay. Signs can be man-made. An arrow can be a sign of the direction to be followed. A flashing light by a level crossing is a sign that a train is coming.

In the sacraments, natural signs also serve as spiritual signs: bread is a sign of human life, the consecrated bread is a sign of spiritual life. Sacramental signs point to or indicate the bestowal of grace: hence the distinction between the outward sign and the inward grace. In addition to being signs or indicators, the sacramental signs are also operative in bestowing the grace they signify.

A *symbol*, on the other hand, is anything used in communication to stand for something other than itself. A symbol conjures up the meaning of something else. Their meaning may have to be explained. The fish was a symbol of Christianity in early times: its meaning was not self-evident and it was intended to be a secret sign. Symbols are conventional, that is they are given a certain meaning by general agreement. We may be able to guess the meaning of some of the symbols on an Ordnance Survey map, but not all of them: we need to consult the key. Symbols represent or typify something.

Both men and animals respond to signs, but they respond rather differently. The animal responds to the stimulus properties of the sign, but man responds not only to the stimulus properties but also to the meaning of a sign. Only man can produce and use symbols. This is part of his ability to be reflective and rational. Man is able to handle meanings, and the use of the symbolic plays a central part in his development of speech, language and concepts.

Religious symbols, such as bread and wine in the eucharist and water in baptism, have both a visible reality and an invisible reality: the visible element puts us in touch with a mystery of our religion which would otherwise be beyond our grasp. Religion seeks expression through symbolism, including the symbolism of art. Many religious truths can only be expressed in symbols or imagery, or in metaphors or analogies. The scriptures are full of poetic imagery, and symbolism is fundamental to Christianity.

It is sometimes said that modern man is less sensitive to the world of signs and symbols. The symbolism of pure running water is more meaningful in the near east, perhaps, than in a country with an abundance of water from the tap. Oil does not have the symbolism it once had: we tend to regard it as an undistinguished commodity hidden away in our larders or in the engine of our car. The light of a candle may seem attractive to us, especially on a dining room table, but in other contexts it is merely an inefficient type of light, only used in an emergency. Yet the symbolism of the paschal candle, and by extension all the other candles in church, is richly significant.

The sacraments are signs of the bestowal of grace. They are also symbols of God's love and his saving power in our lives. Sophisticated urbanised man may need teaching about Christian signs and symbols. Liturgy is highly dependent on imagery, signs and symbolism, not only in the sacramental signs but in gestures, postures, movements, the use of space, the design of furnishings and vessels, the wearing of vestments, and the use of singing and music. Those who have responsibility for these matters must do justice to all aspects of symbolism. The choice of music, the planning of services, the re-ordering of worshipping space, the design of objects used in worship and the decoration of our churches are all symbolic of what we believe we are doing in the liturgy. They all need to be carefully considered not only in aesthetic terms but even more so according to liturgical principles.

Above all, the sacramental signs must be made to appear as authentic and meaningful as possible. Hosts should look and taste like bread, and large hosts (representative of the 'one loaf'), large enough to be broken up into many pieces, should be preferred. The chalice should be offered at every Mass, and intinction, which does not in the least resemble drinking, should only be used for good reasons. The symbolism of the eucharistic meal should not be totally missing from the way Mass is celebrated and perceived.

Celebrants should not be niggardly with the flowing water of baptism, and oil and chrism should be used generously so that it can be seen clearly and even smelt by the people. The minute dab of oil, invisible and imperceptible, seriously depreciates the symbolism, especially if the oil is regarded as nasty dirty stuff to be wiped off the baby's head as soon as possible, and at all costs not allowed to soil its dress!

Modern man may not be open to the more traditional symbolism, but it is unlikely that he is totally unaware of symbolism. Contemporary events suggest that symbolism is as strong as ever in human perception and that modern man uses certain powerful symbols of his own. Is there any scope in the idea that some contemporary symbols should be sought to enrich the liturgy of today and tomorrow?

Notes

1 Use is made here of the classification of rites by J. Cazeneuve in *Les rites et la condition humaine*, 1958.

2 The origin of this saying is a passage in the *De Gratia dei 'Indiculus'* by Prosper of Aquitaine (c.390-c.463): '... sacramenta respiciamus, quae ab Apostolis tradita in toto mundo atque in omni Ecclesia catholica uniformiter celebrantur, ut legem credendi lex statuat supplicandi' [Migne, PL 50:555]. ('... let us look to the sacraments which were handed down to us from the Apostles and are celebrated in the same manner throughout the world and in every Catholic church, so that in consequence the law of worshipping determines the law of believing.')

Prosper was not, however, formulating the principle of *lex orandi, lex credendi*, which was a later development. He was writing about belief in the necessity of grace, and he was arguing that as we have to ask for God's help in prayer we have a duty to hold this belief.

17

Space, Design, and Movement

Architecture and the layout of a church
[GIRM 257; 279-80]
There is no 'natural' style of architecture for a Christian church, despite the claims of A.W. Pugin for a close connection between Christianity and Gothic architecture. In altering, or enlarging, or re-ordering an existing church, respect must be paid to the style of the building and new work must be in harmony with it. Care should be taken not to break up the architectural integrity and visual harmony of the church by insensitive rearrangement or removal of structures or fittings. In the case of a new church, 'the plan of the church and its surroundings should be contemporary' [GIRM 280].

Some historic styles reflect particular emphases in worship. Gothic churches tend to distance the celebration from the people and create a sense of so-called 'mystery' by interposing screens and elevating the mind to heaven by pointed arches and soaring vaults. Baroque churches stress sumptuous decoration, music and ceremonial, with the altar being well open to view and a broad nave to facilitate preaching. Most churches in the past have had a distinct division between the clergy celebrating in the sanctuary and the people installed in the nave, separated by the altar rails. This arrangement has fostered the spectatorial stance of the laity and the popular assumption that the 'sacred' mysteries are celebrated only by the clergy and ministers.

As a result of the Liturgical Movement and the teaching of the Second Vatican Council, we have readjusted our views of liturgical celebration. This has involved a re-examination of the relationship between celebrant and people, not only in the rites themselves, but also in the design and disposition of the total space available for worship. There is a fresh realisation that all liturgical rites are acts of the whole Body of Christ, Head and members. Consequently when a new church is being designed or an existing church is being re-ordered, it is important to plan for this active unity of the whole assembly. The worshipping space is not confined to the area around the altar: it is the entire area occupied by the whole assembly.

This is another aspect of the 'total view' of the liturgy: liturgical considerations encompass all the members present, clergy and people, and all the space, not just the so-called 'sanctuary' [GIRM 273]. The church should not be treated as if it were a theatre in which all the significant action takes place on the stage. It is important, therefore, that the entire worshipping area should be seen as a whole, and not just the major parts, and ordered (or re-ordered) in terms of its suitability for liturgical celebration.

There are three focal points in the worshipping space, the altar, the lectern and the president's chair. These should be distinct and reasonably apart from each other as each symbolises and is concerned with a different part and function of the liturgy. Each of these should be used exclusively for its proper function at the appropriate time during Mass. Ideally the priest should be seen to process from one to another, thus highlighting the different parts of the Mass. There should not be any other focal points in the 'sanctuary' area. All other parts of the church, the seating, the font, the Blessed Sacrament Chapel, the chapel of reconciliation, the organ and space for singers and musicians should be arranged in an appropriate relationship with the three focal points.

(a) *The altar* [GIRM 259-270]

This should be in a central position and not too distant from the people. As far as possible, the people should feel they are gathered around the altar during the eucharistic prayer, rather than facing it as one faces a traditional stage in a theatre. If we could persuade people to do without fixed seating, then the congregation could actually stand around the altar, which would be the most appropriate stance for the eucharistic prayer. Fixed seating imposes many constraints on the creation of an appropriate liturgical 'atmosphere'. In most orthodox churches there are only a few seats and these are intended for the elderly and the weak: the people stand the entire time, although they do not actually stand around the altar. Some churches make very flexible use of movable seats, rearranging them for different occasions and celebrations, and sometimes removing them altogether. An arrangement which might be pastorally beneficial would be to invite the smaller congregation at a weekday Mass to stand around the altar during the eucharistic prayer.

New altars do not necessarily have to be rectangular in shape. The former 'epistle end' and 'gospel end' are not required by the new liturgy. Sometimes a square altar proves to be an effective design. The size of the altar needs careful consideration: cases have occurred of new altars being obviously too large or too small. The size of an altar has to be judged in proportion to its setting, and in relation to the needs of the celebration. A bigger church would probably need an altar large enough to hold several chalices (for communion under both kinds) and to be suitable for concelebration. Whatever the overall size of the church building, every altar should be large enough to hold the altar missal, the chalice(s), and other vessels without appearing crowded. As far as possible, the top of the altar should not be cluttered with other items (e.g. hymn-books) as this detracts from the centrality of the sacred elements in the eucharistic celebration. The altar should not be used to screen amplifying equipment or contain hidden storage areas.

The altar is the place where the Liturgy of the Eucharist *alone* should take place. Apart from kissing the altar at the entry rite, the priest should not approach the altar until the beginning of the Liturgy of the Eucharist; and then he should process with some solemnity to mark the end of the Liturgy of the Word and the beginning of the Liturgy of the Eucharist. He should not creep over to the altar unobtrusively while the people are engaged in other matters such as collections and hymn singing.

The altar is the symbol of Christ as the foundation of the Church, as the spiritual rock (1 Corinthians 10:4). For this reason, it is incensed at various points during the liturgy. The altar should never be used as a general purpose table or counter. It should be free-standing, with ample space around it if possible for incensation, for concelebration, and for special occasions such as episcopal visitations and the Easter Vigil. The altar should be constructed of materials worthy of the sacrament of the holy sacrifice and heavenly banquet, yet simple, complementing the ambo or lectern in materials and design.

There should not be two altars in the 'sanctuary'. This brings about a visual polarity which undermines the unique value of the liturgy. Unless, in cases of re-ordering, the older altar is one of such historic or artistic merit that it cannot or should not be removed or moved to another part of the church, one altar should be the rule. Consequently the older altar should be removed if it cannot be adapted to be the new altar.

(b) The lectern (or ambo) [GIRM 272]
The lectern should be suitably located so that it can be perceived as the focal point of the proclamation of the word. The people should feel a relationship with the lectern comparable to their relationship with the altar, namely a feeling of being 'gathered around' the lectern during the proclamation of the word. In this way they will feel involved with the Liturgy of the Word, and not just listen passively. The impression of the lectern being a professorial rostrum or a place from which people are 'talked at' should be avoided.

The lectern should be a permanent structure, designed with some dignity, symbolising the importance of God's word, and invested with a significance beyond that of a mere book-stand.

The lectern should only be used for proclaiming the word and for the homily. The Introductory Rites, the Concluding Rites, and the giving of notices should not be carried out at the lectern but at the presidential chair. An ambo may be constructed in place of a lectern: this is a type of small pulpit.

(c) The presidential chair [GIRM 271]
This should be carefully sited so that the priest can be seen to be presiding at the assembly, but it should not be more prominent than the altar or the lectern. It should not resemble a throne in appearance. Where there is sufficient width

available, it is best placed to one side of the altar to balance the lectern. It may be placed behind the altar, provided it does not become distanced from the people. It should not be placed immediately in front of the altar or in front of the tabernacle.

(d) *The tabernacle* [GIRM 276-7]

There was a fuller discussion of the tabernacle in Chapter Twelve, with important references quoted. Some of the salient points are repeated here for convenience.

The tabernacle should if possible be housed in a special chapel well suited for private prayer, not too far from the sanctuary, not hidden away in a remote part of the church, and not on an altar. It should be set on a plinth, as an aumbry, in the wall or in a sacrament house. If, however, an existing chapel is to become the Blessed Sacrament Chapel, the tabernacle may be placed on the altar, which then becomes the Altar of Reservation. A lamp should burn continuously before or near the tabernacle.

If the tabernacle has to be sited in the 'sanctuary' area, it should be positioned in such a way that it does not predominate; i.e. it should not detract from the centrality of the eucharistic action. In such cases it is best to place it not in the centre of the 'sanctuary' but to one side. In some churches this would not be possible because of the aesthetic or historical value of the old high altar. In such circumstances, there may be no alternative to keeping the tabernacle on this altar in use.

It should be borne in mind that holy communion should be given from hosts consecrated at that Mass and not normally from hosts reserved in the tabernacle. The people should be reminded of the significance of the Reserved Sacrament and its veneration.

(e) *The baptismal font*

The parish church must have a baptismal font [IRBC

(*Introduction to the Rite of Baptism of Children*) 10]. It should be 'clean and attractive' [GICI (*General Introduction to Christian Initiation*) 19]. The baptistry is the area where the font has been placed, and the church encourages the use of flowing water for its significance. It may be in a chapel or in another part of the church easily seen by the faithful and able to accommodate a good number of people [GICI 25].

In some churches, the fixed baptismal font has been moved to a position in the 'sanctuary' near the altar. The reason given for this is that the font will then serve as a constant reminder of our baptismal status, by which we were given a priestly character, and that it also signifies the intimate relationship between the Sacrament of Baptism and the Liturgy of the Eucharist.

Even if this reasoning can be accepted, there are serious aesthetic and practical objections to placing the font in a permanent position in the sanctuary. A fourth focal point is then created which upsets the balance and harmony of the three focal points. It also usually gets in the way, and there is the temptation to place things on it, which is inappropriate.

The traditional and preferred place is near the entrance to the church as signifying entry into new life in Christ, of which the Church, the gathered community, is his Body. Baptism needs to be seen in relation to entry into the Community of Christ. If the people pass the baptistry, and bless themselves with water at that point, whenever they enter the church, they will be constantly reminded of the importance of baptism. The baptistry should therefore be sited so as to retain the symbolism of entry into the life of the Church. It should also be sited so as to enable the appropriate liturgical processions to take place from door to font, from font into the community, and then with the community to the altar.

Furnishings and decoration
[CL 122-129; GIRM 253-4, 279-80, 287-312]
The structure of the building and the main features of the church should as far as possible all be conceived and designed harmoniously as an integrated whole. This includes the altar, lectern, presidential chair, font and baptistry, tabernacle, chapels of reservation and reconciliation, and the music area. It also applies to the furnishings, statues, pictures, and even the sacred vessels and the vestments, and the entire decoration, both external and internal. The practice of providing the shell of a building, and then deciding afterwards how to allocate the space, adding 'applied' decoration, and buying ready-made statues, furnishings and vestments, is to be avoided whenever possible. It is more satisfactory to commission original works in consonance with the overall design, and it is not necessarily more expensive.

The principle just enunciated does not rest only on aesthetic grounds; it rests on spiritual and liturgical considerations. 'All things set apart for use in divine worship should be truly worthy, becoming, and beautiful, signs and symbols of heavenly realities ... sacred furnishings should worthily and beautifully serve the dignity of worship' [CL 122]. 'Let bishops carefully exclude from the house of God works which offend true religious sense either by their distortion of forms or by lack of artistic worth, by mediocrity or by pretence' [CL 124]. Good design (functionally as well as aesthetically) and an honest use of materials (and not only traditional materials) should be the key to the worthiness and beauty advocated in the Constitution, and not lavishness or sumptuousness. 'Church decor should be noble and simple rather than sumptuous. It should reflect truth and authenticity ... The noble simplicity which reflects authentic art should be a major factor in selecting furnishings' [GIRM 279, 287].

Whether the church building is in an historic style or in modern idiom, it does not simply house the congregation while they worship.[1] It is an expression of the liturgy which takes place within it. The symbolic nature of the church building with its accoutrements is strikingly expressed in the Preface for the Dedication of a Church. Its design must take into account that it is an image of the heavenly and holy city which is the Church and 'a dimension of the way of salvation'. The church and its artworks are part of the liturgy itself, with a liturgical function: they form 'a visual counterpart' to the readings, prayers and hymns of the rite. Father Michael Jones-Frank, on whose ideas this paragraph is based, has this to say about what he calls 'sacred iconography':

> 'Art works are not there to beautify, nor to be memorials to worthy but deceased members of the parish. They are there to concretise, literally to bring into focus the mysteries of faith unfolded in the patterns and rhythms of liturgy. They are the plastic language of liturgy and of faith, as distinct from the performing languages of liturgy.'[2]

The re-ordering of churches[3]

It is important that when a church is to be altered or its sanctuary re-ordered, there should be full consultation at the earliest possible stage not only with the diocesan financial officers but also with the diocesan Liturgical Commission and its Art and Architecture Advisory Committee [GIRM 256]. This consultation should take place before any plans are finalised to ensure that the proposed alterations are satisfactory structurally, aesthetically, and liturgically. Some sanctuaries have been re-ordered quite unsatisfactorily, and it is imperative that expert advice and guidance should be obtained. It is important that the priest should discuss the projected alterations fully with the members of his parish and also have a clear concept of what he wants to achieve. It is recommended that each diocese should have procedures for this which all parishes would have to observe.

This consultation should cover not only structural alterations, but also the suitability of furnishings and artefacts. Artwork and imagery are as much a dimension of the liturgy as music and hymns, and should be integrated into the total structure. It is always preferable to commission furnishings and artwork rather than buy them ready-made. Suitable artists can be consulted through the diocesan liturgical commission, through the Council for the Care of Churches (Anglican), through professional national and county societies of artists, or through the English secretariat of the International Society of Christian Artists. If money is very short, the local college of art and design could give advice on newly-graduated students who are looking for opportunities. An artist should not be commissioned until his previous work has been adequately inspected *in situ*. Artists should be properly paid for their preliminary work, even if it is eventually rejected. Architects should be sought who have an understanding of liturgical requirements.

Lighting needs professional advice. It adds an important dimension to the feel of the liturgy, as does shadow. Light and shadow need to be carefully balanced to give rest to the eyes as well as a true sense of depth. Light and shadow themselves are symbolic of the mystery of our passage from darkness to the light of God. It is important for the lighting system to be as flexible as possible. It should be possible to dim the lights when this is desirable, for example during vigil services or during periods of silent recollection. It should also be possible to 'highlight' some areas, such as the lectern during the reading of the word, and the altar when the Liturgy of the Eucharist commences.

The siting of musicians and the organ needs careful consideration. The choice of a new organ and the position of the organ with regard to acoustics and musical quality are matters for professional advice. The type of organ needed in a church must also be considered: for example, is it required mainly to support good liturgical singing, or is it also required to be a 'performance' organ?

There are also some other liturgical considerations here. The musicians should not be too distant from the assembly and should be part of the worshipping community. Cases have occurred of churches being carpetted to create a relaxed, comfortable, welcoming atmosphere, only to find that the sound of the organ is absorbed by the carpet. This problem must be anticipated by consulting an expert.

Movable artwork and decoration

In addition to permanent artefacts, good use should be made of 'movable' pictures, tapestries, collages and displays, including work produced by members of the parish, which are put up to illustrate a season or festival or occasion (such as a first communion or confirmation). Allied with this is the use of flowers. They should not normally be placed on altars, but in other suitable positions. It is better to have a few effectively placed than an excessive number which would distract from the liturgy. Flower arrangements should not be intended simply to 'beautify' the sanctuary, but should be thematic arrangements, such as white lilies for Easter Day, designed as part of the total liturgy.

Movement

Gestures, posture, and movement are all part of the liturgy. Each of these has a liturgical function. The movement of clergy and ministers needs planning. A procession can be significant and symbolic, especially when it leads to the lectern for the proclamation of the word or the altar for the eucharist or the font for a baptism. Ritual actions should not be obscured or diminished in any way. The pouring of water in baptism, the taking of the gifts at the eucharist, the elevation, the kiss of peace, and the fraction, for example, all have deep significance.

Gestures add meaning to the liturgy: for example, the hand raised in blessing, the triple cross at the gospel, the head bowed at the mention of the incarnation in the creed, and the celebrant's hands outstretched in prayer. Actions such as these concretise the petitions or praise or other prayer statements. Sometimes they are performed without words and in that case are themselves acts of prayer, known as 'movement-prayer' or 'embodied prayer'.

The contribution of physical movement to the totality of the liturgy must not be overlooked. It is, along with the spatial and the iconographic, one of the dimensions of the liturgy. Liturgical dance, drama and mime have undergone considerable development in recent decades. They can enrich the liturgy with their expressive potential, whether telling a story or portraying a theme. At times they can be a homily. Liturgy should relate to the whole person, with all the senses and all the modes of imagery and cognition. There is a tendency to confine the impact of liturgy to one sense, the aural, and to one medium, words. We need to ask ourselves if our revised liturgy is too sophisticated, too verbal, too 'cranial'.

Postures have a meaning: we sit to listen to readings and homilies, stand for the proclamation of the gospel, the creed, and the eucharistic prayer, kneel for private prayer, and so on [GIRM 20-22]. Relative positions in church affect the dynamics of the liturgy. An outstanding example of this is the different liturgical perspective brought about by the 'middle eastward' position of the celebrant, that is, facing the people from the other side of the altar. This brings about a relationship of closer association and sharing in the celebration. Finally, in these various aspects of movement in the liturgy there are many possibilities of furthering that participation which the Second Vatican Council so strongly endorsed.

Notes

1 In this paragraph I have drawn on the following articles by Father Michael Jones-Frank: 'Can we build without the artist?', *Liturgy* 11:3 (Feb.-Mar. 1987), pp. 114-126, and 'Towards a synthesis of sacred art', *Liturgy* 13:6 (Aug.-Sep. 1989), pp. 228-242.

2 'Can we build without the artist?', p. 117.

3 In this section I have drawn on a document compiled for the Diocese of Clifton Liturgical Commission by Father Jones-Frank and myself. Cf. also *Code of Canon Law*, canons 1188-9, 1216, and 1220.

18

Music, Speech, and Language

Music and worship

One of the most striking changes in the average Sunday Mass since the time of the Second Vatican Council is the amount of singing that now takes place, especially of hymns. In most churches, the principle of participation has been implemented largely by hymn singing. Many new hymn books have been published and new hymns composed, many in a 'popular' or 'folk' style. Another great change has been the freedom to use hymns from non-Catholic sources, which has greatly enriched our hymnody. This development of hymn singing in Catholic churches is to be welcomed, but the overall use of music and singing in the liturgy varies greatly in quality and imaginativeness from church to church, and there is a need for a greater degree of musical development in most places.

Music, Speech, and Language

Throughout this book, there have been discussions of the appropriate use of music in connection with each of the various rites. In the present chapter, therefore, liturgical music will be examined only in general terms.

The *Constitution on the Liturgy* [112-121] gave considerable encouragement, albeit rather unadventurously, to the development of music in the liturgy. Church music is described as something 'of immeasurable value, greater than that of any other art' and is to be preserved and fostered. The *Constitution* insists that music is a necessary and integral part of the liturgy, giving it 'a more noble form', and repeatedly associates music with participation. The need for new music is stressed, especially for texts drawn from scripture and from liturgical sources. Implicit here is a criticism of sentimental 'devotional' hymnody which had hindered the growth of authentic liturgical music.

The *General Instruction of the Roman Missal* had a brief but incisive section [19] on the importance of singing. It laid down that singing should be widely used at Mass. In particular the more significant parts should be sung, namely 'those to be sung by the priest or ministers with the people responding or those to be sung by the priest and people together.' The *General Instruction on the Liturgy of the Hours* provided a much more detailed exposition of the place of singing in the office [267-284].

At the outset it seems essential to draw a distinction between music *in* worship and music *as* worship. Much of the singing we hear in church, and especially at Sunday Mass, surely falls under the first of these categories. We have hymns *at* Mass, or Mass *with* hymns, as if a decorative touch were being added to the Mass, or perhaps an attempt made to enliven the Mass and give the people something to do. This is to mistake the reason for having singing at Mass. The justification should be in terms of the liturgy only.

If this argument is accepted, then our aim should be music *as* worship rather than music *in* worship. From this, some important principles can be derived.

(a) All music, both instrumental and vocal, for use at Mass or in any of the rites, should be specifically part of the liturgy, and chosen for its liturgical suitability.

(b) It should be recognised that there are various functions which music can serve in the liturgy, each of which calls for a different type of music. It is inappropriate to have the same tune for the penitential rite as for the *sanctus*.

(c) Some parts of the liturgy are meant to be sung: for example, the gospel acclamation. To sing such parts is the norm, to recite them is a substitute (and in some cases a poor substitute) for singing.

(d) It is important to be clear about who should sing which parts. There are parts meant to be sung by the priest and deacon. There are parts meant to be sung by the whole assembly, clergy and people, and parts sung by the whole assembly except for the celebrant. There are people's parts, and there are other parts which could be sung either by the people or by the choir.

(e) The principle of participation is not satisfied by inserting into the Mass a number of favourite hymns. A hymn should be chosen because it is a good entrance hymn, or a good offertory hymn, or a good hymn for the liturgical season or feast. In addition, hymns are not the only material for singing, and consideration must be given to other material, such as chants, psalms, songs, acclamations, and litanies.

(f) It is highly desirable that each parish has a cantor to lead the people in singing such items as the responsorial psalm and chants. Under the direction of a cantor, a greater variety of relevant material can be sung. One of the most useful functions of a cantor is to sing a simple melody which the people can immediately repeat without a hymn book or music sheet.

(g) Each parish should develop its music and singing as widely and imaginatively as possible. There is much scope for a broad use of instrumental music as well as singing.

(h) Cantors, organists, and leaders of music should if possible attend training courses, and dioceses should organise facilities of various sorts for the promotion of liturgical music in every parish of the diocese. This should be an important function of the Liturgical Commission or of a music advisory committee of the Commission.

Speech and language

We have already referred to the criticism which is sometimes made that our revised liturgy is too wordy, that we rely too much on the verbal element in our worship and do not make enough of other elements, such as signs, actions, gestures, music, singing and so on. There is an element of truth in this claim, and we should be alerted to the dangers of excessive verbalisation. But it is hardly necessary to point out that liturgy is highly dependent on speech and language, and it is illuminating to reflect on the nature and function of these two elements in the liturgy.

It is commonly assumed that the function of language is to communicate information and ideas to other people. But if this were all we ever did with our ability to speak, then our interactions with other people would be very limited indeed. A moment's thought will show that the interactions we have with others are varied and complex, and necessarily so. We use language for many functions apart from conveying information; for example, we express feelings, make requests for help, ask questions, issue orders and prohibitions, and so on. In addition we often use language to make 'performative utterances'. That is, when we say things like 'I promise that ...', 'I agree to do ...', 'I appoint you my executor ...', or 'I admit you to membership of this society ...' we are actually performing the action of promising, agreeing, appointing or admitting.

Many of our speech acts in liturgical rites are clearly not communicative but performative, for example, 'I baptise you ...' is the very act of baptising, and likewise with the spoken formula in each of the sacramental rites; and 'we praise you', 'we thank you' and 'we bless you' are all performative speech acts. The eucharistic prayer is performative, not only in bringing about the transformation of the gifts, but also in that it is in itself an act of remembrance, thanksgiving and offering.

Other speech functions can be discerned in various parts of our liturgy. The Liturgy of the Word is primarily proclamatory: in the scriptural readings we proclaim the word of God. It is also communicatory because God's word is being conveyed to us in the readings. The eucharistic prayer is also proclamatory: whenever we celebrate it, we proclaim the death and resurrection of Jesus Christ. Other functions include the expressive, as in penitential prayers and acts of faith, hope and charity; the intercessory, as in the collects and the Prayer of the Faithful; and professing, as in the creed.

Taken as a whole, liturgical language can also be classed as 'evocative' in that it is designed to elicit certain religious emotions and experiences, such as awe, worship, love, sorrow, and gratitude. It is also evocative in that it leads us to identify certain beliefs. In the liturgy we profess the incarnation, death, resurrection and ascension of Jesus Christ. We affirm our belief in our own salvation and our complete dependence on God; and we believe that the whole Body of Christ under its Head is joined in constant worship of the Father. This aspect of liturgical language is particularly associated with the symbolism discussed in the previous chapter.

It is possible at this stage to pursue this analysis further and discuss the nature of the interaction with God which we call worship or liturgy. Some writers describe the whole of liturgy as a conversation with God: we speak to him in various ways in prayer, we listen to him in the scriptures. The use of this word 'conversation' reminds us that much of the time human language is inadequate to express truths about the infinite God except in metaphorical or figurative language. Religious discourse has, therefore, an affinity with poetic discourse, and this quality can be traced throughout our liturgy.

Any use of language presupposes a body of shared meanings and concepts. This points to the need not only for catechesis in our faith but also for constant reflection on the meaning of what we say and do in worship. Concepts are acquired through the individual's own efforts to grasp meanings in particular situations and in interaction with others. Understanding grows through practice and experience. Liturgy should therefore be an experience as well as an action. Good liturgy begets good liturgy.

Finally, some practical points can be made. Whatever we do, say or sing in the liturgy is a sacred action, and should be carried out with care and reverence. We are dealing with the realm of the holy, and in the early centuries of the Church these holy things were kept hidden from strangers. Words should be said or sung in a manner which accords with their nature or function.

It can be said that we are growing in experience of finding the most suitable style of language to use in translating the liturgical rites from the Latin and in composing new rites. It is easy to criticise particular versions because they are not 'literal' translations of the Latin. Generally speaking, literal translations would be unnatural. Modern English uses structures which are different from Latin, and so a single Latin sentence is often rendered by two or more shorter, less complex sentences. The translations often have to depart from a close adherence to the Latin terminology because it is important to translate the sense or meaning of a passage, not simply the words. The simplicity and directness of style found in the translations have been adopted for pastoral reasons. The meaning of language depends on the community using it and the setting in which it is used. In this sense, liturgy (and liturgical language) is for people. It must enable them to meet God in worship, to find themselves for what they are, namely the worshipping people of God, and to express themselves in genuine corporate prayer.

19

Time and the Liturgical Year

Time and the liturgy
The final dimension of the liturgy which needs to be considered is that of time. Some aspects of this have already been touched on in early chapters. By intervening in human history, the timeless God has linked time with eternity. Christ's saving deeds took place in time and can be assigned dates. Our response to Christ's offer of salvation and everlasting life also takes place in time, and our baptism, confirmation and the reception of other sacraments can also be assigned dates. So while we look forward to life without end, we journey as the pilgrim people of God in a realm of time which has been sanctified by the incarnation.

To this we respond by our own part in the sanctification of time. The passing of each week is sanctified by the remembrance of Christ's death and resurrection in the eucharist on the Lord's Day. Each day is sanctified by continuous prayer, especially that of the Church in the Liturgy of the Hours. Each year is sanctified by commemorating once again the cycle of salvation history. This latter aspect of time, the liturgical year, is the main concern of this chapter.

The evolution of the liturgical year

In the very early Church the resurrection was a recent event. Christ was expected to return soon, and so all life and worship was filled with the spirit of Easter. There was only one real feast, Easter, which was marked by a vigil as well as the celebration on the day itself. Each Sunday was a commemoration of the resurrection, a lesser Easter, so to speak. The only other occasion which could be regarded as a festival, though less prominent, was Pentecost, also marked by a vigil.

In time, belief in Christ's imminent second coming was abandoned and the liturgical year began to evolve. The first step was the development of Holy Week, with the separating out of the main events into Palm Sunday, Maundy Thursday, Good Friday and Easter Day (with its vigil). This took place in Jerusalem in the second half of the fourth century. The holy city lent itself readily to this development, with the holy places, the constant throng of pilgrims, and a greater freedom from the conservative restraints on the liturgy which characterised other centres. These conditions made possible the development of these realistic liturgical celebrations based on the holy places. There was in fact a long programme of services celebrating many events throughout the week, as we know from the detailed eye-witness account by the Spanish nun Egeria.[1] From Jerusalem the observance of Holy Week, that is the observance of Palm Sunday, Maundy Thursday, Good Friday, and Easter (not the many other observances reported by Egeria), spread throughout the Church.

Time and the Liturgical Year

Until the fourth century Pentecost had been a celebration of both the Ascension and the outpouring of the Holy Spirit. Now the two observances were separated, Ascension Day being observed forty days after Easter in accordance with the chronology of Acts 1:3.

Lent evolved quite independently of Holy Week. It was originally the final period of preparation of the catechumens, or more properly the elect, for baptism at Easter. With the demise of the catechumenate, it became a penitential period, not only for those undergoing public penance before being reconciled to the Church on Maundy Thursday and readmitted to communion on Easter Day, but for the faithful generally. In order to imitate Christ's forty days in the desert, Lent was brought forward by four days to start on the previous Wednesday. The six weeks of Lent hitherto only amounted to thirty-six fast days, because Sundays were not observed as days of fasting. The observance of Ash Wednesday can be traced back to the tenth century.

Christmas Day is known to have been observed in Rome by the year 336. The celebration of the nativity may have predated the pagan festival of the Invincible Sun, fixed on this day by the Emperor Aurelian in 274, or it may have been fixed on 25 December to supersede the pagan festival. In the year 1996 BC the Egyptian calendar recorded the winter solstice as occurring on 6 January. The calendar was, however, inaccurate, and by the year 331 BC (the foundation of Alexandria) the solstice (the day when the sun is farthest south from the equator and appears to halt before returning) occurred on 25 December. Christmas and Epiphany are both associated with the winter solstice, therefore, and both these dates were pagan festivals which were christianised.

Epiphany superseded a festival of the birth of a pagan god. It originated as a feast of the eastern Church celebrating both the nativity, including the visit of the Magi, and the baptism of Jesus. During the fourth century the eastern Churches began to celebrate the nativity on 25 December (in imitation of the west), and the feast of Epiphany celebrated simply the baptism. Later the western Church began commemorating the Epiphany on 6 January, and the period between the two feasts constituted the Christmas season. In the eastern observance of the Epiphany, the Church celebrated principally the visit of the Magi. However, the western Church has traditionally celebrated three manifestations of Our Lord on this feast: to the Magi, at his baptism, and at his first miracle at Cana. All three are proclaimed in the office texts in the traditional Roman Breviary. In the recent revision, the Roman rite now has a distinct feast of the Baptism of the Lord.

Advent evolved as a period of preparation for Christmas in imitation of Lent. This began in Gaul in the fifth century and lasted for six weeks, while in Spain and parts of Italy a five week Advent was observed at one time. Eventually the period of four weeks was accepted at Rome and as the Roman rite eventually superseded other customs, this became the norm. Strictly speaking, it is a season lasting for four Sundays, but not necessarily for four full weeks.

In the traditional reckoning of the liturgical year, the remaining Sundays were assigned as follows. The three Sundays before Ash Wednesday were Septuagesima, Sexagesima, and Quinquagesima (i.e. 70, 60, 50 days before Easter: only the last of these is an accurate reckoning!). These Sundays marked a stage before Lent and purple vestments were worn. They originated in the fifth-sixth centuries (but were abolished in the new Calendar which came into effect on 1 January 1970). The remaining Sundays between Epiphany and Septuagesima were 'Sundays after Epiphany', of which there could be up to six, depending on the date of Easter. The Sunday immediately after Pentecost was the Feast of the Trinity, which originated in the tenth century and universally enjoined by Pope John XXII in 1334. The remaining Sundays were numbered as 'Sundays after Pentecost', starting with the second Sunday.

Time and the Liturgical Year

The liturgical year originally commenced at Christmas. Since the introduction of Advent, the liturgical year has begun on the First Sunday of Advent and finished on the Last Sunday after Pentecost (now the Last Sunday in Ordinary Time, Solemnity of Christ the King).

The Second Vatican Council [CL 102-111]

[For the rest of this chapter, reference should also be made to GIRM 313-341 (Choice of Mass Texts); GILH 204-252; and GN (General Norms for the Liturgical Year and the Calendar). The last item is printed in the Roman Missal after GIRM.]

Chapter V of the *Constitution on the Sacred Liturgy* outlines very clearly the importance of liturgical time. It begins by stressing the significance of Sunday and the 'supreme solemnity of Easter', and goes on to remind us of the meaning of the liturgical year.

> 'Within the cycle of a year, the Church unfolds the whole mystery of Christ, not only from his incarnation and birth until his ascension, but also as reflected in the day of Pentecost, and the expectation of a blessed, hoped-for return of the Lord. Recalling thus the mysteries of redemption, the Church opens to the faithful the riches of her Lord's powers and merits, so that these are in some way made present at all times, and the faithful are enabled to lay hold of them and become filled with saving grace' [CL 102].

The Council therefore ordered the following principles to be observed in revising the calendar and the liturgical year:

1 'Other celebrations, unless they be truly of overriding importance, must not have precedence over Sunday',

which is the 'original feast day' and the 'foundation and nucleus of the whole liturgical year' [CL 106].

2   'The liturgical year is to be revised so that the traditional customs and discipline of the sacred seasons can be preserved or restored' [CL 107].

3   'The minds of the faithful must be directed primarily toward the feasts of the Lord in which the mysteries of salvation are celebrated in the course of the year. Therefore the proper of time shall be given the preference which is due over the feasts of the saints, so that the entire cycle of the mysteries of salvation can be suitably recalled' [CL 108].

4   The baptismal and penitential themes of Lent should be more pronounced.

All these requirements have been systematically carried out. The proper texts and the lectionaries used at Mass and the office have been completely revised and greatly amplified. The number of prefaces has been increased so as to enrich the giving of thanks for the mysteries of salvation. Particular attention has been given to the seasons, and there is a proper Mass and office for each day of Advent and Lent. The baptismal theme of Lent has been particularly enhanced by the development of the RCIA.

It is not sufficient, of course, to revise and enrich the texts. Attention has to be paid (a) to the calendar, and (b) to the regulations governing observances. A new calendar was compiled and issued in 1969. This was inserted into the new missal of 1970 and the Liturgy of the Hours (1971). An updated edition of this calendar was published in 1989.[2] The calendar always contains two types of entry: (i) the *temporale* or the proper of time, with allowance for those feasts which are movable; (ii) the *sanctorale* or proper of saints. The new

Time and the Liturgical Year

calendar of 1969 made a drastic reduction in the number of saints' days observed in the universal Church to 182 (by 1989 this figure had risen to 187[3]). The saints selected for the new calendar are much more representative of different times, places, and achievements.

More importantly, the regulations regarding the observance of feasts were made stricter and simpler. Sundays throughout the year and the weekdays of Lent can now only be superseded in the liturgy by other celebrations of the greatest importance. In practice this means that the days of Lent are observed in the fullness of the seasonal liturgy, interrupted at most on only three occasions: the celebration of The Chair of St Peter (22 February), St Joseph (19 March) and the Annunciation (25 March). Other seasons have a degree of 'protection' also, while Holy Week and the Octave of Easter admit of no other celebration.

The classification of feasts is now much simpler and more effective, with only four categories:

(a) *Solemnities*. This is the highest rank of feast, and most other celebrations will yield to a solemnity. A solemnity has certain 'privileges', such as first vespers and the right to be transferred to another date in certain circumstances. There are 10 solemnities of the Lord, 3 of Our Lady, and only 4 of the saints.

(b) *Feasts*. These form the second rank. There are 6 feasts of the Lord, 2 of Our Lady and 25 of the saints.

(c) *Memorials (obligatory)*. The majority of saints' days fall into this or the next category. At present (1990) there are 63 memorials in the general calendar. To this number must be added local celebrations (i.e. saints observed nationally, or in a diocese, a particular place or a religious house). Memorials make only a limited impact on the liturgy, often only the prayer for the day. They do not normally interfere with the course of scriptural readings in the Mass and office. During Lent, all memorials falling on a weekday are reduced to optional memorials.

(d) *Optional memorials.* These are treated exactly in the same way as obligatory memorials except that they are observed or not observed at the free choice of the celebrant or of an individual reciting the office. There are at present (1990) 92 optional memorials in the general calendar. Local calendars also have feasts which are optional memorials, and there is some encouragement for local feasts to be observed as optional to avoid overloading the calendar.

In addition to the above, mention must be made of:

(i) *Sundays.* As we have seen, Sundays have a 'protected' status throughout the year.

(ii) *Weekdays (or ferias).* These are days on which there is no other feast. Outside of seasons, the proper of the Mass will normally be taken from the previous Sunday. On these days, there is some choice of other Masses, and, of course, an optional memorial may be celebrated. But nearly always, the scriptural readings for the day have to be read: this is to maintain the course of readings with as little interruption as possible.

(iii) *Octaves.* There are now only two octaves, those of Christmas and Easter. During each of these octaves, the liturgical celebration continues for eight days.

(iv) *Commemorations.* Commemorations, which once caused much complication, have been abolished. Only one feast can be observed on any one day. If two or more optional memorials are listed for a particular day, only one may be observed.

The Liturgical Year [GN]

To complete the account of contemporary liturgy, we now make a survey of the course of the liturgical year. The *General Norms of the Calendar and the Liturgical Year* provides a thorough account of the pastoral and liturgical aspects of this topic.

(a) Advent

The Church's year begins on the first Sunday of Advent, a season consisting of four Sundays. It has now lost its former spurious character of being penitential, but it is still a period of preparation. We look forward to the celebration of Christ's first coming and think also about Christ's second coming at the end of time. 'It is thus a season of joyful and spiritual expectation' [GN 39]. The weekdays from 17-24 December are more directly oriented to preparation for the nativity, and the second Advent preface is said.

Within the commencement of a new ecclesiastical year on the First Sunday of Advent, a new cycle of the Sunday lectionary begins. The readings for Sundays in Advent are different in each of the three years. On the weekdays of Advent there is one cycle of ferial readings, which are therefore the same each year. There is a Mass proper for each weekday, and votive Masses and daily Masses for the dead are forbidden during Advent.

(b) The Christmas Season

'The Church considers the Christmas season, which celebrates the birth of Our Lord and his early manifestation, second only to the annual celebration of the Easter mystery' [GN 32]. The season includes the Epiphany and finishes on the Sunday after Epiphany. The season has been enriched with prefaces which proclaim different aspects of the incarnation, three for Christmas and one for Epiphany.

(c) Ordinary Time

The first of two periods of 'ordinary time' begins on the Monday after Epiphany. During Ordinary Time, no particular aspect of the mystery of Christ is celebrated, but instead the mystery of Christ in all its fullness [GN 43-4]. A new cycle of the Mass lectionary for weekdays commences on the Monday after Epiphany. There is a choice of Sunday and weekday prefaces. On weekdays when there is no feast, there is considerable choice of Masses which may be said:

- the previous Sunday,
- any other Sunday in Ordinary Time,
- any of the Masses 'for various needs and occasions',
- any votive Mass,
- any Mass of the dead.

(d) Lent

This season is a preparation for Easter and lasts from Ash Wednesday to the Mass of the Lord's Supper on Maundy Thursday (exclusive). The catechumens who are to be baptised and those who are to be received into full communion at the forthcoming Easter Vigil attend the Rite of Election at the beginning of Lent and then pass through the various stages of preparation. The rest of the faithful recall their own baptism and do penance for their sins [GN 27]. There are four prefaces for Lent and two for Passiontide, and in addition some Sundays have their own preface. There is a special lectionary for the whole of Lent, both for Mass and for the office.

(e) Holy Week

Holy Week refers to the period from Passion Sunday (Palm Sunday) to Easter, and it overlaps, therefore, the last five days of Lent and the three days of the Triduum. During this week we recall the passion of Christ, beginning with his messianic entry into Jerusalem [GN 31].

(f) The Easter Triduum

These three days, Maundy Thursday, Good Friday, and Holy Saturday, are the culmination of the entire liturgical year, commemorating the paschal mystery: by dying Christ destroyed our death, by rising he restored our life. 'What Sunday is to the week, the solemnity of Easter is to the liturgical year' [GN 18]. The high point of the Triduum is the Easter Vigil, the 'mother of all vigils'. 'During it the Church keeps watch, awaiting the resurrection of Christ and celebrating it in the sacraments' [GN 21].

(g) The Easter Season

'The fifty days from Easter Sunday to Pentecost are celebrated as one feast day ... The singing of the alleluia is a characteristic of these days' [GN 22]. 'The first eight days of the Easter season form the octave of Easter and are celebrated as solemnities of the Lord' [GN 24]. The importance of this season may be judged from the provision of five prefaces for Easter and two for the Ascension.

'The weekdays after the Ascension to the Saturday before Pentecost inclusive are a preparation for the coming of the Holy Spirit' [GN 26]. The coming of the Holy Spirit is now seen as the completion of the Easter mystery and the beginning of the Church formed by Christ to continue his mission on earth. Henceforth the Church makes constant remembrance of the paschal mystery and joins with the Son in offering everlasting praise to the Father. Accordingly, Pentecost no longer has an octave.

(h) Ordinary Time

When Eastertide has ended, the paschal candle is moved next to the font, and the candles of those being baptised are lit from it. It may be placed next to the coffin at a funeral to symbolise the paschal mystery.

The second period of ordinary time begins on the day after Pentecost. The people of God commemorate the mystery

Catholic Worship

of Christ in all its fullness, living out the new dispensation in their liturgical worship and in their daily lives. The final Sunday of the Church's year is the Solemnity of Christ the King, when we celebrate that God has made all things new in his Son Jesus Christ, the King of the Universe. It is a joyful and triumphant ending to the Church's year.

Notes

1 The best translation with much interesting commentary is that of John Wilkinson, *Egeria's Travels* (London: SPCK, 1971). There is a summary of the programme of the Great Week on pp. 73-77.

2 The *Calendarium Romanum* was published on 14 February 1969 and came into operation on 1 January 1970. When this was inserted into the *Missale Romanum* (1970) a few minor changes were made. In 1989 a revised version of the *Calendarium Romanum* was issued by the Congregation for Divine Worship and the Discipline of the Sacraments [see *Notitiae* 275 (June 1989), pp. 489-503]. The changes in the latter are not many, but it brings the calendar up to date.

3 The following saints' days have been added to the Universal Calendar since 1969:

14 February   Ss Cyril and Methodius (Memorial) [1980]

14 August	St	Maximilian Kolbe (Memorial) [1983]
20 September	Ss	Andrew Kim Taegon, Paul Chong and companions (Memorial) [1985]
28 September	Ss	Laurence Ruiz and companions (Optional Memorial*) [1988]
24 November	Ss	Andrew Dung-lac and companions (Memorial) [1989]

*In 1979, the observance of St Stanislaus (11 April) was upgraded to an obligatory memorial. So (in 1990) the number of optional memorials is still 92.

20

The Liturgy Today and Tomorrow

Progress

Although over twenty-six years have elapsed since the *Constitution on the Sacred Liturgy* was promulgated by Pope Paul VI on 4 December 1963, the task of liturgical revision is still continuing. Apart from ongoing work on new and revised rites taking place in Rome, in the English-speaking world we are now in a second round of translation and adaptation of texts. The revisers were set a mammoth task by the Council Fathers, and for the most part their achievements have been outstanding. These achievements have been reviewed in Chapter Eight and in the detailed discussions of the various rites in the subsequent chapters. To sum this up in one sentence, even a long one, is not easy. But it could be said (with certain qualifications) that the revision has been thorough and comprehensive, imaginative and sensitive to pastoral needs, and conducive to greater simplicity and meaningfulness.

However, an important distinction has to be made between liturgical revision and liturgical development. While the achievement in the former sphere has been outstanding, the progress of the latter has been rather patchy in this country. Some parishes have a lively, living and enthusiastic liturgy, and make every effort to develop all the possibilities for its effective celebration. At the other extreme, there are parishes where the observances are dull, unimaginative and perfunctory. Many parishes, of course, come somewhere between these two extremes: in such parishes there are good initiatives, but more could be done with a little thought and planning.

This chapter will conclude with some detailed suggestions for what needs to be done. But before this is attempted, a more fundamental factor needs some consideration. There seems to be, unfortunately, a widespread failure on the part of many Catholics to understand the need for ongoing liturgical renewal and development. The spirit of the Constitution and of subsequent documents is not fully appreciated because so many people have not read them and have not been taught about them. Until there is a sounder grasp of what liturgy means and why it is important, it will be difficult to convince those who need convincing about the necessity for more liturgical development.

Pope John Paul II on liturgical development

The present Holy Father has recently addressed this problem cogently and specifically. He has written an Apostolic Letter on the 25th Anniversary of the promulgation of the *Constitution on the Sacred Liturgy*.[1] This was published on 4 December 1988, and deserves to be widely read.

In the first chapter of his letter, he reminds bishops and priests of the importance and significance of the *Constitution*.

The renewal of the whole life of the Church is very closely linked with the renewal of the liturgy, and the liturgy has therefore been renewed in accord with tradition and with openness to legitimate development.

He goes on (in Chapter II) to emphasise that the guiding principles of reform as laid down by the *Constitution* were (a) the re-enactment of the paschal mystery, (b) the presence of the word of God, and (c) the self-manifestation of the Church as one, holy, catholic and apostolic. 'Thus it is especially in the liturgy that the mystery of the Church is proclaimed, experienced and lived' [9].

Chapter III offers guidelines for the renewal of liturgical life, saying 'the pastoral promotion of the liturgy constitutes a permanent commitment to draw ever more abundantly from the riches of the liturgy ...' [10].

The Pope quotes his own words written in 1980: 'It is therefore necessary and urgent to actuate a new and *intensive education* in order to discover all the richness contained in the liturgy.' He pleads for 'an ever deeper grasp of the liturgy of the Church' and states quite unequivocally 'The most urgent task is that of the biblical and liturgical formation of the people of God, both pastors and faithful' [15].

Chapter VI is concerned with the institutions responsible for liturgical renewal. The Pope deals in turn with the Congregation for Divine Worship, the episcopal conferences, and the diocesan bishop. Speaking of the role of the bishop in his diocese, he has this to say about the need for more instruction in the liturgy:

> 'Much still remains to be done to help priests and the faithful to grasp the meaning of the liturgical rites and texts, to develop the dignity and beauty of celebrations and the places where they are held, and to promote, as the Fathers did, a "mystagogic catechesis" of the sacraments. In order to bring this task to a successful conclusion, the Bishop should set up one or more

diocesan commissions which will help him to promote liturgical activity, music and sacred art in his diocese. The diocesan commission, for its part, ... should be able to count upon his authority and his encouragement to carry out its particular task properly' [21].

The Pope concludes thus:

'The time has come to renew that spirit which inspired the Church at the moment when the Constitution *Sacrosanctum Concilium* was prepared' [23].

Present needs and future prospects

The Pope's analysis of the present state of liturgical development is very apposite. There is a need for continual effort to make the most of the liturgy in every way. Parishes vary greatly in their development of musical resources, in the use of lay ministries, and in the adoption of communion under both kinds.

There is a danger of complacency, of getting into a rut, so to speak, and of not seeing the importance of ongoing development. Some diocesan liturgical commissions are either ineffective or even moribund. The appointment of diocesan directors of liturgical formation and of liturgical music would greatly assist parishes to develop their liturgy. The establishment of diocesan liturgical centres to provide courses for priests and laity, and especially for lay ministers, parish musicians, and catechists, is greatly to be desired. Deaneries also should be active in promoting liturgical development, and most parishes would benefit from having a liturgy committee.

It is in the dioceses that the main thrust of renewal and development should take place. At the same time, there is a good case for having a national liturgy centre to provide longer and more advanced courses. A national centre would organise both pastoral and academic courses in liturgy. It would also house a reference library and a reference collection of resource material, although diocesan centres would have their own smaller collections of resource material, perhaps offering borrowing facilities. One of the most important functions of a national centre would be to 'train the trainers', that is, those who would take up the task of catechesis and development in their own dioceses. It is sad that there is still no national liturgical centre to serve the dioceses of England and Wales. The few persons, clerical, religious or lay, who take more advanced courses in pastoral liturgy are at present compelled to go to centres overseas.[2]

Meanwhile, development on three fronts is indicated. Firstly, in the area of pastoral liturgy, there must be more liturgical catechesis in the parish. Much could be achieved if pastors would give or organise simple talks about various aspects of the liturgy, such as the meaning and structure of the Mass. It is particularly important that parish catechists and lay ministers should have training in liturgy. Facilities for day (or short) courses should be made available.

Secondly, lively and imaginative liturgical music should be fostered by means of courses and by the appointment of diocesan advisers or directors of music. Parish musicians should be encouraged to attend courses and to develop the facilities and expertise available in the parish.

Thirdly, the area of art and architecture needs adequate attention. All dioceses should have clearly articulated procedures for consultation and advice regarding the re-ordering of sanctuaries and other alterations to churches to prevent work being carried out which is unsuitable either liturgically or aesthetically. Each diocese should establish a commission for art and architecture in liaison with the liturgical commission, or perhaps a sub-committee of the liturgical commission would be preferable.

Conclusion

The record of the last quarter-century is impressive. Lay participation and involvement have progressed. We have new rites and new books, and an ongoing programme of revision. We also have some liturgical documents of outstanding importance. There is, however, further potential and scope for meaningful and effective development. While it is essential to consolidate and enrich what we have already achieved, the task of renewal must continue. The key to this development, both in the immediate future and in the long term, lies, surely, in enhancing the general understanding of liturgy among clergy and laity and encouraging lively and imaginative celebrations in our churches.

Notes

1 Apostolic Letter *Vicesimus quintus annus*, published in *Acta Apostolicae Sedis* lxxxi:8 (10 August 1989), pp. 897-918. An English translation has been published by the CTS entitled *Love Your Mass* (Do 591, 1989). As most of the letter is about the spirit of the liturgy and what still needs to be done for the fullest implementation of the Constitution, a more apt title for the translation might have been 'Love Your Liturgy'.

2 There are only very limited facilities in this country for advanced study and research in liturgy, and almost no such facilities available in any Catholic institution. Most students seeking higher degrees in the field of liturgy have to go to centres such as Rome, Paris or the USA.

Further Reading

J.D. Crichton. *Christian Celebration*, London: Geoffrey Chapman, 1981

Cheslyn Jones, Geoffrey Wainwright, Edward Yarnold (eds). *The Study of Liturgy*, London: SPCK, 1978

A.G. Martimort and others (eds). *The Church at Prayer*, London: Geoffrey Chapman, 4 vols 1986-8

James F. White. *Introduction to Christian Worship*, Nashville: Abingdon Press, 1980

Raymond Moloney. *The Eucharistic Prayers*, Dublin: Dominican Publications, 1985

R.C.D. Jasper and G.J. Cuming (eds). *Prayers of the Eucharist: Early and Reformed*, New York: Pueblo, 1987

E.C. Whitaker (ed). *Documents of the Baptismal Liturgy*, London: SPCK, 1970

George Guiver. *Company of Voices: Daily Prayer and the People of God*, London: SPCK, 1988

J.G. Davies (ed). *A New Dictionary of Liturgy and Worship*, London: SCM, 1986

Hugh Wybrew. *The Orthodox Liturgy*, London: SPCK, 1989

Index

Adaptation to local cultures, 107
Advent, 258, 263
Altar, 236, 237-9
Ambo
see Lectern
Anamnesis, 37, 144, 146
Anointing of the Sick,
 Council of Trent on, 89
 Second Vatican Council on, 108, 217-8
 Rite (1972, 1983), 217-8
Architecture and liturgy, 235-7
Artwork in church, 242-3, 244, 245
Ascension, 57, 257, 265

Baptism, origins, 17-18, 40-2
 later history, 40-52, 64-9
 Council of Trent on, 88, 192
 Second Vatican Council on, 108, 192-3
 infant/child baptism (1969), 108, 198-202
 adult baptism (1972), 108, 193-8
  see also Catechumenate and RCIA
 sacrament of, 17-18, 190-2
Bell, 75, 80
Berakah (-koth) (Jewish blessings), 24-7, 34, 143
Books, liturgical, evolution of, 59, 71-2

Calendar, 103, 112, 260-3
Canon, Roman, 57
 silent, 58-9, 73, 113
Catechumenate, 48-52, 67, 193-6
Ceremonial, 226
Chalice, Council of Trent on, 89-90
Children, the rite of baptism of, 198-202
Christmas, 57, 257-8, 263
Church buildings, 56
 see also Architecture and liturgy
Communion Rite [at Mass], 149-52
Concluding Rite [at Mass], 150-2
Confirmation, emergence as a separate sacrament, 58, 66-7, 68-9
 Council of Trent on, 88
 Second Vatican Council on, 108, 203
 Rite (1971), 204-5
 Sacrament of, 203-5
Congregation for Divine Worship, 108, 109-10
Congregation of Rites (1588), 94-5, 100, 109
Constitution on the Sacred Liturgy, the, 105-7
 implementation of the Constitution, 108
 on the Mass, 118, 134, 142
 on the Liturgy of the

276

Hours, 171-3
on the sacraments, 192-3, 198, 203, 230
on funerals, 219
on church furnishings, 242
on music in the liturgy, 249
on liturgical time, 259-63
Pope John Paul II on, 269-71
Council of Trent 86-96
Creed, the, [at Mass], 131-2

Dance, liturgical, 246
Didache, the, 34, 43
Divine Office
see Liturgy of the Hours
Drama, 246

Easter, 31, 57, 256, 265
Triduum, 112, 265
Vigil, 49, 51-2, 65
restored (1951), 97
English Language Liturgical Consulation (ELLC), 111
Epiclesis, 37, 146-7, 154
Epiphany, 257-8, 263
Eucharist, origins, 20-1
early history, 29-39
Council of Trent on, 88
Liturgy of the, 102-3, 113, 116-8, 138-55
Eucharistic Prayer (or *Anaphora*), 141-8
Eucharistic Prayers I, II, III, IV, 152-3
Eucharistic Prayers for Masses of Reconciliation, 153

Eucharistic Prayers for Masses with Children, 153
Evening Prayer, 175
Exposition and Benediction, 163
Extreme Unction, 88-9
see also Anointing of the Sick

Flowers, 245
Font, 240-2
Funerals, history of, 219
Second Vatican Council on, 219
rite (1969, 1975), 219-21
revision of rite, 220-1
music at, 221-2
Furnishings, 242-3

Good Friday, 256, 264-5
Gregory, 59, 61, 71-2

Hadrianum, the, 72
Hippolytus, 36-8, 45-6, 49, 57, 152
Holy Communion
outside Mass, 162
under both kinds, 149-50, 158-9
Holy Water, rite of blessing and sprinkling, 122
Holy Week, 256-7, 264
new order of (1955), 97-104
Homily, 113, 130

International Commission on English in the Liturgy (ICEL), 109

International Consultation on English Texts (ICET), 111
Introductory Rites [at Mass], 119-23

Jewish blessings
see Berakah (-koth)
John XXIII, 99
John Paul II, 269-71
Joint Liturgical Group (JLG), 111
Justification, 84, 89
Justin Martyr, 35-6, 43-4

Last Supper, 20-7
Latin, 57, 73, 91, 101, 102, 113, 153, 170, 253
Lay led services, 164-6
Lectern, 123-4, 236, 239
Lectionary for Mass (1969, 1981), 112, 134-6
Lent, 57, 257, 264
Lentini, Anselmo, 178
Lex orandi, lex credendi, 226-7, 234
Lighting, 244
Liturgical Movement, the, 96-7, 105
Liturgical year, 57, 256-9, 263-6
Liturgy, general principles of, 54, 142, 224
Liturgy Consilium, the, 108, 155
Liturgy of the Eucharist
see Eucharist
Liturgy of the Hours (1971), 108, 113, 167-89

Liturgy of the Word, origins, 18-19
(1970 Missal), 113, 116-8, 126-34

Marriage Rite
see Matrimony
Mass, origins of, 18-20
later history, 29-39, 54-63, 70-80, 81-98
private, 76, 83
stational, 59, 61-2
the sacrifice of the, 90-1, 144
see also Introductory Rites, Liturgy of the Word, Eucharist, Communion Rite, Concluding Rite
Matrimony, Council of Trent on, 92
Second Vatican Council on, 108
rite (1970), 210-1
revision of the 1970 rite, 211-2
sacrament of, 209-10
music at weddings, 212-3
Maundy Thursday, 57, 256, 264-5
Mediator Dei, encyclical (1947), 97, 104
Ministers of Communion, 159-60
Missal, 71-2, 92
the first printed (1474), 94
see also Roman Missal
Morning Prayer, 175
Movement, 245-6

Music, general principles,
    248-51, 272
  at Mass, 120-4, 129, 131-3,
    141, 148, 151-2
  in eucharistic worship
    outside Mass, 164
  in the Liturgy of the
    Hours, 185-7
  during the rites of
    initiation, 206-7
  at weddings, 212-3
  at funerals, 221-2
Mystery, 228-9

National liturgy centre, 271-2
New rites, list of, 108
Newman, John Henry, 170
Night Prayer, 176-7

Office hymns, 177-9
Order, the sacrament of,
  Council of Trent on, 91-2
Ordinary Time, 264, 265-6
Ordination of Deacons,
  Presbyters and Bishops
  (1968), 213-4
Ordo Romanus Primus, 59, 61-2
Organ, 244-5

Palm Sunday, 256
Parisian Breviary (1736), 96
Participation in liturgical
  celebrations, 83, 101, 103,
  106, 112, 113, 186-7, 227-8,
  246, 250
Paschal Vigil
  see Easter Vigil
Passover, 21-3
Peace of the Church, 64-6

Penance
  see Reconciliation
Penitential Rite [at Mass], 122
Pentecost, 57, 265
Posture, 245-6
Prayer, 15-17
Prayer of the Faithful, 113,
  132-4
Preparation of the Gifts [at
  Mass], 138-41
President, 123
Presidential chair, 123-4, 236,
  239-40
Priesthood and the Mass,
  56-7, 142-3

RCIA
  see Rite of Christian
    Initiation of Adults
Re-ordering of churches,
  243-5, 272
Readers, 127-8
Readings, Office of, 176
Reception into the full
  communion of the Church,
  196-7
Reconciliation (Penance), the
  sacrament of, 215
  Council of Trent on, 88-9
  rite (1973), 215-7
Reformation, the, 84-6
Reservation of the Blessed
  Sacrament, 157-8
Rite and ritual, 224-6
Rite of Christian Initiation of
  Adults (RCIA), 48, 67,
  193-6
Rite, Roman, 59-60, 71
Rites, liturgical, 60-1

Index

Ritual (*Ritual Romanum* 1614), 95
Roman Breviary (1568), 93-4, 170
Roman Canon
 see Canon, Roman
Roman Missal (1570), 94-5
 (1970), 108, 113-4, 116-25, 126-37, 138-55
Roman Pontifical (1595), 95-6
Rubrics, simplification of (1955, 1960), 97, 104

Sacramentaries, 59, 71-2
Sacramentary, Gregorian, 59, 71-2
Sacraments, Council of Trent on, 86-8
 significance of, 229-31
Sarum Mass, 78-9
Sarum Use, 76-77
Second Vatican Council, 99-115, 170-1, 259-63

Signs and symbols, 231-3
Silence, 102, 130-1, 151, 228-9
Society of Saint Gregory, 97
Speech and language, 251-4
Sunday, 31, 112, 259-60, 262
Synagogue, 18-19

Tabernacle, 157-8, 240
 hosts from, 103, 149, 155, 158, 240
Tertullian, 44-5
Time, 57, 255-6
Trent, Council of, 86-96, 101

Vatican Council, Second, 99-115, 170-1, 259-63
Vernacular languages, 91, 107

Worship, 223-4
Worship of the Eucharist outside Mass, 161-3
Worshipping space, 236

www.ingramcontent.com/pod-product-compliance
Lightning Source LLC
Chambersburg PA
CBHW050842230426
43667CB00012B/2108